Economic Development,
Climate Change, and the Environment

Economic Development,
Climate Change, and the Environment

Editors

Ajit Sinha and Siddhartha Mitra

Routledge
Taylor & Francis Group

LONDON   NEW YORK   NEW DELHI

First published 2006
by Routledge
512 Mercantile House, 15 Kasturba Gandhi Marg
New Delhi 110 001

Simultaneously published in UK
by Routledge
2 Park Square, Milton Park,
Abingdon, Oxon, OX14 4RN

Routledge is an imprint of the Taylor & Francis Group

Transferred to Digital Printing 2006

© Ajit Sinha and Siddhartha Mitra

Phototypeset in 10.5/12.5 Sabon by
Star Compugraphics Private Limited, Delhi
1626 Suiwalan
Daryaganj
New Delhi 110 002

HD
75.6
.E2947
2006

British Library Cataloguing in Publication Data
A catalogue record for this book is available from the British Library

ISBN   0-415-424100

Contents

List of Figures

List of Tables

Environment and Development: Introduction

Ajit Sinha and Siddhartha Mitra

One of the greatest, if not *the* greatest, challenges facing humanity in the 21st century is the problem of environmental degradation. If a solution is not found soon and economic policies of nations do not change fast enough to reverse the trend, then future generations might not have much of a future to look forward to. We simply cannot go on eroding and depleting the life-sustaining powers of the environment. It must however be recognised that the problem is much bigger than the usual scope of economists. At the same time, it cannot be denied that the problem is largely due to the economic activities of human beings. Therefore, it would be prudent for policy makers to give a patient hearing to the analyses and policy recommendations of economists on this issue.

It is well known that the state of the environment is intricately linked with economic development, though it is not always clear what one means by 'economic development'. Usually, it is considered to be positively related to per capita income. From this perspective, the relationship between economic development and environment boils down to a relationship between affluence and environment. Given that the process of economic development in modern times is powered by the use of energy, which is, in most cases, associated with pollution, does it mean that the greater the affluence the greater will be the level of pollution? The matter is not so straightforward. Very low levels of incomes are often associated with the use of inferior cooking fuels with very high emissions of particulate matter and carbon monoxide. For example, the poor rural population in developing countries use dung cakes, crop residue and firewood as cooking fuel. Indoor smoke pollution is a significant hazard, and in India alone it accounts for as many as half a million deaths every year. Table 0.1 compares these sources of cooking fuel with LPG, which is used by the rural elite and the affluent in the urban areas of developing countries. In such cases, it is quite clear that the data on per capita income hide as much as they reveal, as evidently an equitable distribution of income, leaving the per capita income constant, could considerably reduce such pollution. Moreover, an increase in incomes of people near the poverty line should lead to a decrease in pollution as they switch to better fuels. If we use the pollution coefficients in Table 0.1, then it is clear that an increase in the income of one million poor families, which enables them to shift from crop residue to LPG, will lead to a reduction in the annual emissions of carbon monoxide by 132 million kg and of particulates by 14.1 million kg. Consider the case of India, which has 52 million families below the poverty line. These families primarily use dung cakes or crop residue as cooking fuel. The vastly higher pollution coefficients associated with these fuels in comparison to LPG implies that poverty alleviation or income increase in the lower half of the income distribution should have a cathartic effect on the environment.

On the other hand, high incomes can also be a reason for high pollution, given the obvious relationship between income and high energy consumption. But again, it may not be so straightforward after all. Affluent people might put higher premium on a cleaner environment and thus be willing and able to put in resources for a clean environment as well as pay for environmentally-friendly technologies that might be too expensive for poor people. This is the premise of the well-known inverted U-shaped Environmental Kuznets Curve hypothesis (EKC) on pollution. In a nutshell, it argues that environmental pollution rises with rise in income from a low level to a moderate one, and then eventually falls after a high income threshold is reached. Some empirical works (for example, Grossman and Krueger 1995) have shown that the EKC hypothesis stands the test for some local pollutants such as sulphur dioxide and particulate matter. Does this mean that we should not worry about pollution and leave it to economic growth to take care of it in the long run? Again, the matter is not

Table 0.1

Cooking Fuel Expenditure and Pollution (by Source per Household per Month) in Rural India

	Firewood	Dung Cakes	Coal	LPG	Residue
Estimated Required Expenses on Cooking	0	0	213.41	175.65	0
Average Carbon Monoxide Emission (kg)	6.71	8.73	12.11	1.50	12.513
Average Particulate Emission (g)	370.54	177.51	119.58	3.92	1178.55

Source: Ahuja et al. (1987).

so simple. The question of who gains from economic development and who pays for the resulting pollution cannot simply be swept under the rug on the grounds that economic development will take care of it in the long run.

Leaving aside the question of ethics and social justice, we know that productive activities do not create only local pollutants. They also create global pollutants. In the case of carbon dioxide and other greenhouse gases, the EKC hypothesis has been found to fail the test. Table 0.2 lists the carbon dioxide emissions per capita for the nine highest polluters and the nine lowest polluters. The data reveal a remarkable positive correlation between carbon dioxide emissions and income. The reason for this could be fairly simple: the harm caused by local pollutants is felt in the close vicinity of the source. This is not the case for global pollutants—emitters capture the entire benefits but suffer only a fraction of the harm. As a result, local pollution leads to correcting action whereas global pollution does not.

The positive relationship between global pollution and income is ominous for the environment given that the populous countries of the world such as India and China, which are still at a relatively low level of per capita income, are now developing very fast. These two countries account for 40 per cent of the world's population. The rest of the world, the United States, China and India had per capita annual emissions of 3.8, 19.8, 2.2 and one metric tons respectively in the year 2000. In purchasing power parity terms the Indian and Chinese per capita incomes are around one-tenth and one-fifth of the US figure respectively. At their present growth rates these countries should catch up with the present-day US figure in 40 and 30 years respectively. If we assume that they will display a per capita emission equal to the 2006 US standard, then when they catch up the increase in their emissions in the intervening period alone will raise world per capita annual emissions by around 200 per cent of its current level. This is a terrifying thought and increases the urgency of getting all developed countries to reduce their emissions so that these large countries also feel the obligation to temper their tendency to grow by polluting the global environment.

If income increase is associated with poverty alleviation, then it leads to a decline in local or indoor smoke pollution. The incidence

Table 0.2
Carbon Emissions per Capita by Country:
Highest and Lowest Polluters

Country	Anthropogenic Carbon Emissions in 1999 (Metric Tons per Capita)	Per Capita Income in Current Dollars (2000)
1 Qatar	91.5	N.A.
2 United Arab Emirates	31.3	N.A.
3 Bahrain	29.4	10,420
4 Kuwait	24.9	16,290
5 United States	19.7	34,400
6 Trinidad and Tobago	19.4	5,220
7 Luxembourg	18.6	43,550
8 Australia	18.2	20,090
9 Canada	14.4	21,820
10 Rwanda	0.1	260
11 Tanzania	0.1	280
12 Malawi	0.1	170
13 Central African Republic	0.1	280
14 Ethiopia	0.1	110
15 Mozambique	0.1	210
16 Burkina Faso	0.1	250
17 Niger	0.1	180
18 Sierra Leone	0.1	130

Source: World Bank, World Development Indicators: http:// www.fao. org//docrep/003/3 × 8054e/ × 8054e 05.htm; and Grossman and Krueger (1995).

of cancer and diseases of the respiratory system can be averted. On the other hand, as mentioned before, an increase in incomes of the affluent countries leads to an increase in emissions of global pollutants. Many of these pollutants, such as carbon dioxide, nitrous oxide, methane and fluorocarbons, are classified as greenhouse gases. They are so named because of a similar effect produced by the glass panes of a greenhouse. These gases allow short wavelength radiation to pass through but trap long wave-length radiation. Thus, the blanket of gases enveloping the earth allows free passage to shorter wavelength solar radiation. When such radiation hits the earth's surface, the latter reflects some of it back as long wave infrared radiation. As a result, heat is absorbed by the gaseous blanket. A higher concentration of such gases in the atmosphere implies greater absorption of heat (http://www.eb.com:180). This could result in a rise in the average temperatures on our planet, particularly as we move towards the poles. Higher temperatures could result in oceans expanding and land being submerged. There might be a proliferation and greater occurrence of diseases such as malaria and dengue. Thus, a rise in the incomes of already affluent people/countries might not be a good thing as it could be associated with neutralising welfare losses. The only way that such growth can be environmentally friendly is if technological change (much of it being consciously driven by research) can reduce the amount of carbon used by the production of a dollar of output. A lot of such research is being motivated not by the effects of global pollution, but by the shortage of carbon-based minerals such as crude oil, which forms the basis of petroleum and diesel. The focus of current research is on increasing the fuel efficiency of vehicles and development of plant-based fuels. Such fuels should be associated with very little increase in the earth's concentration of carbon dioxide. If plants are cultivated for the purpose of fuel, then any carbon dioxide generated by using such fuels may be neutralised by the carbon dioxide absorbed by such plants during their growth process.

Another way to keep global pollution in check is to have agreements among countries, prescribing quotas for emissions. The Kyoto Protocol (KP) is such an attempt. However, it is just a beginning. The rejection of the KP by the United States, the single largest greenhouse gas producer, has already put a serious question mark on the success of the Protocol. It is imperative that we learn from the strengths and weaknesses of the KP to develop a more comprehensive agreement that includes most developing countries and such developed countries as the United States. But a global agreement is not the only possible way of controlling trans-border pollution. In many cases it could also be checked by bilateral or regional agreements between countries where each country specialises in the production of the product or service in which its technology is relatively clean. For example, a country might provide hydel power to its neighbour in return for clean bio-diesel. With the globalisation of the world economy, the question of the relationship between environment and trade, as well as transfer of technologies, also needs to be scrutinised closely.

The other link between environment and economy is through natural resources, often referred to as national capital. The indispensability of natural resources to the human production process cannot be disputed. Natural resources fall into two categories: renewable, characterised by a positive rate of recharge, and non-renewable. Economic development has been heavily dependant on the use of non-renewable sources of energy, but its rapidity has led to the fast depletion of these. This has given rise to the possibility of cessation of economic development if new reserves of these resources or renewable substitutes are not found. In this context, the rapid decline of old growth rainforest is of particular concern. This destruction is not only threatening the environment, but also affecting human life through destruction of biodiversity. It is again incumbent on us to analyse the economic dynamics of this development and find ways to stop or reverse the trend to the extent possible.

But the problem with non-renewable resources does not start or end with old growth rainforests and an alarming rate of extinction of several species, both on land and in water. Take the case of petroleum, for example. The known reserves of petroleum are around 15,960 billion litres. At the current rate of world consumption these would be exhausted in about 36 years (http://strata.geol.sc.edu). There is a wide disparity in petroleum consumption with countries like India consuming only 9 litres per capita per annum, and others like the US consuming as much as 1,800 litres per annum. Given that developing countries like India and China are looking to increase their energy consumption, this estimate of 36 years seems over-optimistic. Even when we take into account the large reserve of coal and the possibility of converting it into petroleum, the known reserves of coal will be exhausted in 16 years at the rate of current consumption of petroleum. This is an ominous sign given the heavy reliance of the modern world economy on oil. In order to decrease world consumption of gasoline, leading world companies have been experimenting with hybrid cars—cars that run off a rechargeable

battery and gasoline, rather than just gasoline. (see http://www.
care2.com/channels/ecoinfo/hybrid). They yield around 25 km
per litre as opposed to a standard car, which yields around 12 to
15 km per litre. Employment of hybrid models on a large scale
should reduce gasoline consumption by 30 per cent. However, we
should keep in mind that greater fuel efficiency usually leads to
greater propensity to travel. Thus, the savings might not materialise unless travel is made expensive through appropriate tax policy.

Given the scenario with the total reserve of oil and its contribution to greenhouse gases and other particulate pollution, it is
no wonder that the world is now turning to plant sources of
energy such as vegetable oils. It is now fairly well accepted that
cooking oils can be used to power cars and machines. India, being
a net importer of edible oils, is looking to tap the potential of a
non-edible oil-bearing plant called *jatropha*, which grows in all
sorts of agro-climatic conditions. It is felt that India's wasteland
acreage of around 10 million hectares can be used to plant this
crop. But at a yield of around 1.5 tonnes per hectare, this would
yield less than 50 per cent of the total annual diesel demand of
42 million tonnes. Research, therefore, has to be targeted towards
increasing the yield of the *jatropha* plant.

One drawback of most economic analyses of this kind, however, is that it either bases its future projections on the *ceteris
paribus* assumption or the assumption of a constant rate of
change. But, of course, in a real dynamic world all other things
neither remain constant nor change at the same pace over time.
This is considered to be a constant source of forecasting errors.
But the problem could be more subtle. Economic analyses look
at change in quantitative terms only, but the perceived quantitative changes might entail qualitative changes as well. If the nature
of the beast is changing continuously, then it is not easy to predict
how it is going to behave in the future. For example, a policy of
introducing energy-efficient technologies might lead to more
energy consumption rather than less (as it might create an increase in real income), a new set of possibilities in consumption,
and a fall in the derived prices of services such as travel.

These are the broader issues around which an international
conference on environment and development was organised by
the Gokhale Institute of Politics and Economics, Pune, India, in

2005. Several of the contributing authors to this book participated in the conference. As the deliberations threw new light on development and environment linkages, it was felt important to publish a book that would make a significant contribution to the existing literature. What follows is a brief description of the papers in the book, which includes some revised articles presented at the conference as well as others especially solicited for the book.

In Chapter 1, Barkley Rosser argues that the relationship between environmental quality and pollution is critically dependant on human institutions. This is true for deforestation, which exhibits no discernible relationship with income. Similarly, he cites recent works to show that political and institutional factors are more important than income levels in determining the threat to endangered species. Community management of renewable resources has often been successful in sustaining the levels of these resources. Two types of social capital are important in determining the success of management: (*a*) 'bonding capital', which bonds the members of the community and ensures that communal laws and norms are observed by all; and (*b*) 'bridging capital', which ensures effective communication with the outside world. For isolated communities, effective management of common property resources requires the presence of just 'bonding capital,' but when such communities come in contact with others 'bridging capital' is also needed. It is possible that a degree of income equality might be needed for both these forms of social capital to exist. Rosser also points out that local pollutants exhibit the EKC pattern to a greater extent than global pollutants, the reason being that nations do not factor in transnational externalities into their regulatory decisions. Finally, he stresses the success of traditional institutions in poorer countries in preventing environmental degradation and urges the replication of such institutions at higher levels of economic development.

While the discussion in Rosser's paper is basically policy oriented, Siddhartha Mitra in Chapter 2 concentrates on the theoretical aspects of the relationship between environmental quality and income. He concludes that a unique theoretical relationship in the form of an inverted U between emissions and income does not result in a unique relationship between income and environmental quality. This is because environmental quality does not just depend upon current emissions, but also on stocks of pollutants that might have accumulated in the atmosphere. Accumulation takes place whenever the concentration of pollutants is in excess of the absorptive capacity of the environment. Clearly, the pace at which an economy grows in the 'dirty income range' (that range over which emissions exceed absorptive capacity) is crucial in determining how much pollutant is accumulated as the economy traverses that range. Thus, a unique income–environmental quality relationship might not exist as many empiricists have assumed.

In Chapter 3 a well known French environmental economist who had personal experience of negotiating the Kyoto Protocol from the French side, Jean-Charles Hourcade, discusses the problem in his essay. He speculates on the chances of success of the KP, pointing out that it would depend on the correlation between reduction in carbon emissions and local environmental problems, which in turn might lead to problems of local health and productivity. Moreover, the chances of success would increase if high emissions by developed countries adversely affecting developing countries are seen to be a source of economic and political instability, which ultimately results in propagation effects (like climatic refugees) impacting developed countries themselves.

In Chapter 4, leading French economist Roger Guesnerie provides an analysis of the KP. Though he highlights some of the weaknesses of the Protocol, such as its bias in favour of emission reduction and not enough emphasis on the development of clean technology, he argues that the Protocol should be kept alive and improved. According to Guesnerie, developing countries could be brought into an expanded Kyoto by offering them not only some short-term 'carrots', but, more importantly, by following more or less 'egalitarian' principles such as assignment of 'hot air' on the basis of population that guarantees a long-term advantage to the developing countries. However, it should also take into account the geography and exposure to adverse climatic change of a country such as Russia. Inclusion of developing countries with real transfer of income from developed countries to the developing countries would be beneficial to the former countries as well, since it considerably reduces the cost of abatement to them. It is, thus, politically feasible to arrive at such an agreement. Guesnerie does not support the, so-called, more efficient mechanism of regulation through prices compared to rigid quantity regulation as followed by Kyoto. He believes that the price mechanism has several technical problems and that the short-comings of the quantity regulation could be largely overcome by developing an ingenious 'safety valve' by introducing a 'flexible' ceiling and floor prices for emission permits. The Kyoto Protocol is, however, prone to the adverse effects of free-rider behaviour like other public goods. Countries like the USA can only gain if they do not sign the Protocol and free-ride on the reduction of emissions by other countries. Guesnerie argues that some sort of insurance mechanism could be devised by clubbing Kyoto-like agreements with other international trade and diplomatic agreements where free-riding may not be so easily possible.

M.N. Murty and S.C. Gulati in Chapter 5 pursue the objective of finding the net positive effect of development after taking into account its negative environmental effects. This objective is attained by valuing emissions caused by economic development at their abatement costs. The result is a net measure called Green GDP or environmentally corrected net national product (ENNP). The authors estimate that this measure is 2.18 per cent less than the conventional measure of GDP for their study of the state of Andhra Pradesh. This implies that the benefits of economic growth might be considerably overstated if we only look at the conventional measures of well-being such as per capita GDP.

In Chapter 6 Ngo Van Long posits some hopeful results. He points out that there is no contradiction between the absence of inter-generational altruism (selfishness) and sustainable development, that is, the continuous rise of per capita utility over time. He emphasises that any production or growth is usually accompanied by some depletion of the environment. Given that such depletion is associated with a lower production of amenities such as clean water and clean air, people do not extract resources from the environment beyond a point. Moreover, when natural capital has a natural appreciation rate, which is reasonably high compared to the community's love for consumption, it is possible that growth in material production is accompanied by growth in environmental amenities.

Next, Arghya Ghosh and Partha Sen spell out a model of a small open economy with a monopolistically competitive export sector. They argue that in the short run with a fixed number of brands, overall dirty output might increase with trade liberalisation. However, in the long run, competition provided by new clean firms might actually lead to a decline in dirty output. The authors caution against generalisations based on short-term analysis which might lead to a bias against trade liberalisation.

In Chapter 8, Merry and Amacher examine one approach to check deforestation—smallholders who practice slash-and-burn cultivation entering into a contract with logging companies. The contract makes them realise the value of standing trees, which yield revenue, and have to be harvested optimally for future gain. Moreover, the infrastructure created by the logging companies provides the smallholders a pathway to the outside world and reduces their dependence on agriculture and the accompanying land degradation.

In the following chapter, Tuli looks at the development of bio-diesel in India, which might serve as a substitute for conventional diesel and even gasoline. Bio-diesel is currently being made from seeds of the *jathropa* plant. This plant grows in any type of soil and in any climate. Rearing costs are almost nil. Tuli reckons that adequate use of wasteland in India in growing the plant might be helpful in overcoming fuel shortage and in meeting the increase in the demand for fuel as the country develops economically.

In Chapter 10 Giampietro and Mayumi illustrate the use of complex adaptive systems (CAS), which use a type of circular reasoning to verify the truth of hypotheses. The particular phenomenon that they analyse is the Jevons' paradox whereby any increase in energy efficiency of a machine leads to such an intensive use of the machine that energy expenditure increases.

In the end, we wish to express our sincere gratitude to all the authors who made this book a possibility. Our queries were always answered promptly and this has enabled us to publish this book within a reasonable amount of time. We wish to thank the entire staff of the Gokhale Institute and particularly our student volunteers who took up the job of organising the conference with great gusto and supreme efficiency. Last, but not the least, a generous grant of Rs 100,000 by the Indian Council for Social Science Research (ICSSR) to partially meet the expenses of the conference is most gratefully acknowledged.

References

Ahuja, D.R., V. Joshi, K.R. Smith and C. Venkataraman. 1987. 'Thermal Performance and Emission Characteristics of Unvented Biomass-burning Cookstoves: A Proposed Standard Method for Evaluation', *Biomass*, 12: 247–70.
Grossman, Gene M. and Alan B. Krueger. 1995. 'Economic Growth and the Environment', *Quarterly Journal of Economics*, 110: 353–77.

1

Institutional Evolution and the Environmental Kuznets Curve

J. Barkley Rosser, Jr.

Introduction

Half a century ago Simon Kuznets argued that there is a general path during economic development wherein income becomes more unequally distributed as an economy moves from a low to an intermediate level of income, and then becomes more equal again as it moves into a higher level of income and development (Kuznets and Simon 1955). This pattern has come to be known as the *Kuznets curve*, an inverted U-shaped curve one would observe under these assumptions, with the level of real per capita income on the horizontal axis and a measure of income inequality, such as the Gini coefficient, on the vertical axis. While there have been many examples that fit this pattern, others do not seem to have followed it as much or even at all. Individual national circumstances and institutional characteristics within specific historical contexts appear to play a large role in whether or not the curve represents the historical trajectory of a given nation. Thus, economies that moved into a strongly socialist orientation during their development process may have seen greater equality during the intermediate stage of development than previously, as perhaps in the Soviet Union, although it can be argued that the initial take-off in Russia occurred prior to the Bolshevik Revolution during the Tsarist period when inequality may have increased. Likewise, during the past decade and a half both China and India have seen substantial growth, moving up from a low level of development, and have seen increasing income inequality, although this may also reflect movements away from a socialist system in both countries to varying degrees.

This issue of historical specificity and institutional idiosyncracy may also arise in relation to the environmental equivalent of the Kuznets curve, the *environmental Kuznets curve*, in a similar way. This idea posits that during the process of economic development, the quality of the environment initially deteriorates as pollution emissions increase, and then after some time the environment improves again as the economy achieves higher levels of income and development. It was first labelled the 'environmental Kuznets curve' by Panayotou (1993, 1997) and was empirically observed in several studies (Grossman and Krueger 1991, 1995; Selden and Song 1994; Shafik and Bandyopadhyay 1992). It has also proven controversial, although it may have a stronger foundation than the original Kuznets curve due to the nature of industrial technologies that tend to predominate at certain stages of development. With pollution emissions more strongly influenced by this than is the nature of social class relations and income distribution during the same process, the latter maybe more readily altered by politics. Both these concepts have been invoked to argue that developing countries must accept a degradation of social and environmental conditions as the price of 'taking off' into sustained economic development, but that there is an ultimate pay-off when these countries are able to succeed in reaching their higher stages.

Besides reviewing the arguments related to the environmental Kuznets curve (EKC) itself, we shall consider different institutional formations that can affect how environmental concerns might be managed at different stages of economic development. We shall deal in particular with such formations in relation to the management of biological resources, with an eye to their equivalents operating in the management and control of pollution emissions and at different hierarchical levels.

The Environmental Kuznets Curve

As a result of the Club of Rome studies (Meadows et al. 1972) during the 1970s, there was a widespread view that material throughput rose with industrial growth and that this material throughput would result in pollution; hence, pollution would also rise with industrial growth and more generally with economic growth. This led to the view that the only way to halt pollution and preserve the environment was to halt population and economic growth, and bring about a steady state economy (Daly 1977). A criticism of this solution came from other ecological economists who noted the impossibility of a steady state because of the degradation process implied by the law of entropy (Georgescu-Roegen 1979).[1]

The major argument against the pessimistic view of the Club of Rome group came from technological optimists who argued that over time technological change would bring about the development of ways to produce goods that would require less material throughput and thus generate less pollution (Simon 1981). Even in the 1970s evidence began to emerge that as incomes rose the rate of metal usage per output would begin to decline after some point (Malenbaum 1978), a view that came to be called the 'intensity-of-use hypothesis' and first inspired the notion of an inverted U-shaped curve associated with growth (Auty 1985), albeit for material inputs. This view did not depend precisely on a Simonian argument of technological change over time per se, although it was consistent with such a view, combined with a composition effect argument that higher-income economies begin to shift more to services from industry, thus reducing their demand for material inputs relative to output, even without technological change.

Another important factor came to be recognised as the environmental movement in higher-income countries such as the US

---

[1] Ironically, Georgescu-Roegen (1971) was more generally an advocate of strong limits to growth position based on his emphasis on the law of entropy, even as he saw it ruling out the possibility of a steady state.

began to introduce and enforce environmental regulations that imposed clean-up activities and less polluting techniques of production in the 1970s. It was argued that this political pressure reflected a high-income elasticity of demand for environmental quality (Beckerman 1992; Dasgupta et al. 2002). In poorer societies the emphasis is on basic survival, the production of food, and other basic necessities. Only as these are satisfied do people become more concerned with broader environmental quality. Also, it becomes easier for higher-income societies to fund pollution control activities and techniques (Magnani 2000) as well as to fund research and development in better pollution control technologies (Komen et al. 1997).

Thus, as noted in the previous section, empirical studies began to emerge that appeared to show inverted U-shaped curves relating pollution emissions and levels of income, both in the aggregate and for various specific pollutants, with most of these studies being based on cross-sectional data across countries and using reduced form equations models. Specific air pollutants that most clearly seemed to fit the pattern included air pollutants that have strong local effects: sulphur dioxide (SO_2), nitrogen oxides (NO_x), suspended aerosol particulates and carbon monoxide (CO), with the national income 'turning points' ranging from US\$ 3,000 to 10,000 (1985 rates) (Grossman and Krueger 1995; Selden and Song 1994).[2] These are important in that they are associated with some of the most serious negative human health impacts from any kind of pollution. Several of these, especially sulphur dioxide, largely arise from coal burning, associated with simpler industrial processes with easily identified point source emitters that can be controlled relatively easily through end-of-pipe methods.

Also fitting the conventional EKC story fairly well tend to be heavy metal industrial hazardous wastes such as arsenic, cadmium, lead, mercury and nickel (Gawande et al. 2001), as well as biochemical oxygen demand (BOD) and faecal coliform

[2] Some locally impacting air pollutants have estimated turning points outside this range, such as hydrocarbons at around US\$ 35,000, associated with inefficient automotive combustion (Kahn 1998).

contamination in water. However, while some such as lead have turning points within the more common range at around US$ 7,000 (Hilton and Levinson 1998), more general hazardous waste seems to have a much higher turning point level around US$ 23,000 (Wang et al. 1998). Efforts to estimate aggregate EKCs have also sometimes appeared to fit the story that has been told so far, especially to the extent that aggregate measures of pollution become heavily weighted by some of these pollutants that are especially hazardous to human health, such as sulphur dioxide.

However, many caveats have appeared regarding this story. The first and most obvious is that not all pollutants obey this empirical regularity. A few, notably basic sanitary water-borne wastes, appear to be inversely related to income, to be improved monotonically as economies develop (Dinda 2004). This coincides with the observation that infant mortality tends to decline rapidly with early stages of economic development as these very basic water pollutants are brought under some degree of control, thereby preventing very young infants with undeveloped immune systems from drinking untreated sewage.

At the other extreme are pollutants that do not seem to have a turning point, that seem to fit the original scenario of the Club of Rome group, with emissions appearing to increase with income without limit, or at least to some very high level of turning point income. Some of these are global, with the most important being carbon dioxide (Holtz-Eakin and Selden 1995), important as the major ingredient in global warming. This underlies the difficulty in getting the United States to go along with the Kyoto Accord on global warming as its carbon dioxide emissions have continued to rise sharply as its economy has continued to grow. Others that seem to increase monotonically with national income include solid municipal waste, traffic volumes and general energy consumption (ibid.; Horvath 1997).

Another caveat involves scattered evidence that some of the pollutants that appear to follow the EKC may in fact exhibit *re-linking* at higher income levels with a subsequent upswing again in emissions, and hence show an 'N curve' rather than the Kuznets inverted U curve. Shafik (1994) claims to have found this for faecal coliforms in water, and de Bruyn and Opschoor (1997) claim to have found it for sulphur dioxide. The argument they make is that after a while efficiency improvements are used up and the increase in production effect again predominates. Figure 1.1 shows the four possible relationships that have been identified between national income and pollution emissions.

Figure 1.1
Possible Relations Between GDP and Pollution Emissions

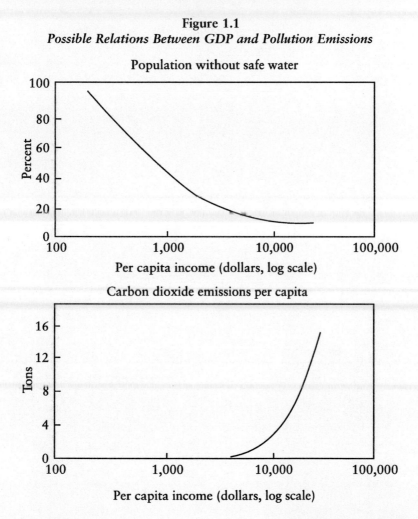

Population without safe water

Per capita income (dollars, log scale)

Carbon dioxide emissions per capita

Per capita income (dollars, log scale)

(*Figure 1.1 continued*)

(*Figure 1.1 continued*)

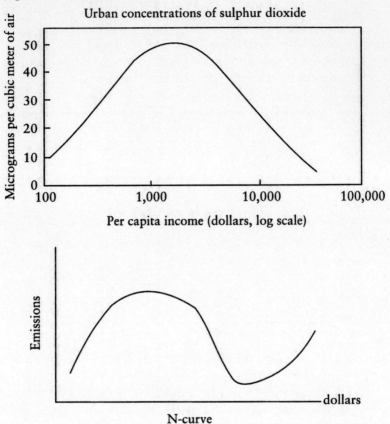

N-curve

Following up on this point, even though many pollutants appear to fit the EKC hypothesis with regard to emissions, they may not do so with regard to accumulations over time, which becomes important when it is accumulated quantities that matter for environmental quality. Of course, carbon dioxide does not even appear to follow the EKC, but it is an example for which aggregate, undissipatged accumulation in the atmosphere is what matters (Arrow et al. 1995). Besides those with global impact, some of the hazardous wastes exhibit such an accumulation effect as well, especially those that concentrate as they move through food chains, such as mercury.

Then there is the problem that for quite a few environmental factors there seems to be no discernible relationship at all between environmental damage and national income across countries or even within countries. This appears to be the case for deforestation (Bhattarai and Hammig 2001; Koop and Tole 1999). Regarding endangered species, it appears that political and institutional factors are more important than income levels, especially the issue of civil liberties (McPherson and Nieswiadomy 2001).

This brings up a broader problem—that many of these studies were carried out on a cross-section of countries rather than on a more careful panel or time-series basis within specific countries. Efforts to do the latter have found wide variations across countries regarding these relationships for many pollutants (Stern and Common 2001; Stern et al. 1996). Differing ecological and geographic situations, and how they interact with the economy, can bring about such variations (Ezzati et al. 2001). Some of these variations have to do with varying enforcement effects, which can be seen even within the US across states (Selden et al. 1999). These in turn reflect political and cultural factors (Magnani 2000), with such obvious factors as corruption playing an important role (Lopez and Mitra 2000). This leads us to the next stage of the analysis: how different institutional patterns may affect and interact with income levels in particular contexts to inform policy making.

Cooperative and Non-cooperative Management of Renewable Resources

In a classic study, Gordon (1954) argued that 'common property' institutions would lead to fisheries being overexploited in a bio-economic sense that rents would be dissipated as individual agents confused average marginal revenue with their own private marginal revenue. Failing to understand the implications of their actions on the system and on others, agents would generate negative externalities on each other and overharvest the fishery.[3]

[3] Problems of open access fishery manifest themselves in the form of a backward-bending supply curve of fish (Copes 1970), which opens

Considering grazing commons and the history of the enclosure movement, Hardin (1968) declared common property to be the source of the 'tragedy of the commons' endemic to many resources, both biological such as fish, grazing animals and forests, as well as non-biological such as pools of oil. Figure 1.2 depicts this situation where the optimum will be at marginal revenue = marginal cost.

Figure 1.2
Open Access Resource Overuse

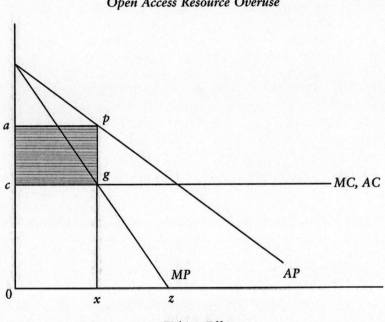

Fishing Effort

---

fisheries up to catastrophic collapses and even more complex dynamics (Clark 1990; Hommes and Rosser 2001). In an optimally managed fishery, the supply curve will tend to bend backwards as the discount rate increases, with the open access solution being equivalent to optimisation with an infinite discount rate, and the supply curve the most backwardly bent and thus susceptible to various catastrophic or dynamically complex solutions.

Since Ciriacy-Wantrup and Bishop (1975) it has been known that the problem is not common property but open access. If a well-defined group owns the resource and is able to control access to it, the group may be able to establish institutional arrangements within itself to manage the commonly-owned resource in an optimal manner (Bromley 1991; Ostrom 1990). However, even a privately-owned resource will not be managed optimally if its owner cannot control access to it.[4]

Whereas open access involves a situation in which the number of agents can increase indefinitely and thus drive rents to zero, managing common property with controlled access implies a fixed population of agents who must arrive at a mutually satisfactory set of arrangements. Sethi and Somanathan (1996) have provided an analysis of the general problem within an evolutionary game theoretic context, which broadly resembles a prisoner's dilemma situation. Let X = labour effort and K = resource stock, with $f(X)$ being concave and $A(X) = f()(X)/X$ be the average product of labour, assumed to be strictly declining in X. Let w be the wage of labour, and π_i be the pay-off to the ith agent (who is hiring labour). This can be given by:

$$\pi_i = x_i(A(X) - w)$$

which will be a share of the aggregate pay-off

$$P = X(A(X) - w)$$

Sethi and Somanathan (ibid.) establish that for a fixed n agents for a one-shot game there will exist a unique Nash equilibrium that will involve a lower extraction effort (and a higher resource stock) than the open access solution, although still a higher extraction effort (and lower resource stock) than the optimal level.

---

[4] Thus, in the American plains it took the invention of barbed wire for farmers to be able to keep cowboys and their grazing cattle out of their farm fields (Libecap 1981), and the collapse of the Soviet Union led to the collapse of the Beluga sturgeon fishery in the Caspian Sea as the now privatised fisheries could not control access from each other's fisheries (Rosser and Rosser 2004: 34–35).

They then consider a dynamic game in which there may be three types of agents, cooperators, defectors and enforcers. When enforcers punish defectors, they experience a cost of γ while the defectors suffer a cost of δ. Let there be only two harvest levels, a lower x_l of the cooperators and a higher x_b of the defectors, with both these between the optimal and one-shot Nash equilibrium levels. If there are $s_1 n$ cooperators, $s_2 n$ defectors and $s_3 n$ enforcers, their respective pay-offs will be given by

$$\pi_1 = x_l(A(X) - w)$$
$$\pi_2 = x_b(A(X) - w) - s_3 \delta n$$
$$\pi_3 = \pi_1 - s_2 \gamma n$$

They then show that there will be two asymptotically stable equilibria, one in which everyone ends up as a defector, the D equilibrium, and one in which everyone ends up as either a co-operator or enforcer, the C-E equilibrium. There will be an interval (s_1, s_2) such that the C-E equilibrium will result, with the length of this interval given by

$$1 - [(x_b - x_l)(A(nx_l) - w)]/\delta n$$

The possible dynamic cases are depicted in Figure 1.3, in which the horizontal axis represents K, the resource stock, and the vertical axis represents X, the aggregate labour effort. All these involve critical depensation in which if the resource stock is below a critical level it will collapse to zero. In all cases the stable C-E equilibrium will exceed the stable D equilibrium in resource stock, and the stable D equilibrium will exceed the stable C-E equilibrium in labour effort, to the extent that both exist.

In 1.3(a) and 1.3(b) the marginal rewards begin to exceed the wage at stock levels that are below the minimum necessary to maintain the stock. In the case of 1.3(b) there is no D equilibrium and the stock can go to zero. Thus, in that case, if social norms break down and defection dominates cooperation-enforcement, the system will collapse. In 1.3(c) and 1.3(d) the marginal rewards begin to exceed the wage at a stock level that is now sustainable. Hence, in the case of 1.3(d) the domination by defectors will

Figure 1.3
Cooperative vs Non-cooperative Resource Management

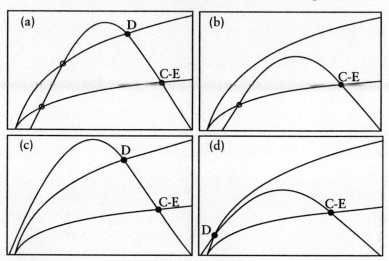

(Some Possible Configurations of Equilibria [● Stable ○ Unstable])

only lead to a decline of the stock to some much smaller but still positive level.[5]

Unsurprisingly, examples of sustained common property cases are more likely within relatively homogeneous groups that are able to communicate well and have been stable over long periods of time. Among fisheries, successful examples include the Icelandic cod fisheries (Durrenberger and Pàlsson 1987) and the Maine lobster fisheries (Acheson 1988). The list of failed fisheries that have suffered catastrophic declines is long and includes, among others, blue whales, Antarctic fin whales, Hokkaido herring, Peruvian anchoveta, South-West African pilchard, North Sea herring, California sardine, Georges Bank herring and cod, and Japanese sardine (Clark 1985: 6).

An example of the collapse of a forest is given by Sethi and Somanathan (1996: 781–82), that of the Kumaon and Garhwal in northern India. These had been divided up among villages

[5] A variety of more complicated dynamics under alternative assumptions are studied in Bischi and Kopel (2001, 2002), as well as Hommes and Rosser (2001) and Rosser (2001).

which managed their portions according to internally evolved rules of allocation. Between 1911 and 1917 the British took over management to extract logs for railroad construction. Protests by the villagers led the British in 1925 to end all restrictions on use and the forests became open access. By 1931 an observer noted that 'the oak is melting away in Kumaun like an iceberg on the equator'. Bromley (1991) has documented similar cases in Africa where herds of wildlife well managed under traditional arrangements fell apart as a result of colonial imposition of higher-level controls that resulted in essentially open access outcomes.

Forestry management becomes substantially more complicated because there are so many different outputs from forests beyond simply timber, including grazing, hunting, fishing, recreation, pharmaceuticals, preservation of endangered species and aesthetics, which can result in multiple optimal equilibria for rotation periods (Swallow et al. 1990) and multiple optimal methods of management (Rosser 2005). These problems are exacerbated in the context of less developed economies with self-sufficient indigenous groups living in the forests, with the associated potential conflicts over property rights and income distribution (Kant 2000).

The Struggle for Cooperative Institutions

In studying how cooperation can evolve within repeated prisoners' dilemma games, Axelrod (1984) found that the tit-for-tat strategy performed better than others. In this approach an agent begins by preparing to cooperate, but retaliates by defecting if another agent does so, thereby presumably punishing the defector and enforcing cooperation. The tit-for-tat agent is then prepared to cooperate again if the other agent does so, although if the other agent is a stochastic 'tit-for-tatter', they may also shift to enforcing-defecting until their stochastic trigger puts them back into a cooperative stance. Problems of this sort and the study of more complicated games than just those involving two parties and two strategies have undermined the earlier findings of Axelrod.

Thus, Lindgren (1997) has shown how in such more complicated contexts there may simply be an ongoing evolution of strategies with no settling down to any equilibrium or any set pattern.

Clearly, fundamental to fostering cooperation in the management of common property resources and more general environmental quality problems is reasonably high levels of trust. Without doubt trust is something that is learned and earned over time through repeated interactions in which trust has been fulfilled on all sides, in which no party has defected. Several analysts have identified this build-up of trust over time with the notion of accumulation of *social capital*, an idea that has many problems of definition and conceptualisation,[6] but which has come to dominate much of this discussion, although in practice many observers end up identifying social capital with trust, or use indexes of 'generalised trust' as measures of social capital. Some have found that such generalised trust is associated with economic growth (Dasgupta 2000; Fukuyama 1995; Knack and Keefer 1997; Woolcock 1998; Zak and Knack 2001), although many note that this may not hold for cases where trust is just within specific groups and not more generalised, what Putnam (2000) labels 'bonding' social capital in contrast with the presumably more productivity-enhancing 'bridging' social capital associated with generalised trust that can reduce transactions costs.

The problem of bonding versus bridging social capital is more complicated when we are dealing with the management of common property natural resources. This may be a case where the usually looked-down-upon bonding form within a specific group may be what is needed, especially for resources located in a particular locale such as the Icelandic cod fishery or the Kumaon forest of northern India. All that may matter is that there be strong relations within the local group, these being sufficient to

---

[6] Among alternatives are the accumulation of 'social debt' by giving others gifts (Bourdieu 1977) or widespread membership in many social organisations (Putnam 2000). See Durlauf and Fafchamps (2004) for more pointed critiques of the concept of social capital and its definitional problems.

induce the cooperation necessary to manage the resource. Indeed, these local group bonding social capital relations may be very strong, with a high ability to enforce sanctions on defectors (Svendsen and Svendsen 2004). In the lobster fisheries of Maine, those who do not follow the agreed-upon management practices are likely to find their lobster pots damaged, with similar management practices and results holding for the Icelandic cod fishery. Those who violate local rules will find their boats damaged. In such locales it may be hard to conceal the defecting behaviour.

While this can be a positive factor in maintaining cooperative practices within a traditional setting or even a modern setting, this can also make it harder for the practices to survive interaction with outsiders or higher-level authorities. Fishing communities are particularly insular and isolated from the surrounding society. Often the people belong to distinct ethnic groups, or at least speak unusual dialects different from those around them, even if they are technically of the same ethnic background (Charles 1988). While this may enhance the functioning of their own internally generated cooperative practices, it can lead to major problems if outsiders attempt to impose rules or practices, even if these are needed. As has already been seen, outsiders may be able to destroy the practices of the group and their social capital, but they may not be able to substitute anything effective in its place due to an inability to enforce their rules. The bonding social capital may remain strong enough for the local group to resist and undermine the rules of outsiders, but may not be strong enough to preserve their own cooperative practices.

When we move to the level of controlling pollution in industrial settings in the mid-stages of economic development, the central focus of the EKC debate, it is not immediately obvious that this discussion of how small groups do or do not cooperate to manage common property natural resources is really relevant. However, it may be in several ways. Some approaches to managing pollution, such as marketable emissions permits, may involve elements of cooperation, although in principle these can be managed in an 'arms-length' market context, assuming that the parties are honest with the government that is overseeing such an artificially created market. Certainly there are technological aspects of pollution control that are largely independent of these social and institutional factors and arrangements.

However, at this higher level the more generalised trust associated with bridging social capital comes into play. In his study of Italy, Putnam, with Leonardi and Nanetti (1993) observed that in low social capital southern Italy, there is a nexus of corruption, lack of generalised trust, and a general breakdown of law and order, in contrast with higher social capital northern Italy, with its more entrenched civic associations and generalised trust (and better overall economic performance). Both the ability to formulate widely acceptable environmental policies and to enforce them would appear to depend strongly upon this more generalised social capital, which is known to be linked with democratic and inclusive structures.

More recently, these factors have been seen to be linked with a deeper set of elements in a more general pattern of social cohesion. An element that appears to be involved in the complex interaction of trust, corruption and lawlessness is income equality (Ahmed et al. 2005; Uslaner and Badescu 2004). Indeed, Ahmed et al. have studied a global data set and observed econometrically that there appear to be strong and direct relations between the degree of income equality, levels of generalised trust, a lack of corruption, and the propensity not to participate in the underground economy. Presumably, therefore, the ability of a society to decide upon and enforce environmental regulations at any level of economic development should be easier in societies with greater income equality and generalised trust, as well as open and democratic structures. There is perhaps not an accidental link here between the two different Kuznets curves, that the increase in equality with higher development may help feed into the implementation of environmental regulatory policies that bring about the environmental Kuznets curve, ideas that have been emphasised by Magnani (2000), and also by Lopez and Mitra (2000).

A further aspect that is important for the management of environmental problems is the level of hierarchy in the ecologic-economic system that we are dealing with. Thus, we have already

seen the argument that forms of pollution that seem to exhibit
the EKC pattern more are ones that are more local in their impact
rather than global. This may be a reflection of the fact that at
the national level regulation can bring about the internalisation
of the relevant externalities. For those of more global impact,
such as carbon dioxide, national-level regulation fails to internal-
ise the externalities. A global-level pollutant must be regulated
at the global level. But it is harder to obtain national-level adher-
ence, just as a higher level of government may have trouble getting
a fishing community to go along with its rules. The failure to enforce such global regulations may be an important factor in why
such pollutants have not exhibited the sort of EKC pattern seen
more by those pollutants impacting more strongly at the national
level (although sulphur dioxide has been a matter of controversy
and diplomacy across national boundaries).

Whereas it is clear that problems arise when lower-level entities attempt to regulate pollutants or processes that are transpir-
ing at a higher level of the ecologic-economic hierarchy, there
can also be problems when higher-level entities attempt to manage
pollutants or processes operating at lower levels. Besides the sort
of enforcement problems that can arise in dealing with local communities, as in the case of the fisheries, there can be inappropriate
controls decided upon. Wilson et al. (1999) have shown that
managing fisheries at too high a scale of hierarchy can lead to
overfishing of crucial local stocks. Thus, Rosser (1995) argues
that there should be a coordination of property rights and levels
of ecologic-economic hierarchies.[7]

Final Observations

Although it has had a label for only a dozen years, clearly the
environmental Kuznets curve has become a much-studied and

[7] Usually higher levels of hierarchical systems constrain lower-level
ones, but when change moves from below to above, substantial changes
in the system may arise, such as in the 'revolt of the slaved variables'
scenario of synergetics theory (Diener and Poston 1984).

influential idea. It does not seem to apply to some pollutants and may not hold more generally for some countries, but it seems to hold for many important pollutants in many countries. The general tendency for material throughput to be associated with economic output, and for pollution to be associated with material throughput, leads to the tendency for many pollutant emissions to increase with economic growth. However, the high-income elasticity of demand for environmental quality combined with the increased ability of higher-income countries to implement pollution control technologies leads those that have political systems able to respond to popular opinion to move to reduce emissions of many pollutants. This basic outline lies behind the apparently widespread relevance of the environmental Kuznets curve. However, some pollutants seem to become less of a problem with any economic growth; others simply get worse with economic growth without any apparent limit; and some that look like they obey the EKC may stop doing so and follow an unpleasant N-curve pattern instead.

The responsiveness of a system to the desires of its people to attain high environmental quality depends on the levels of trust and cooperativeness within society. Multiple equilibria may exist between more cooperative states and states without cooperation. Many factors are involved in bringing about institutions that reinforce cooperation rather than defecting conduct with regard to environmental and natural resource contexts. Greater social cohesion may be enhanced by greater income equality and broader social and political conditions, including the ability to bring corruption under control and the willingness of citizens to participate in the legal economy and in democratic political processes. One Kuznets curve helps the other.

It is perhaps ironic that in resolving their environmental problems, high-income countries might find a model in the traditional institutions and practices carried out in poorer countries in their local and communal management of common property resources. However, it will always remain easier to act locally even when one is trying to think globally in any society.

References

Acheson, J.M. 1988. *The Lobster Gangs of Maine*. Hanover: University Press of New England.

Ahmed, E., J.B. Rosser, Jr. and M.V. Rosser. 2005. 'A Global Perspective on the Non-observed Economy, Inequality, Corruption, and Social Capital'. Mimeo, Programme in Economics, James Madison University.

Arrow, K.J., B. Bolin, R. Costanza, C. Folke, C.S. Holling, B. Janson, S. Levin, K-G. Mäler, C. Perrings and D. Pimentel. 1995. 'Economic Growth, Carrying Capacity, and the Environment', *Science* (reprinted in *Ecological Economics*, 15: 91–95).

Auty, R. 1985. 'Materials Intensity of GDP: Research Issues on the Measurement and Explanation of Change', *Resource Policy*, 11: 275–83.

Axelrod, R. 1984. *The Evolution of Cooperation*. New York: Basic Books.

Beckerman, W. 1992. 'Economic Growth and the Environment: Whose Growth? Whose Environment?' *World Development*, 20: 481–96.

Bhattarai, M. and M. Hammig. 2001. 'Institutions and the Environmental Kuznets Curve for Deforestation: A Cross-country Analysis for Latin America', *World Development*, 29: 995–1010.

Bischi, G.-I. and M. Kopel. 2001. 'Equilibrium Selection in a Nonlinear Duopoly Game with Adaptive Expectations', *Journal of Economic Behavior and Organization*, 46: 73–100.

———. 2002. 'The Role of Competition, Expectations and Harvesting Costs in Commercial Fishing', in T. Puu and I. Sushko (eds), *Oligopoly Dynamics: Models and Tools*. Heidelberg: Springer-Verlag.

Bourdieu, P. 1977. *Outline of a Theory of Practice*. Cambridge: Cambridge University Press.

Bromley, D.W. 1991. *Environment and Economy: Property Rights and Public Policy*. Oxford: Blackwell.

Charles, A.T. 1988. 'Fishery Socioeconomics: A Survey', *Land Economics*, 64: 276–95.

Ciriacy-Wantrup, S.V. and R.C. Bishop. 1975. '"Common Property" as a Concept in Natural Resources Policy', *Natural Resources Journal*, 15: 713–27.

Clark, C.W. 1985. *Bioeconomic Modelling and Fisheries Management*. New York: Wiley-Interscience.

———. 1990. *Mathematical Bioeconomics: The Optimal Management of Renewable Resources*. New York: Wiley-Interscience.

Copes, P. 1970. 'The Backward-bending Supply Curve of the Fishing Industry', *Scottish Journal of Political Economy*, 17: 69 –77.

Daly, H.E. 1977. *Steady-state Economics*. San Francisco: W.H. Freemen.

Dasgupta, P. 2000. 'Economic Progress and the Idea of Social Capital', in P. Dasgupta and I. Serageldin (eds), *Social Capital: A Multifaceted Perspective*. Washington, DC: World Bank.

Dasgupta, P., B. LaPlante, H. Wang and D. Wheeler. 2002. 'Confronting the Environmental Kuznets Curve', *Journal of Economic Perspectives*, 16(1): 147–68.

de Bruyn, S.M. and J.B. Opschoor. 1997. 'Developments in the Throughput–Income Relationship: Theoretical and Empirical Observations', *Ecological Economics*, 20: 255–68.

Diener, M. and T. Poston. 1984. 'On the Perfect Delay Convention or the Revolt of the Slaved Variables', in H. Haken (ed.), *Chaos and Order in Nature*. Berlin: Springer-Verlag.

Dinda, S. 2004. 'Environmental Kuznets Curve Hypothesis: A Survey', *Ecological Economics*, 49: 431–55.

Durlauf, S.N. and M. Fafchamps. 2004. 'Social Capital.' NBER Working Paper No. W10485.

Durrenberger, E.P. and G. Pàlsson. 1987. 'Resource Management in Icelandic Fishing', in B.J. McCay and J.M. Acheson (eds), *The Question of the Commons*. Tuscon: University of Arizona Press.

Ezzati, M., B.H. Singer and D.M. Kammen. 2001. 'Towards an Integrated Framework for Development and Environmental Policy: The Dynamics of Environmental Kuznets Curves', *World Development*, 29: 1421–34.

Fukuyama, F. 1995. *Trust: The Social Virtues and the Creation of Prosperity*. New York: Free Press.

Gawande, K., R.P. Berrens and A.K. Bohara. 2001. 'A Consumption-based Theory of the Environmental Kuznets Curve', *Ecological Economics*, 37: 101–12.

Georgescu-Roegen, N. 1971. *The Entropy Law and the Economic Process*. Cambridge, MA: Harvard University Press.

———. 1979. 'Comments on the Papers by Daly and Stiglitz', in V.K. Smith (ed.), *Scarcity and Growth Reconsidered*. Baltimore: Johns Hopkins Press.

Gordon, H.S. 1954. 'The Economic Theory of a Common Property Resource: The Fishery', *Journal of Political Economy*, 62: 124–42.

Grossman, G.M. and A.B. Krueger. 1991. 'Environmental Impacts of the North American Free Trade Agreement', NBER Working Paper 3914.

———. 1995. 'Economic Growth and the Environment', *Quarterly Journal of Economics*, 110: 353–77.

Hardin, G. 1968. 'The Tragedy of the Commons', *Science*, 102: 1243–48.

Hilton, F.G.H. and A. Levinson. 1998. 'Factoring the Environmental Kuznets Curve: Evidence from Automotive Lead Emissions', *Journal of Environmental Economics and Management*, 35: 126–41.

Holtz-Eakin, D. and T.M. Selden. 1995. 'Stoking the Fires? CO_2 Emissions and Economic Growth', *Journal of Public Economics*, 57: 85–101.

Hommes, C.H. and J.B. Rosser, Jr. 2001. 'Consistent Expectations Equilibria and Complex Dynamics in Renewable Resource Markets', *Macroeconomic Dynamics*, 5: 180–203.

Horvath, R.J. 1997. 'Energy Consumption and the Environmental Kuznets Curve Debate'. Mimeo, Department of Geography, University of Sydney, Sydney, Australia.

Kahn, M.E. 1998. 'A Household Level Environmental Kuznets Curve', *Economics Letters*, 59: 269–73.

Kant, S. 2000. 'A Dynamic Approach to Forest Regimes in Developing Economies', *Ecological Economics*, 32: 287–300.

Knack, S. and P. Keefer. 1997. 'Does Social Capital have an Economic Payoff? A Cross-country Investigation', *Quarterly Journal of Economics*, 112: 1251–88.

Komen, R., S. Gerking and H. Föllmer. 1997. 'Income and Environmental R&D: Empirical Evidence from OECD Countries', *Environment and Development Economics*, 2: 505–15.

Koop, G. and L. Tole. 1999. 'Is There an Environmental Kuznets Curve for Deforestation?' *Journal of Development Economics*, 58: 231–44.

Kuznets, S. and P. Simon. 1955. 'Economic Growth and Income Inequality', *American Economic Review*, 45: 1–28.

Libecap, G.M. 1981. *Locking Up the Range: Federal Land Control and Grazing*. San Francisco: Pacific Institute for Public Research.

Lindgren, K. 1997. 'Evolutionary Dynamics in Game-theoretic Models', in W.B. Arthur, S.N. Durlauf and D.A. Lane (eds), *The Economy as an Evolving Complex System II*. Reading: Addison-Wesley.

Lopez, R. and S. Mitra. 2000. 'Corruption, Pollution, and Kuznets Environment Curve', *Journal of Environmental Economics and Management*, 40: 137–50.

Magnani, E. 2000. 'The Environmental Kuznets Curve: Environmental Policy and Income Distribution', *Ecological Economics*, 32: 431–43.

Malenbaum, W. 1978. *World Demand for Raw Materials in 1985 and 2000*. New York: McGraw-Hill.

McPherson, M.A. and M.I. Nieswiadomy. 2001. 'Sliding Along the Environmental Kuznets Curve: The Case of Biodiversity'. Mimeo, University of North Texas.

Meadows, D.H., D.L. Meadows, J. Randers and W. Behrens. 1972. *The Limits to Growth*. New York: Universe Books.

Ostrom, E. 1990. *Governing the Commons: The Evolution of Institutions for Collective Action*. Cambridge: Cambridge University Press.

Panayotou, T. 1993. 'Empirical Tests and Policy Analysis of Environmental Degradation at Different Stages of Economic Development'. ILO Technology and Employment Programme, Geneva.

———. 1997. 'Demystifying the Environmental Kuznets Curve: Turning a Black Box into a Policy Tool', *Environment and Development Economics*, 2: 465–84.

Putnam, R.P. with R. Leonardi and E. Nanetti. 1993. *Making Democracy Work: Civic Traditions in Italy*. Princeton: Princeton University Press.

Putnam, R.P. 2000. *Bowling Alone: The Collapse and Revival of American Community*. New York: Simon & Schuster.

Rosser, J.B., Jr. 1995. 'Systemic Crises in Hierarchical Ecological Economics', *Land Economics*, 71: 163–72.

———. 2001. 'Complex Ecologic–Economic Dynamics and Environmental Policy', *Ecological Economics*, 37: 23–37.

———. 2005. 'Complexities of Dynamic Forest Management Policies', in S. Kant and R.A. Berry (eds), *Sustainability, Economics, and Natural Resources: Economics of Sustainable Forest Management*. Dordrecht: Springer.

Rosser, J.B., Jr. and M.V. Rosser. 2004. *Comparative Economics in a Transforming World Economy*. Cambridge, MA: MIT Press.

Selden, T.M. and D. Song. 1994. 'Environmental Quality and Development: Is There a Kuznets Curve for Air Pollution Emissions?' *Journal of Environmental Economics and Management*, 27: 147–62.

Selden, T.M., A.S. Forrest and J.E. Lockhart. 1999. 'Analyzing the Reductions in US Air Pollution Emissions: 1970–99', *Land Economics*, 75: 1–21.

Sethi, R. and E. Somanathan. 1996. 'Evolution of Social Norms in Common Property Resource Use', *American Economic Review*, 86: 766–88.

Shafik, N. 1994. 'Economic Development and Environmental Quality: An Econometric Analysis', *Oxford Economic Papers*, 46: 757–73.

Shafik, N. and S. Bandyopadhyay. 1992. 'Economic Growth and Environmental Quality: Time Series and Cross-country Evidence', Background Paper for the *World Development Report*, World Bank, Washington, DC.

Simon, J. 1981. *The Ultimate Resource*. Princeton: Princeton University Press.

Stern, D.I., M.S. Common and E.B. Barbier. 1996. 'Economic Growth and Environmental Degradation: A Critique of the Environmental Kuznets Curve', *World Development*, 24: 1151–60.

Stern, D.I. and M.S. Common. 2001. 'Is There an Environmental Kuznets Curve for Sulfur?' *Journal of Environmental Economics and Management*, 41: 162–78.

Svendsen, G.L.H. and G.T. Svendsen. 2004. *The Creation and Destruction of Social Capital: Entrepreneurship, Co-operative Movements and Institutions*. Cheltenham: Edward Elgar.

Swallow, S.K., P.J. Parks and D.N. Wear. 1990. 'Policy-relevant Nonconvexities in the Production of Multiple Forest Benefits', *Journal of Environmental Economics and Management*, 19: 264–80.

Uslaner, E.M. and G. Badescu. 2004. 'Making the Grade in Transition: Equality, Transparency, Trust, and Fairness'. Mimeo, Department of Political Science, University of Maryland.

Wang, P., A.K. Bohara, R.P. Berrens and K. Gawande. 1998. 'A Risk Based Environmental Kuznets Curve for Hazardous Waste Sites', *Application of Economics Letters*, 5: 761–63.

Wilson, J., B. Low, R. Costanza and E. Ostrom. 1999. 'Scale Misperceptions and the Spatial Dynamics of a Social-ecological System', *Ecological Economics*, 31: 243–57.

Woolcock, M. 1998. 'Social Capital and Economic Development: Toward a Synthesis and Policy Framework', *Theory and Society*, 27: 151–208.

Zak, P. and S. Knack. 2001. 'Trust and Growth', *Economic Journal*, 111: 295–321.

2

Environmental Degradation: Bridging the Gap in EKC Literature

Siddhartha Mitra

Introduction

The literature on the environmental Kuznets curve (EKC) is incomplete in one way. While the theoretical literature looks at the effect of income on the level of pollution (see Andreoni and Levinson 2001), much of the empirical literature looks basically at the effect of income on environmental degradation (see Grossman and Krueger 1995; Harbaugh et al. 2002). Some exceptions to this trend have occurred in recent times, and economists have also looked at the empirical relationship between emissions and per capita income (for example, De Bruyn et al. 1998).

Environmental degradation is defined for the purposes of this paper as the concentration of a certain pollutant in the environment. However, their concentration in the atmosphere may not be governed just by the current level of net emissions (gross emissions minus abatement). If the net emissions in a past period exceed the absorptive capacity of the environment, the excess is accumulated by the environment. Otherwise there is no accumulation (see Tietenberg 2001 for details). The concentration of a pollutant in the environment in the present period is equal to net present emission plus the net accumulation of excesses in past periods. If net emissions in the present period are exceeded by the absorptive capacity[1] of the environment, then the environment not only absorbs the net emissions, but also a part of the previous baggage of excesses, which is equal to the difference between absorptive capacity and current net emissions. In this way current environmental degradation, though related to current net emissions, is not solely determined by it, and also depends on the stock of excesses from the past. In other words, the state of the environment is not just determined by what is happening now (the current level of pollution), but is history-dependant. Thus, an inverted U-shaped relationship between net emissions (pollution) and per capita income (as captured in Figure 2.1) need not always imply a similar inverted U-shaped relationship between environmental degradation and income. In fact, this paper shows that for given consumer preferences, there is no unique relationship between the two even if there is one between pollution (net emissions) and income. Which of the multiple paths of environmental degradation with respect to income actually materialise depends on the growth path of income over time.

Figure 2.1
Relationship between Pollution and per Capita Income

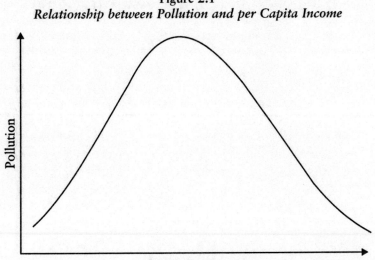

[1] By absorption is meant decomposition of a pollutant into its harmless constituents.

If we look at the literature linking environmental quality to per capita income, there is hardly any agreement among the contributors to this literature. Grossman and Krueger (1995) base their analysis on the Global Environmental Monitoring System's (GEMS) data set. According to their analysis, the turning points (peaks) for sulphur dioxide and smoke occur at $4,053 (PPP)[2] and $6,151 (PPP) respectively. In their work, Harbaugh et al. (2002) replicate the Grossman and Krueger analysis with the same data set and obviously get the same results. However, when they repeat the estimation with the data set of the Aerometric Retrieval System (AIRS), which is obtained from the GEMS data set by including some new observations and deleting some others, the peak for sulphur dioxide is obtained at $20,081 (PPP), whereas that for smoke is at $5,399 (PPP). The large differences in estimates while estimating the same relationship with different data sets cannot be ignored.

The present theoretical literature also ignores the build-up of environmental stock while postulating the existence of an environmental Kuznets curve. However, this error is less serious. Under certain restrictive assumptions (as employed by Harbaugh et al.), the structure of the curve and the location of the turning point remain unchanged after the incorporation of the level of the stock.

This discussion implies that empirical and theoretical literature on EKC are imperfectly linked. This paper attempts to bridge the gap between these two segments in EKC literature by developing an accounting framework for environmental degradation and the consequent implications of the present theoretical EKC literature for the relationship between environmental degradation and per capita income.

The following section of this paper develops an accounting framework that takes into account the build-up of the stock of pollutants. The next section re-evaluates the relationship between environmental degradation and per capita income on the basis of the Kuznets curve for net emissions and the accounting framework developed in the previous section. Following this we look at the impact of internalisation of the stock effects on the consumer's

---

[2] All PPP estimates are in 1985 US dollars.

maximisation problem and, therefore, on the theoretical relationship between net emissions and per capita income.

The Accounting Framework

The relationship between environmental degradation and current pollution is mathematically depicted as follows:

$$E_t = \max (E_{t-1} - a, 0) + x_t$$

where the subscript is used to refer to periods, E denotes environmental degradation and x denotes net emissions. If the first term on the left hand side is zero, then $E = x$. Therefore, it follows that,

$$E_i \equiv x_i \text{ when } x_i \leq a \ \forall i < t$$

where t refers to the first time period in which net emissions equal the absorptive capacity.

The Mechanism

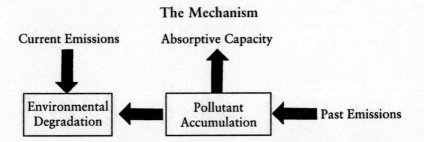

Now consider the case where net emissions (often just called pollution) displays an inverted-U relationship with respect to per capita income. Let us consider a situation where income grows continuously over time. If we think of continuous time, let t_0 and y_0 be the smaller values of t and y (income) where net emissions equals the absorptive capacity of the environment, and t_1 and y_1 be the other values of t and y where the same holds true. Between the two values of time, pollution always exceeds the absorptive capacity of the environment. After t_1, however, pollution falls below the absorptive capacity. Environmental degradation for any t which is greater than t_0 can be captured by the formula:

$$E_t = x_t + \max(\int_{t_0}^{t}(x_t - a)dt, 0)$$

Figure 2.2
Derived Relationship between Pollution and Time

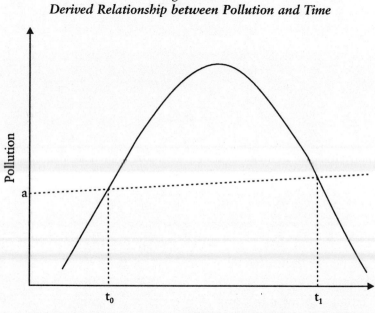

At the turning point of the Kuznets curve for pollution, x is maximised but the second term is still increasing. Therefore, the environmental degradation function does not exhibit stationarity at the turning point of the Kuznets curve for pollution. Stationarity towards the left of this turning point is also ruled out because in that case x is increasing and the second term is increasing. It therefore follows that the turning point for environmental degradation always lies to the right of the turning point for pollution, provided, of course, that the pollution at the turning point is greater than the absorptive capacity of the environment. This is because the derivative of the first left-hand-side term is negative and that of the second term is positive provided $t < t_1$. The turning point will definitely lie to the left of t_1 as at t_1 the derivative of the first left-hand-side term with respect to time is negative and that of the second term is zero, implying that environmental degradation is declining at that point. If the turning point for pollution is sufficiently high then the turning point for environmental degradation might not be reached at any feasible level of per capita income.

Economic Growth and Environmental Degradation

What is the effect of the rate of economic growth on environmental degradation? Note that the environmental Kuznets curve is a relationship between pollution and per capita income. Therefore, it can be expressed as a function $x(y)$. A function $x(t)$ which expresses pollution as a function of time will be given by $x(y(t))$. The rate of growth of pollution is therefore given by

$$\dot{x} = x'(y)\dot{y}$$

This implies specifically that the rate of increase in pollution will be higher if economic growth is higher for the income range $y_0 < y < y^*$ where y^* is the level of income corresponding to the turning point. On the other hand, for any income greater than y^* a higher rate of economic growth[3] will also imply that the rate of decline in pollution too is higher. These two conclusions mean that faster growth between y_0 and y_1 implies that the gap between t_0 and t_1 is smaller. Therefore, the unabsorbed stock of pollution accumulated at any level of income between y_0 and y_1 is also smaller. For a given income less than y^* the pollutant accumulation approximates the area of a triangle, which always has the

[3] By the rate of economic growth we mean the time derivative of y with respect to income. It is assumed that the population is constant in order to abstract from demographic effects.

same height and a base that is smaller if rate of growth is higher. In Figure 2.3 the shaded triangular areas under the two inverted U-shaped curves are the accumulated stocks of pollution for two income paths. The curve, which is steeper, corresponds to a higher rate of economic growth between y_0 and y_1. Given that the shaded triangle corresponding to the steeper curve has a smaller base, the accumulation of pollution stock is smaller for a higher rate of economic growth. For incomes greater than y^*, the pollutant accumulation is captured by Figure 2.4. In Figure 2.4:

$$\text{Ar } (ABC) < \text{Ar } (ADE) \tag{2.1}$$

$$\text{Ar } (BIJK) < \text{Ar } (EFGH) \tag{2.2}$$

$$\text{Ar } (IJC) < \text{Ar } (DFG) \tag{2.3}$$

Equations (2.1), (2.2) and 2.3 imply

$$\text{Ar } (ABC) + \text{Ar } (BIJK) + \text{Ar } (IJC) < \text{Ar } (ADE) \\ + \text{Ar } (EFGH) + \text{Ar } (DFG) \tag{2.4}$$

Figure 2.3
Effect of Higher Growth Rate for Incomes above those Corresponding to Absorptive Capacity on the Pollution–Time Relationship

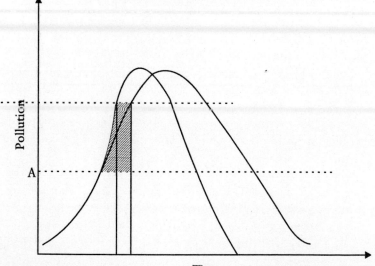

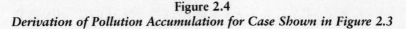

Figure 2.4
Derivation of Pollution Accumulation for Case Shown in Figure 2.3

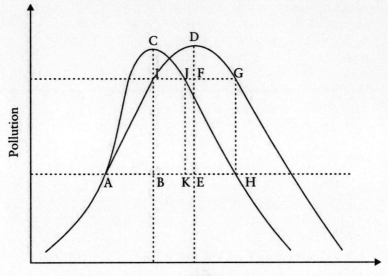

Note that the first inequality holds because the two mentioned triangles have the same height (the maximum level of pollution corresponding to each curve is the same as they are derived from the same EKC for net emissions). However, triangle ABC has a smaller base because of faster growth. A similar reason determines the nature of the inequalities in (2.2) and (2.3). Equation (2.4) says that the amount of pollution accumulation is greater on the low growth path than the high growth path for any income greater than y^* and less than y_1. This implies that the level of emissions being the same irrespective of the rate of growth, environmental degradation at any level of income in the mentioned range is lower on the high growth path.

Similarly, it can be shown that all other things remaining constant, slower growth after y_1 implies faster loss in the excess stock of pollutants. Thus, environmental degradation (the sum of stock of excess pollutants plus current pollution) reaches the level of current pollution in shorter time but at a higher level of income. Note that there is a trade-off. Faster growth implies faster decline in pollution over time. Thus, at any point of time $t > t_1$ the absorption of excesses from the past is higher in the case of higher growth as current pollution is lower. However, since any given income range to the right of y_1 on the number scale is traversed in shorter time, the absorption of pollution over the income range is smaller. Thus, environmental degradation reaches the current level of pollution at a higher level of income. Thus, there is no unique correspondence between income levels and environmental degradation even if there is a unique relationship between income level and net emissions for given preferences.

Consider two growth paths A and B, where the latter is asso-ciated with a higher rate of economic growth (the time derivative of y) at all points of time. Figure 2.5 (A) plots the pollution tra-jectories corresponding to the two growth paths over time. Fig-ure 2.5 (B) plots the corresponding trajectories for environmental degradation. In this case, if we plot the environmental degrad-ation trajectories over time, we note that when pollution is below the absorptive capacity, the environmental degradation for both

Figure 2.5 (A)
Effect of Higher Rate of Economic Growth at all
Points of Time on the Pollution–Time Relationship

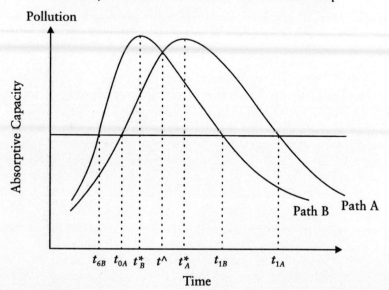

Figure 2.5 (B)
Derived Relationship (from 2.5A) between
Environmental Degradation and Time

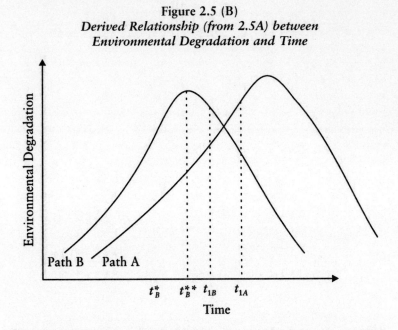

growth paths equals the current level of pollution. The positive relationship in the early phases of income growth implies that the higher growth path will correspond to a higher level of pollution at each point of time. This will definitely be true till the pollution level corresponding to the higher growth path reaches absorptive capacity.

Let t_{0A} be the point of time when absorptive capacity is reached from below for path A. Let the corresponding point of time for path B be t_{0B}. For $t_{0B} < t < t_{0A}$, environmental degradation in path A will correspond only to current pollution, whereas that in path B will correspond to current pollution plus environmental degradation. Given that current pollution for path B is higher in this time range, environmental degradation is higher. Let t_B^* be the point of time where pollution reaches its turning point for path B. This value is obviously smaller than t_A^*, the corresponding value for path A. For $t_{0A} < t < t_B^*$, stock build-up as well as pollution is lower for growth path A. Thus, environmental degradation is lower. For $t_B^* < t < t_A^*$, current pollution in path B is declining. For growth path A it is increasing. At $t^\wedge$ the current pollution in both paths is the same. However, note that addition to stock is higher in the case of path B for every t in this range, which is smaller than $t^\wedge$ and equal to that for path A when $t = t^\wedge$. Therefore, at $t^\wedge$ or any value smaller than it, environmental degradation is higher for growth path B. Let t_{1A} and t_{1B} be the values of t_1 for growth paths A and B. For $t^\wedge < t < t_{1B}$, current pollution on path B is smaller. However, because stock build-up till $t^\wedge$ is larger on path B, it is certain that environmental degradation will be larger for at least a part of the period mentioned and possibly the entire period. Between t_{1B} and t_{1A} stock build-up is negative for path B and positive for path A. Moreover, the current pollution is lower for path B. Given that the total pollution stock built up between t_{0B} and t_{1B} for path B is smaller than that built up between t_{0A} and t_{1A} for path A, it follows that environmental degradation for path B definitely falls below that in path A before t_{1A}. Thus, we can conclude that environmental degradation equals that of path A from above and falls below it somewhere in the time period $t^\wedge < t < t_{1A}$. For $t > t_{1A}$, environmental degradation in path B continues to be less than that of A.

It is seen that the high growth path initially leads to both higher environmental degradation and higher pollution than the low growth path. Later the relationship is reversed for both variables. The duration of the initial phase is higher for environmental degradation.

Does the stock effect actually exist in real life? According to the US-based Environmental Protection Agency (EPA), sulphur dioxide emissions in the United States are declining less rapidly than its concentration in the environment. Average ambient concentration of sulphur dioxide in the US environment has decreased 31 per cent between 1993 and 2002, whereas concentration has decreased by 39 per cent during the same period (http://www.epa.gov/air trends/sulfur.html). What does this imply?

The concentration of a pollutant in the environment can be expressed as:

$$c = p + e$$

where p is net pollution (emission) and e is stock of pollutant carried over from the past.

Proportionate or percentage change in concentration can be expressed as:

$$\frac{\Delta c}{c} = \frac{\Delta p}{p} \frac{p}{p+e} + \frac{\Delta e}{e} \frac{e}{p+e}$$

This implies that the percentage change in concentration is a weighted average of percentage changes in net emission and stock of pollutant. The weights are the proportions of these two components in the total concentration of the pollutant. If the percentage decline in concentration is greater than the percentage decline in emissions, it implies that: (*a*) the stock of pollutant carried over from the past is positive; and (*b*) the percentage decline in the stock is greater than the percentage decline in concentration. Thus, the stock effect is shown to be positive in at least the American case. Moreover, statement (*b*) implies a positive percentage decline. This obviously means that current pollution levels in the United States are below absorptive capacity.

Theory and Stock Build-Up

The model in this section is based on the work of Andreoni and Levinson (2001). Assume that the gross pollution in the one consumer economy is given by C, where C is consumption. The economy spends either on consumption or on abatement. The expenditure on abatement is given by E. The level of abatement is a homogenous function of E and C given by $A(C, E)$. The level of homogeneity is greater than one. Let the utility function be given by:

$$U = C - P \qquad (2.5)$$

where P is concentration of pollutants. P is given by:

$$P = C - A\,(C, E) + e \qquad (2.6)$$

Substituting (2.6) in (2.5) yields

$$U = A(C, E) - e$$

The consumer maximises utility subject to the budget constraint:

$$\frac{C}{M} + \frac{E}{M} = 1$$

Because the abatement function is homogenous, we can write it as:

$$A = M^{\lambda} A(\frac{C}{M}, \frac{E}{M})$$

Note that in this case the utility function becomes an increasing monotonic transformation of $A(C/M, E/M)$ at a given level of income. Therefore, the levels of C/M and E/M ($(C/M)^*$ and $(E/M)^*$), which maximise this function, also maximise the utility function at any given level of income. Moreover, these levels are independent of the level of e. Let these levels be denoted by c^* and d^* respectively. Therefore, the optimal pollution at any level of income can be given by:

$$p^*(M) = c^* M - M^{\lambda} A(c^*, d^*)$$

This too is independent of the level of e. Therefore, the pollution path with respect to M is the same at $e = 0$ and a positive e. This proves that in the case of a constant marginal disutility, incorporation of the stock effect of pollution does not change the postulated optimal pollution path.

However, this conclusion arises from the assumption of constant marginal disutility of environmental degradation. We now explore the case of increasing marginal disutility of environmental degradation, that is:

$$U = C - P^{\gamma}$$

In this case we have:

$$\frac{\partial U}{\partial C} = 1 - \gamma P^{\gamma-1} \frac{\partial P}{\partial C}$$

The first term is the marginal utility from consumption. The second term after the minus sign is the disutility/utility associated with an increase in consumption caused by a change in pollution/ environmental degradation. Let us assume that the abatement function is such that, *ceteris paribus*, net pollution/pollutant concentration increases with an increase in consumption.[4] In that case the second term denotes the marginal disutility associated with polluting effects of higher consumption. Given that P is increasing in e, a shift from $e = 0$ to a positive e would result in an increase in the marginal disutility from pollution at all levels of C (an upward shift in marginal disutility), leading to a decrease in optimal consumption (see Figure 2.6). This would imply a lower level of optimal

Figure 2.6
Pollution Stock Effects and the Marginal Disutility Associated with Pollution that is a Result of Consumption

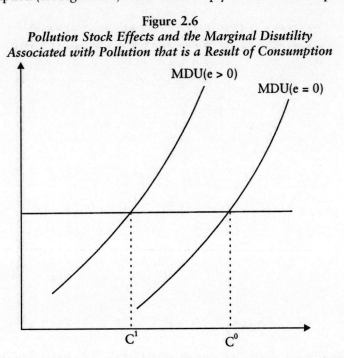

[4] This is a perfectly reasonable assumption. Let us say that a factory employs an electrostatic precipitator. In the beginning let consumption of its products be equal to C. Assuming that production/consumption of unit leads to a gross emission of 1 unit of pollution and that the electrostatic precipitator manages to absorb 80 per cent of the particulates passing through it, the net pollution is $0.2C$ and abatement is

pollution for any given level of income. This shift also captures the transition from the theory presently in vogue for prediction of net emissions to a theory incorporating the stock effect. The latter is seemingly a more complete theory and shows that the former over-predicts the level of net emissions at any point of time.

In sum, there is no one-to-one correspondence between the environmental Kuznets curves for net emission and those for environmental degradation. A single EKC for net emissions based on stated preferences can correspond to an infinite number of EKCs for environmental degradation. This is because of the effect of accumulation of pollution stock if pollution exceeds the absorptive capacity of the environment. However, the turning point among the latter set would never lie to the left and would many a time lie to the right of the turning point for the former. Even with given preferences and a unique EKC for net emissions, the environmental degradation at any level of income over the range, which gives rise to pollution levels above absorptive capacity, would be lower if, *ceteris paribus*, the rate of economic growth over this range is higher. For income levels to the right of this range, environmental degradation at any level of income would be lower if, *ceteris paribus*, the rate of economic growth over such incomes is lower. In effect, therefore, the existing empirical formulation of the EKC is incorrect as the rate of economic growth is not one of the control variables. This is perhaps the reason why different studies show very different estimates for the turning point level of income for a given pollutant. Moreover, our discussion implies that the existing empirical studies are inadequate tests of the existing theoretical models.

The theoretical literature also suffers from the neglect of the stock accumulation effect. However, under certain assumptions, such as the constant marginal disutility of environmental degradation, the incorporation of the stock effect is critical neither to the shape of the EKC for net emissions nor to the location of

---

0.8*C*. On doubling of consumption to 2*C*, even though abatement increases to 1.6*C*, net pollution also increases to 0.4*C*. Therefore, if we keep abatement expenditure constant or make it decline, in all realistic situations net pollution in absolute terms will go up.

the turning point. In other words, we end up with the same EKC for net emissions, irrespective of whether or not we incorporate the stock effect. However, the more realistic assumption of increasing marginal disutility implies that incorporation of the stock effect in the consumer's maximisation problem would imply lower emissions at any given level of income.

References

Andreoni, James and Arik Levinson. 2001. 'The Simple Analytics of the Environmental Kuznets Curve', *Journal of Public Economics*, 80: 269–86.

De Bruyn, S.M., J.C.J.M. Van den Bergh and J.B. Opschoor. 1998. 'Economic Growth and Emissions: Reconsidering the Empirical Basis of Environmental Kuznets Curves', *Ecological Economics*, 25: 161–76.

Grossman, Gene M. and Alan B. Krueger. 1995. 'Economic Growth and the Environment', *Quarterly Journal of Economics*, 110 (May): 353–77.

Harbaugh, William T., Arik Levinson and David Molloy Wilson. 2002. 'Reexamining the Empirical Evidence for an Environmental Kuznets Curve', *Review of Economics and Statistics*, 84 (3): 541–51.

Tietenberg, Tom. 2001. *Environmental Economics and Policy*. Addison Wesley Longman.

3

Disentangling the Climate–Development Gordian Knot: Towards an Integrated Blueprint

Jean-Charles Hourcade

This paper deals with the many facets of the climate–development debate, while at the same time not organising these facets into too strict a hierarchy. Instead, the attempt is to help the reader understand the interplay of these facets. We will also accept as a matter of fact the differences in the perceptions of issues of developed and developing countries while providing elements of a dispassionate analysis. This double ambition will perhaps result in a text too complex and not focused enough. However, this is necessary in order to make an exploratory first attempt to cut the development environment Gordian Knot which might be illustrative for future researchers in this field.

Two points deserve mention at the outset. While using the words 'North' and 'South', 'developed' and 'developing', we are fully conscious that, economically and socially, there is no longer one Third World but a plurality of situations in the G-77. We are also conscious of the diversity of the North even if this North is restricted to the OECD. Second, one assumes that state policies are the outcomes of the selfish interests of their constituents as well as pressures mounted by various lobby groups.

Environment and Development:
Perceptions of the Gordian Knot

Difficulties of climate policy are the result of two contradictions that have been present since the attempts made in Stockholm (1972) and Rio (1992) to reconcile environmental objectives with those of development. First, the participation of developing countries in environmental negotiations is necessary, but these countries will not cooperate as long as they perceive environmental issues as a new form of Malthusianism and not as an opportunity for a leverage effect on their development. This challenge cannot be taken up in isolation from broader issues such as world trade regulation, energy and food security. However, countries fear that new negotiations on environmental issues might endanger the outcome of ongoing negotiations on non-environmental issues.

In Stockholm a hypothesis emerged about disruptions of local environments (soils, water quality, deforestation, disarticulated urban environment) being stumbling blocks to the development process (Indira Gandhi). This diagnosis reinforced questions about the tendency of dominant growth patterns to generate a dualistic development through distorted choices of technique. The results are structural unemployment, unfulfilled basic needs, drift from the land, urban congestion and exhaustion of local resources, as captured by Myrdal's *Asian Drama*, Sen's early contributions, R. Dumont's *Afrique Noire Est Mal Partie* and the UNCTAD group (R. Prebisch). Twenty years later, after the mobilisation of many groups in the North around issues such as the ozone layer, climate change and biodiversity, the focus has moved from local to global pollution. Despite the extensive use of Brundtland's expression of 'sustainable development', there has been a tendency to disconnect discussions on climate regimes from debates on development. There is no point in developing a catch-all rhetoric that tilts the balance towards a heavier focus on local environment. Rather, one should search for a dynamic synthesis between inevitable contradictions, and this cannot be made without an in-depth examination of the interface between climate, development and other dimensions of global governance.

Reality of Development Deadlocks;
Questions about the Development Baselines

A repeated intellectual bias in development–environment debates
is to consider development scenarios that neglect the constraints
placed by the environment. Typically, many prospective exercises on developing countries extrapolate high growth rates over
a long time period. This is politically correct, but comes to assume
that resource and environmental obstacles to economic development have been ruled out. A more efficient approach should
be to assume these constraints at the outset. These obstacles prevent countries from exploiting existing endogenous potentials
and developing human capital and empowerment capacities, and
can be grouped into three interrelated clusters:

1. **Capital scarcity and technical choices:** For building infrastructure in energy, transportation or water distribution,
   developing countries cannot easily repeat the experience
   of the Western world in the 19th and 20th centuries because of a higher gap between internal saving capacities
   and the capital needs imposed by modern techniques. Failure to modify technological patterns has resulted in a debt
   trap not only in the less developed countries (LDCs) but also
   in countries such as Brazil.
2. **Basic needs and social dualism:** This social dualism is
   probably one of the sources of non-sustainability of development in some areas. It results in political instability,
   downgrades self-reliance, hinders empowerment of economies, and fosters informal economies. In many cases a
   social and technological lock-in has been formed and re-
   medies suggested by economic considerations without
   considering pre-existing conditions result in equity problems.
   This is the case for electricity, gasoline and water tariffs,
   which are subsidised for equity reasons, but foster technical
   choices that ultimately prove unsustainable and inequitable.
3. **Endogenous development and economic globalisation:** The
   Seattle syndrome conveys an increasing concern that development issues will not be resolved by trade liberalisation and structural adjustment programmes only. Further,

liberalising infrastructure sectors may not suffice to attract private investors and close the shortage of capital, and export-oriented agricultures may fail to maintain local food productions. In total, the globalisation movement is associated with: (*a*) readymade recommendations that neglect the fact that, far from being *tabulae rasae*, real economies are formed of various development spaces differing according to their size, their underlying economic rationale (public services governed by local communities versus the car industry), and their interplay with local human dynamics; (*b*) generalised free trade weakening the capacity of political powers to protect the interests of their country; (*c*) a world governance that is in the hands of a bureaucracy dominated by Western interests and very sensitive to the influence of large international private companies; and (*d*) constraints (including the reduction of public aid) in contradiction with both sustainable development objectives and demands expressed in the name of global environment. As questionable as the presuppositions of the anti-globalisation movements are, these critics cannot be ignored any longer. One needs to take into account three points in this regard:

i. **Extent of synergy between curbing carbon emissions and reducing local environmental problems:** The synergy might involve improving energy security, tailoring the use of local resources to allow for spatially balanced development, reorienting technical choices in order to avoid the debt trap, removing direct (subsidies), and indirect incentives for unsustainable consumption patterns over the long run. The question is whether these options make sense from the point of efficiency.

ii. **Removal of obstacles to welfare maximisation in the long term:** Countries often feel an urgency to grow quickly and, therefore, do not consider the long-term benefits of policies that prevent climate or other damage only in the distant future but lead to costs in the short term.

iii. **Coordination between national and international policies:** The necessity of developing coordination tools more apt to take into account the huge diversity of situations (from informal economies to internationalised activities) should lead us to reconsider the appropriate level of subsidiarity.

What Issue Linkages, If Any?

Beyond the 'only one earth' mantra, the globalisation of (mostly local) environment affairs had a clear geopolitical dimension in the early 1970s, that is, there was competition between the two blocs to attract developing countries into their influence area (Mc Namara). Things have changed after the collapse of the USSR and the increasing integration of economies of the Third World into the world market system. However, the rapidity of the early Bush Sr administration (Schlessinger) or of the European Commission in putting conjectures about global warming on the diplomatic agenda (only three years after the first numerical experiments through tri-dimension models), cannot be understood independently from its linkages to energy security and the geopolitical implications of the petroleum game.

Even today the reasons why developed countries are really concerned by climate change and the factors influencing the will to act will determine their capacity to open a dialogue with the South. There is a school of thought that interprets climate damages falling on developing countries as an additional source of economic and political instability, with possible propagation effects that are hard to control (including climate refugees). In this case damages falling on developing countries would be included in the objective function of the North, not for reasons of empathy, but for reasons of well-understood self-interests.

The question of issue linkages has also to be clarified from a South perspective. The bottomline seems clear. In the absence of a political push to take care of long-term climate damages, decision makers in developing countries cannot but try and benefit from climate negotiation to obtain significant reforms of the international economic order in exchange for their contribution.

But this general statement involves choice from a larger menu of options and depends on their degree of concern about global warming. Political teams who give no attention to climate risks will require higher direct incentives than those who do. The nature of the obstacles to development and development priorities are crucial.

Managing Global Commons

Climate negotiations between the North and South are intrinsically difficult because of substantive stakes. But past experience suggests that they can be made far more difficult by the very language used in these matters, either because the employed concepts do not entail the same semantics in each country, or because they relate to unsolvable issues.

Equity, Common but Differentiated Responsibilities, Property Rights

Most analysts of climate policies refer to burden sharing, with the idea that it should be equitable and should translate into a principle of common but differentiated responsibilities. It is easy, however, to demonstrate the difficulties relating to these concepts. The very concept of burden sharing is no longer relevant in case of a leverage effect of climate policies on development; the real problem relates rather to the funding for structural transitions. To be more specific, an enterprise benefiting from CDM (Clean Development Mechanism) credits through projects that facilitate its access to certain domestic markets (for example, to enhance energy efficiency, waste disposal and purification, rural electrification) will not entail a 'burden'. No consensus exists as to whether equity should be measured in the policy space or outcome space. In both cases the question arises whether criteria grounded in uncontroversial data can be found. Moreover, an embarrassing question arises when passing from the equity amongst countries (assessed at the aggregate per capita level) to equity amongst citizens of various countries, given existing discrepancies in the distribution of incomes. A poor citizen of a rich country can contribute far less to global warming than rich citizens of developing countries, and this may constitute a solid stumbling block to climate policies.

The principle of common but differentiated responsibilities is in large part a response to the legitimate concerns of developing countries and the recognition by developed countries that their responsibility was to make a demonstration effect, given their historical contribution to the problem and their higher economic and technical potential. However, it is difficult to derive direct consequences from this principle. The perverse effect of this principle is that only the incremental costs of measures are to be covered. Ten years of experience with the GEF (Global Environmental Facility) tell us that such incremental costs are extremely difficult to define, and that this out-measures with net social benefits.

Disconnecting the question of emissions quota allocation from the issue of property rights does not eliminate the discussion on equity and responsibility. Rather, it gives more flexibility in resolving this through an explicit debate about the perceived fairness and acceptability of the outcome of various institutional devices. It also leads the global community to expand the menu of 'future commitments' beyond the 'Kyoto style' quotas.

Market-based Instruments, Technological Transfers and Public Aid

The Kyoto framework is based on the idea that a world carbon market will generate funds to abate carbon cheaply in developing countries through the use of more efficient techniques. The CDM is one way to achieve this result in a more cumbersome manner in which countries do not make commitments on binding quotas. The attraction of the resulting financial and technological transfers has been supposed to be strong enough to spur developing countries into action. This framework presents a lot of advantages. However, its potential will remain underexploited as long as some misunderstandings remain. The basic reluctance of developing countries stems from the felt compulsion to sacrifice short-term growth and growth-generating projects such as rural electrification in order to maximise carbon abatement if they join the CDM. A few attempts have been made to demonstrate the capacity of the CDM to generate a leverage effect on development, but these attempts are inhibited by the permanence of other misunderstandings. One suspicion is that the CDM would be used as a pretext to decrease public aid. This is why it was increasingly presented as functioning on the basis of private funds and totally separated from public aid. The price to pay for this suspicion is that without synergy with public funding, the CDM will never be able to modify technological patterns in infrastructure sectors. This hunch was reinforced by the environmental additionality imperative, since in structural projects it is very difficult to ascertain what is 'additional'. There is an awareness that the heterogeneity of pre-existing economic and legal conditions and basic needs (rural electrification, water purification, etc.) matter. This leads some to prioritise project -based reductions with a focus on firms as a more realistic approach better suited to the heterogeneity of local conditions.

Industrial Competition and Carbon Leakages

The absence of commitments by developing countries to industrial competition is probably one of the key obstacles to making climate policies acceptable to Northern public opinion. In fact, economic analysis is weak on this point for reasons that cannot be developed here: the compensating effect of terms of trade; role from transportation costs for low value-added industry; role of recycling of revenue of carbon taxes or auctioned permits; and difficulty of capturing the impact of asymmetrical carbon constraints; and so on. However, whether it is necessary to have a consensus as well as a diversity in forms of commitments is a three-fold question: (*a*) should the rules for industry be harmonised while heterogeneity is preserved for other sectors? (*b*) will the Southern industry have a strategic behaviour independent from the Northern industry (given their interpenetration in many cases)? and (*c*) if yes, will the Southern industry (and their governments) accept some form of common rules even if their country has no binding targets.

Reforming the Negotiation Process

The very negotiation process is critical as an obstacle to disentangling the climate–development Gordian Knot. Some of the dimensions of this process that need due attention are:

1. **No representation without taxation:** Some developed countries are unhappy about giving representation to developing countries without any corresponding decrease in carbon emissions. This issue needs to be resolved. Moreover, the quality and level of representation of countries is very imbalanced in climate negotiations. This means that there is always uncertainty about each delegation representing the choice ultimately made by the country.
2. The lack of administration devoted to these issues, which are sometimes still perceived as exotic, is another problem area.
3. There is a gap between the discourses of development NGOs and those of governments, not to mention the gaps between development NGOs and environmental NGOs, which generates masking effects regarding the actual interests of developing countries.
4. There is a problem of capacity building and of allowing real experts on local development to have their say at each step of the process.
5. Last but not least is the difficulty arising from the heterogeneity of the G-77 plus China. This political group encompasses totally divergent interests, but represents a tool for developing countries to reinforce their diplomatic position against the North on other dimensions of international affairs.

Terms of the Negotiation and Nature of the Commitments

The importance of the prices and quantity dilemma was underestimated in the mid-1990s. This mistake should not be repeated when considering developing countries, because of the level of uncertainty concerning their emissions baseline and abatement costs (all transactions costs included). The first response is to accept the long-term coexistence of Kyoto type commitments in Annex B countries and commitments with a programmatic character (policies and measures). However, for reasons of both political credibility and of facilitating the emergence of a meaningful price signal, it would be useful to explore in greater depth the advantages of coupling new forms of quantity commitments (quotas plus price caps, non-binding targets, sector commitments) with diversified accompanying measures, including reforms of international funding. This would mean that the concept of commitment would run parallel with the concept of partnership. One step further in that direction would be to drop the concept of commitments for developing countries to retain only the partnership perspective.

Questions of Linkage to Other Regimes

Rather than elaborate much on this obvious issue, it will suffice to simply rank three problems, which are characterised by the same degree of importance and difficulty, but which cannot be discarded without further examination:

1. **Biodiversity convention:** Not only because of the possible trade-offs and/or synergies between carbon sequestration and protection of biodiversity, but also because developing services provided by the forest, either through new markets or through new forms of public intervention, may be one of the only sources of synergies between climate policies and development in some regions.
2. **Reforms of international public funding organisations.**
3. **Link with the WTO:** This link is natural as a part of the only means to secure real compliance. In the absence of war, trade barriers are the only direct means to force a reluctant country to comply. This is also, in principle, a place to resolve the question of distortions in international competition among countries with and without commitments or having different sorts of commitments.

The progress on these three issues has so far been inhibited by various of taboos. Their sources should be explored further.

References

Gandhi, Indira, Declaration by the then Prime Minister of India delivered at the UN Conference on Human Development and Environment. *http://www.unep.org/Documents.multilingual/Default.asp? Document1D-97&ArticleID*.

Myrdal, G. 1968. *Asian Drama: An Inquiry into the Poverty of Nations and the Challenge of World Poverty.*

Prebish, R. 1964. 'Towards a New Trade Policy for Development', Report of the Secretary General of the UN Conference on Trade and Development, New York.

Sacks, I. 1987. *Development and Planning.* New York: Cambridge University, Press and Paris: Maison des Sciences de l'Homme.

Schlesinger, J.R. 1989. 'Energy and Geopolitics in the 21st Century', Montreal: World Energy Conference, 14th Congress.

Sen, K. 1984. *Resources, Values and Development.* Oxford: Blackwell, and Cambridge, Mass.: Harvard University Press.

4

A Future for the Kyoto Protocol?

Roger Guesnerie*

Kyoto: Present Flaws

It has been established that the incentives to reduce emissions and stimulation to technical progress are complements rather than substitutes (see Guesnerie 2003a). On that basis, we argued for a division of given economic and financial efforts between R&D and emission reductions[1] according to some principles that need to be refined. Whatever it may be, the relative weight of the total collective efforts planned in Kyoto is too biased in favour of emission reduction initiatives and, therefore, unsatisfactory. The flaw of the Kyoto scheme in this regard is obvious and already calls for action. For instance, the countries that have ratified Kyoto, or at least some of them, should involve themselves in

* This text is based on the English translation of extracts from a report for an advisory economic group to the French Prime Minister (Conseil d'Analyse Economique). The report was presented in July 2002 and published in 2003 (Guesnerie 2003a).

A first translation from French to English was made by Dr J.J. Boillot and M. Labbouz. I thank in particular J.J. Boillot for his contribution to the translation and also for his suggestions and encouragement. I am also most grateful to Ajit Sinha for long discussions on the language and on the content.

[1] Ideally, part of the effort should be devoted to adaptation (to global warming), but action on this front today may be quite premature.

collective research on carbon-free technologies.[2] On this matter
a European initiative proposing cooperation on the basis of costs
and benefits sharing would be particularly welcome.

Another urgent problem, however, concerns developing countries. Non-participation of Southern countries, while limiting the
'carbon tax' base, increases costs to the Northern countries, at
first because it increases the level of tax to attain a given quantitative objective, and then it increases the incentive to move activities abroad. From this point of view, the Clean Development
Mechanism (CDM) is not very satisfactory even if the arrangement succeeds in keeping the South in the negotiation. Second,
Southern countries are rightly refusing a costly effort for the
moment. To ask India to pay for reducing its emissions per capita,
which is considerably lower than the figures for the United States,
is shocking.

Nevertheless, mutually advantageous solutions do exist, the
participation of developing countries with attractive conditions
for them also considerably reduces the abatement costs for developed countries. Most analyses have converged on this conclusion. A simulation exercise done by using the model GEMINI
E3[3] on an enlarged Kyoto at the world level with the initial emission rights distributed on a per capita basis shows, in a speculative
but spectacular manner, a possible middle-run reconciliation of
equity and efficiency. For example, on a worldwide market for
permits with rights proportional to population and a given target,
the price of the permits would be two or three times lower in the
year 2040 compared to the price on the assumption of an extended Kyoto scheme with the same target but without the participation of developing countries. The cost for Annex B countries
(the list of Annex B countries is given in the Appendix to this
chapter) would be three times lower, while the transfers from
Annex B countries to the rest of the world would be about 0.5
percentage points of the Annex B GDP. Even if the situation is
less simple in the long run, we would like others to share our

[2] These actions would eventually involve the private sector, but
could make creation of some ambitious collective institutions, such as
an International Commission for Research on Free Carbon Energies,
meaningful, bypassing the too narrow national scope.
[3] See Criqui, Vielle and Viguier (in Guesnerie 2003b), as well as
Bernard (2001) and Criqui et al. (1999).

conviction that *participation in the fight against climate change can be made attractive to developing countries*. Without going into detailed technical discussions, the proposal (see also Philibert 2002) could be based on either:

1. generous national quotas of 'hot air' such that as soon as the beneficiaries make some minimal efforts it assures them a positive transfer; or
2. non-binding quotas, which implies that exceeding them does not entail any penalties, whereas any improvement gives access to the international market for permits.

This alternative scheme could replace rather than be juxtaposed to the current CDM. Without doubt they would have to be linked with an increase in the objectives of the Annex B countries in order not to exacerbate the difficulties of implementing an international market for emissions rights to which the United States would not participate. In this case, the cost of observance would decrease in the end and the system would provide significant transfers towards the 'virtuous' Southern countries. Last, to avoid the legitimate mistrust of developing countries regarding some highly temporary 'carrots', these schemes should provide guarantees in the medium run; for example, by accepting the principles that in the medium or long run reflect an egalitarian logic, such as quotas on the basis of population, at least until a definite level. This point is discussed in detail later.

The exploration of the track that has just been suggested should be given high priority today. In our earlier work (Guesnerie 2003a) we have discussed the predictable effects on development of the total greenhouse gas (GHG) emissions, the narrow feature of the Kyoto framework, the limits that competitiveness puts on the effectiveness of an environmental policy with a too restricted base. All this and the mutually advantageous character of the suggested extension indicate how decisive this question will be for the future of policies against climate change. Let us also point out that even though this paper does not deal with the geopolitical aspects of the question, the position of the three big partners of this negotiation, India, China and Brazil, who could be affected in the future by some notable damages linked to climate change, offers hope for a realistic treatment of the question suggested here.[4]

Of course, it would be desirable to have the United States come back to the bargaining table. In the light of *a posteriori* judgement and better information, it is clear that Kyoto asked too much from the United States.[5] The late concession of the EU on the issue of market for permits might have been the first acknowledgement of this error. It is astonishing that the well-known extreme reluctance of US citizens to reduce their energy consumption did not make the negotiating partners recognise how difficult it was for them to 'swallow' the Kyoto potion, leaving aside the electoral contingencies. Naturally, it does not appear unreasonable to ask the the biggest polluter in the world (6 tons carbon equivalent per capita) to reduce 7 per cent of its emissions. To evoke its responsibility as both the biggest polluter and the richest country is not out of place. But this is a 'moral' argument and it does not take account of core economic issues such as the cost, and what we have called, the 'willingness to pay'. Let's note that today the American trend of the emissions between 1990 and Kyoto phase I is about +25 to +30 per cent due to inaction and demographic and economic growth. To reduce the emissions by 30 to 35 per cent even between 1997 and 2012 would have meant a rate of decarbonisation of 2 per cent per year, which is a very difficult task given the inertia of equipment and institutions, even if some strong reduction potentialities exist in the USA with weak or negative costs. The strategy that seems most reasonable now is to attempt, by negotiation, to convince developing countries

[4] We may, however, note the success of the first Chinese efforts regarding reduction of the emissions, despite the effective and potential role of coal in the Chinese economy.

[5] Despite the apparent contradiction between the positions of the candidate Al Gore and the elected president George W. Bush, most observers think that a different result of the American elections might not have changed the situation much. One might argue that this American position reflects a bad interpretation of their interests, in view of the rate of substitution between moral leadership and military leadership, and the economic cost of the latter.

to rejoin the Annex B countries as soon as possible. Paradoxically, the absence of the United States, which is apparently suspicious of solutions implying advantageous transfers to developing countries in the short run or an egalitarian agreement in the long run, could make this negotiation easier.

Kyoto: Can the Basic Design be Improved?

The Kyoto protocol has been designed around two basic dispositions: first, it sets quantity objectives (for participating nations that are given individual quotas, but consequently for the set of participants as a whole); second, it organises a world market for exchanging quotas. We come back successively to these two central features of the arrangement and pose the question: Is this basic design flawed, and can it be improved?

Most experts agree that the function that links global damages to the concentration of GHG, in the relevant intervals of carbon concentration, is linear in the short run. Therefore, the marginal damages would be relatively constant. Many economists think that in such a context regulation through a *price instrument* (to give a price signal in accordance with the expectation of marginal damage) should be preferred over regulation by *quantity* (to set a quantitative target according to the calculation of mathematical expectation) from an efficiency point of view (see Weitzman 1974; Philibert 2002). The argument can be explained intuitively: as the marginal cost of reduction, expressed in the variable stock, is rapidly increasing, while the marginal benefit is relatively constant, the rigidity of the quantitative objective entails an important and socially useless increase in costs in the case of unfavourable realisation of hazard on the cost, while it does not allow exploitation of the opportunities of welfare gains in the favourable case.

This argument was used either to refute the whole architecture of the Kyoto Protocol or to propose amendments to it. Here it is necessary to discuss the nature of the argument first and its scope next. We must note that quantity policy with market for permits constitutes a first insurance mechanism for participants against internal specific shocks. The argument in favour of a 'price' solution applies, therefore, to a structural mid-term uncertainty on costs rather than to a temporary one. Moreover, it raises a lot of technical issues,[6] and one has to keep in mind a more fundamental criticism for the long run; namely, the argument neglects one of the possible factors of ineffectiveness of a price instrument—it transfers the rent linked with the fossil energies without necessarily reducing their rate of extraction, a remark that pushed to its limits would invalidate all policies of taxation.

The invoked argument in favour of the 'price' solution, therefore, is not a devastating criticism of the whole architecture of Kyoto as some people think. If, however, a lesson has to be recommended from this discussion, it is that *a quantity policy is likely to increase the variability of costs beyond what is desirable.* This is because an insufficient smoothening has negative effects on welfare, but also perhaps because economic agents are risk-averse. Therefore, in order to limit the certainty equivalent of the costs, it is desirable to reduce their exposure. A combination of this argument with the one concerning the pattern of the damage function then suggests the usefulness of *a ceiling price* on the emissions permit market. Nevertheless, the analysis just sketched raises some questions about the adequacy of the recommended measures given the objectives. One may wonder, shouldn't the ceiling price apply to the 'total' price of GHG, a price that adds to the permit itself the market price of the underlying resources (for example, oil, gases or coal for the carbon dioxide), rather than to the price of the permits? In that case, instead of being ideally rigid, the

[6] The technical argument of Newell and Pizer (2000) in favour of a price solution should be seen with some reservations. It relies on a formalisation of costs, some convex cost functions in each period, which raises the question of inter-temporal aggregation. See Guesnerie (2003a) for details. Finally, regulations by quantities have advantages that are not taken into account in the model. For example, one could argue that a price fluctuation around the average value will have a positive effect on the incentive to research (the 'convexity in prices' of the revenue function of the innovator does not, however, seem to be empirically validated).

ceiling price of a permit might be ideally fluctuating to help stabilise the global ceiling price.[7]

To summarise: reducing intervention costs to the minimum helps in the success of any environmental policy. In this respect, the implementation of a policy that sets exclusively quantitative targets triggers cost variability; hence, it calls for some insurance mechanism. This is why one may regret *the absence of any safety valve* in the Kyoto scheme and wish for its inclusion in the future (Kopp et al. 1997). 'Safety' would be obtained by a guaranteed supply of permits at a ceiling price whenever the market price goes over it. As said before, such a ceiling price should ideally vary in certain cases in order to partially offset significant although possibly irrelevant variations in energy prices. In any case, the corresponding revenues could be recycled by an international institution following methods experienced at national levels, although they may be more difficult to implement at the international level. Similarly, an introduction of a *floor* price of the permits would help limit the randomness of the market value of abatements beyond national quotas.[8]

Apart from these flaws of quantitative regulation, the performance of the instruments set by the Kyoto Protocol is uncertain. For example, *the prejudgement in favour of the markets*

[7] This suggestion deserves a greater theoretical discussion as well as a more practical precision—on the one hand because it raises the question of the relevance of spot price signals for the energy market, and on the other, since the prices of the various GHG sources are themselves likely to vary in a different manner.

[8] Some suggestions were made by Victor (2000) to avoid 'junk permits' coming from countries not respecting their commitments. Let us also note the requirements of already adopted solutions, for example, that of a reserve for the commitment period. This is an unrecognised but essential mechanism: every country must keep in reserve an important part of its initial emissions. But the buying countries can also sell (temporarily) a part of their assigned quantity (10 per cent). The environmental integrity of the market is preserved (one cannot flood the market with permits that the country would later need to cover its emissions), while assuring its liquidity. A firm that is located in a net buying country, but surpasses its target, would nonetheless have access to the international market.

for emission permits relies on the relative empirical success of experiments, especially experiments done in the sulphur dioxide market in the United States. But the scope of the international market implemented by the Kyoto Protocol is completely different and nothing guarantees that an adjustment that has appeared as effective in a special context will still be as effective in a more general context. For instance, the 'banking' or emission credit accruals that allows a temporal smoothening of the effort may compromise in certain circumstances an effective stabilisation of expectations. Despite the favourable precedent of the sulphur dioxide market, the time that has been historically required to implement such adjustments in some of the existing financial markets should not be forgotten. There is, therefore, an *experimental* dimension in the implementation of the Kyoto mechanisms (which may be considered a merit and not a defect).[9]

In this respect, a band with a ceiling and a floor price, within the logic discussed, would have other virtues beyond the intertemporal smoothening of the costs emphasised so far (Cournède and Gastaldo 2001). First, it would contribute *to framing expectations,* which tackles the risk of market volatility, the reality of which has been confirmed by our few experiences so far. Second, a safety valve, which introduces a price regulation in a system based on quantitative objectives, is not a denial of the Kyoto principles. The ceiling price can be seen as a penalty for exceeding the quotas (it had been discussed as such in the previous negotiations without being adopted). The safety valve would be a substitute for the supervision mechanisms that Kyoto succeeded in making compulsory, but in a framework that leaves some grey areas. In the absence of a ceiling price, any country that finally grumbles about the required effort could simply postpone the foreseen reductions and undergo, as planned in the Marrakech agreements, a penalty involving a multiplier effect, which requires that 1.3 tons must be 'recovered' for each lacking ton during the second commitment period. However, despite the ban on participation in the permits market that the failure would entail,

[9] The price volatility observed on the American market for sulphur dioxide is somewhat disturbing.

environmental debts could be accumulated until it becomes irre-
coverable without a sharp cutting date in place.

Can Kyoto-like Arrangements be Made Durable?

The proposed improvements deal with the architecture of the
Kyoto Protocol, especially with its static aspects. To answer the
question of the 'durability' of Kyoto-like arrangements we need
to return to the inter-temporal dynamics of the agreement and
to the legitimacy of the international 'grandfathering' clause that
Kyoto phase I introduces.

Kyoto lends to two extreme interpretations. At the minimum
it is *a mutually advantageous agreement* that takes into account
the differences of costs and exposure to the greenhouse effect,
and does not necessarily call for universal participation. Apart
from the difficulties of the initial negotiations, the renegotiation
of the agreement after the contractual period is subject to much
potential inefficiency, as all sequential negotiations are. We will
not give an exhaustive list here, but simply underline a type of
Achilles' heel quite common in such cases, *the ratchet effect* (see
Freixas et al. 1985). First, let us ask the just evoked question of
how to punish a country that fails to fulfil its commitments. This
question, however, masks a less visible but more fearsome problem, that is, what will be the starting point for later renegotiations? The response, in principle, is crystal clear: to do as if the
previously accepted objectives had been met. It is, however, not
very realistic to think that it will be so: the 'default' would, of
course, be an argument for future discussion.[10] It will probably

[10] Even if some dispositions envisage an early renegotiation that
would limit this risk at the early steps. In that way the Kyoto Protocol
specifies in its item 3.9 that 'Commitments for subsequent periods for
Parties included in Annex I shall be established in amendments to Annex
B to this Protocol …. The Conference of the Parties serving as the
meeting of the Parties to this Protocol shall initiate the consideration
of such commitments at least seven years before the end of the first
commitment period.'

increase the de facto bargaining power and then, through successive agreements, give an increasing part of the surplus to the defaulting party.

A more ambitious or a more utopian interpretation of Kyoto is to read it, like many commentators have, as the first step towards *a progressive cancellation of the historic rights* (grandfathering) that give advantage in the short run to the biggest GHG polluters.[11] One would thus substitute for the logic of the historic rights a more 'egalitarian' logic, entailing, for instance, an allocation of national emission rights based on population criteria. Such a formula cannot claim to be 'fair' in a deep sense, and even less a solution to the general and widely indefinite problem of implementation of international justice. However, economic development today has generated a need to limit the use of a former free good, and calls for a definition of new rights on *a worldwide scale*. An egalitarian distribution seems to be, all things being equal, a basis for the allocation of rights that is quite natural and is a step forward in the direction of 'equity', whatever the exact meaning one gives to this word. Without discussing further this formula, we might believe that this utopia was implicit in the Kyoto Protocol. It might have contributed in setting up a high required effort for the US beyond what was politically realistic. On the contrary, an explicit recognition of an egalitarian principle could have contributed to the consent of developing countries by ascribing to them some 'hot air' today and offering them some good perspectives in the long run.

This brief analysis suggests two conclusions:

1. In the long run the sustainability of an international agreement like Kyoto would have considerably improved if it had incorporated an agreement *on the principles of burden sharing in the long run*. Such an agreement should focus on the implicit or explicit property rights that will emerge

[11] The Bonn Agreement stipulates that the Annex I countries will have to implement some domestic actions that aim to reduce emissions such that it reduces the per capita differences between developed countries and developing countries, while working towards the ultimate objective of the Convention.

at the end. In the absence of such an agreement, which might be linked to *an indicative target* of the long-term objective (and also perhaps with indicative trajectories), opportunistic behaviours that reduce the effectiveness of the action will be recurrent. Even if the adopted scheme must remain simple, it should be flexible so that in particular the transition trajectories may react to a set of considerations absent from the long-term target. For instance, *transitional indexation* on growth (as an insurance mechanism) is compatible with a certain equality of registered rights in a long-term perspective.

2. The arguments of simplicity, equity and political consent on a worldwide scale give a 'focal' status to *the egalitarian solution*. Egalitarian solutions, which allow for real transfers to the developing countries, also bring advantages to the Northern countries: they are hence more politically realistic than appears at first sight. The efficiency surplus that these solutions determine in the short run, since they entail the consent of the developing countries, has a counterpart in the long run.[12]

However, there are two reasons to believe that a purely egalitarian policy, in spite of its focal position, is not the 'solution'. First, the residual inequality of emissions distribution will remain important for long. This inequality is clearly shown in the graph (Figure 4.1) depicting cumulated emissions according to cumulated population and to their Gini index for different scenarios of property right allocation.[13] Second, it should be noted that egalitarian solutions, however, entail unacceptable costs to certain parties (for example, Russia), given their expected 'willingness to pay', as is shown by the study by Criqui et al. (see Guesnerie 2003b), which indicates the middle-term efforts required for North

[12] In the long run, the political acceptability of per capita emissions convergence scenarios can be improved by the fact that the 'veil of ignorance', even if incomplete, reinforces the acceptability of the distributive argument that they incorporate.

[13] One of which integrates the convergence objective of per capita emissions at the planetary scale and leads to the curve nearest to the bissectrix.

Figure 4.1
Cumulated Emissions According to
Cumulated Population Under Different Scenarios

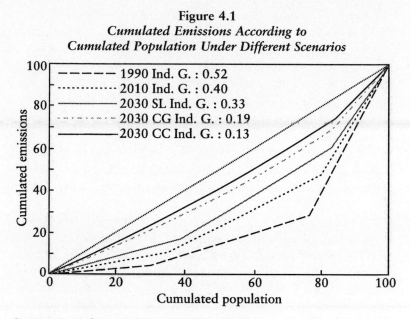

Source: Complément Criqui, Vielle et Viguier à ce rapport. Voir le complément pour la signification des scénarios.
Notes:
Scenario SL: Soft landing
Scenario CC: Contraction and convergent
Scenario CG: Global compromise
Ind. G: Gini index

America and the former Soviet Union countries under the scenario of convergence of per capita emissions (also see Germain and Van Steenberghe 2001).

The combination of these two remarks leads us to recommend a widening of short- and mid-term agreements like Kyoto and to assign them an agreement not on the amount but on the principles of allocation of the emission rights till 2050–70. Whatever the exact formulation of this principle, the allocation formula should remain simple and strike a compromise between egalitarian logic and one of acceptability.[14]

[14] One can, for example, define for each country a fictitious population, taking account of its present and future population and its degree

One cannot deal with the question of acceptability without returning to a more basic problem of participation. The permanence of an environmental agreement like Kyoto, as well designed as it could be, is constantly threatened by the free-rider problem. It means that it is impossible to exclude someone from the use of collective goods produced by the agreement. Each country's most likely best interest is not to join an agreement when others already have.[15] This problem does not disappear even in the framework of limited action and increases with increase in the efforts demanded. It is difficult to build an international order when the reasons to participate are so fragile. To reinforce it, do we need to widen the framework of the agreement?

The earlier reflection on the relations between international trade and global collective goods started with the necessity to preserve the efficiency of environmental efforts undertaken by a group of countries (the signatory countries) and led to the reconsideration of the well-founded separation between the fields of trade and global environmental goods. But the issue is wider: in the absence of any world governmental institution, should ideally international agreements on trade or any global public goods be globalised? We will make only a few remarks here. Economic analysis suggests that the widening scope would increase the range of mutually advantageous agreements, a conclusion that does not invalidate, it seems, most realistic theories of negotiations available today. This suggestion, which of course should be established by more studies, does not imply that the preparatory works for a global agreement cannot or should not be separated. It does not at all imply that technical agencies such as the WTO and a future possible agency for the environment should merge. Let us admit that the compromises are better, from the efficiency point of view, when made global on both trade and environmental policies. Still, it cannot be denied that such a solution also changes

---

of exposure to the greenhouse effect (Russia thus having a fictitious population that is greater than its real population).

[15] One can envisage penalties, of which Aldy et al. (2001) suggest a list, including the most anecdotal ones like exclusion from the Olympic Games or Football World Cup.

the bargaining powers of the partners. In the context of the con-
tention of Kyoto it would, without doubt, modify it in favour of
Europe and to the detriment of the United States.

The assessment of the feasibility and diplomatic opportunities of such actions is of course out of the scope of this paper. It
is nevertheless worth mentioning the fact that an environmental
compromise like Kyoto is necessarily fragile and that it can be
reinforced only by coupling it with some other international
agreements (trade, other environmental agreements, etc.) that
are less subject to free-riding. It means that a widened space for
compromises is beneficial and is likely necessary for the viability
of an ambitious environmental agreement.

Some Final Words on Perspectives

Our complete report (Guesnerie 2003a, 2003b) renders an overall judgement in favour of the initial action envisaged in Kyoto
regarding both its scope and methods. Let us recall the reasons
adduced for this judgement.

First of all, given the present state of scientific knowledge, it is
difficult to come to terms with climatic risks while postponing
significant action to an indeterminate date. The timeliness of
implementing the 'hardware' and the 'software' of a policy of
worldwide control of greenhouse gas emissions is not very doubt-
ful. The scope of the initial effort envisaged in Kyoto can be
discussed. It takes place within a reasonable range, in the sense
that there are good reasons, but no convincing proof, to think
that Kyoto does too much or too little. The nature of the uncertainty and the temporal horizon make cost–benefit analysis difficult. But the arguments that conclude that the pace of reductions
in Kyoto are too quick rely on simplistic economic calculations,
and are rather less convincing than those that conclude (for example using option values arguments) in favour of insufficient
present abatement. The truth is that our comprehension of the
climatic consequences of the growth of GHG concentration is
insufficient, and this position pleads for prudence. Prudence and

86 *Roger Guesnerie*

credibility, as aimed for in Kyoto, recommend going well beyond symbolic actions.

The flexibility mechanisms notably aim at lowering the implementation costs of policies. Markets for tradable emission permits constitute a major innovation, which most likely would considerably increase the efficiency of the action, even if the scheme has never been experimented on this scale before. On the other hand, however, this paper points to some reservations about the implementation of the Clean Development Mechanism. More generally, the architecture envisaged in Kyoto is based on rigid quantitative commitments that should ideally be more flexible. But this quantitative frame is excessively criticised. The implementation of alternative mechanisms, considering probable supply reactions in the energy market, is more difficult than generally expected. Nevertheless, some form of price supervision, like the safety valve mechanism alluded to earlier, is desirable. Besides, the Kyoto architecture allows renegotiations and opens the door to limited transfers between nations. It is an improvable evolving scheme that could possibly lead to other 'Kyoto-compatible' architectures.

Even though this paper does not evaluate most of the political aspects of the subject, in particular the political willingness of Europe placed in a position of ecological leader, it underlines the costs of renunciation of Kyoto and argues in favour of keeping it alive and improving it. Nevertheless, before recapitulating the principal suggestions that were made in this direction, it is useful to evoke several scenarios of the post-Kyoto period, starting with two extreme scenarios, an idealised Kyoto, and a weak and frayed Kyoto.

A vigorous and 'idealised' post-Kyoto governance could include:

1. Some quantitative Kyoto-like targets, agreed upon by sovereign entities. But the agreement would be widened to the definition of long-term allocation principles for national emission rights. It would match with the provisional perspectives of the implementation of these principles. Equality of rights for all inhabitants of the world would be the focal position of the discussion, even though long-term principles

should necessarily compromise to reconcile it with mobilisation capacity and economic and political realism. Therefore, the agreement would also reflect the exposure of the protagonists to climatic risk.

2. An assignment of binding objectives to be fulfilled within a period together with some indicative paths coherent with long-term perspectives.

3. The possibility of meeting targets of the period not only by internal reduction efforts but also by trade on international markets for emission. In this respect, the regulation of these markets by a floor price and a ceiling price would operate, according to the circumstances, as a tax or subsidy, and would help provide insurance and entail at least a minimum incentive for abatement. Such a regulation, however, should aim to frame user prices of fossil fuels, that ultimately determine GHG emissions, and not only the price of permits. The expected receipts of the scheme could be collectively managed and could help implement some specific assistance to developing countries, and also finance an international research network.

4. The solidity of the agreement would be guaranteed by its inclusion in a *packaged deal* of international agreements including trade agreements, and defining rules of the game for an interdependent and supportive international order.

The idealised Kyoto sketched here, which can be pleaded at least from the point of view of efficiency, is likely to be utopian. One essential obstacle to such a Kyoto utopia may be the reluctance on the part of the international community, not only the US, to agree to solutions implying a significant, although still very modest, redistribution of the planet's income. The state of things today, therefore, makes this utopia improbable. But a spectacular increase of the danger of climatic change, if it was proved, would make an increasing number of people aware of it and thus could give the Kyoto utopia a chance. Nevertheless, in the short run, the situation is less favourable, and the danger of seeing Kyoto become more and more weak is real.

The demonstration effect of a limited club of nations who have been unsuccessful in convincing the international community to join them and who represent a minority both in terms of number and volume of emissions may neither be very productive nor rewarding. In order not to lose the political support of their citizens worried about a low value of benefit–cost ratio, it may lead to limited efforts by their governments. Moreover, these countries may find their competitiveness weakened in some segments of the world market of goods and services. In a nutshell, the 'demonstration effect' risks being highly limited.

One fears that another kind of frayed Kyoto stands out today, that is, Russian 'hot air' rather than the political erosion of European determination. Russia, due to its recent deindustrialisation, is in possession of excess permits for 'hot air' and may lower the price of permits on the market to the extent that it deters abatement efforts by other countries. Furthermore, both the credibility of the climate policy and incentives to research on clean technology that a significantly high carbon price insures, and that are the cardinal virtues of the international permit market, disappear with it. Until the end of the first commitment period in 2012, the European Union has the responsibility to contain these risks. It must proceed in an effective manner to a significant reduction of its emissions, while managing the question of Russian 'hot air'.

Finally, the action taken within the Kyoto framework will be fully meaningful only if it can continue after 2013, for which it is necessary to prepare now. Therefore, the ambition of the Kyoto Protocol will be lasting only if at least some important developing countries are associated with the extension of the agreement. For that the Annex B countries will have to present economically attractive solutions to developing countries, which they have the capacity to do.

These solutions could be more or less inventive. However, to be mutually advantageous, that is, to lower the cost for rich countries and trigger significant income transfers on a sufficiently long period to developing countries, they will have to be generous in the short run and give solid guarantees on the rules of the game in the middle run. Without broaching diplomatic and geopolitical questions, our larger report (Guesnerie 2003a) expresses the conviction that an agreement on the basis of the suggested solutions is possible as soon as the two conditions that have just been underlined are met. Supporting the implementation of efficient systems of measurement for emissions in developing countries is also a concrete priority today.

Still in the middle run, together with quantitative control, some form of control of the GHG price, that comes within a *safety valve* and/or sets an inferior bound to the incentive with a price floor, should be integrated in the scheme. But, although this point deserves elaboration, the mechanism might be all the more satisfactory if it stabilises the total price of carbon and not only the 'carbon tax'. Moreover, the agreement could evolve towards adopting architectures that are 'Kyoto compatible', either more effective or more adaptable to the political economy of negotiation. It is necessary, in whatever manner, to solve the problem of the inter-temporal inefficiencies that come with the ratchet effect more satisfactorily than we do today. It is also necessary to widen the space of carbon tax to the whole planet. In strict Kyoto logic, the solution to these problems is likely to require an agreement on the principles of a long-run distribution of emission rights on the one hand, and, on the other hand, a coercive participation, of which the privileged mean could be the merging or logrolling of international compromises outside the lone field of environment. However, these problems have other Kyoto-compatible solutions, the understanding of which future studies must imperatively deepen.

Appendix

List of Annex B Countries

***Party Quantified Emission Limitation or Reduction Commitment
(percentage of base year or period)***

Australia	108	Liechtenstein	92
Austria	92	Lithuania*	92
Belgium	92	Luxembourg	92
Bulgaria*	92	Monaco	92
Canada	94	Netherlands	92
Croatia*	95	New Zealand	100
Czech Republic*	92	Norway	101
Denmark	92	Poland*	94
Estonia*	92	Portugal	92
European	92	Romania*	92
Community		Russian Federation*	100
Finland	92	Slovakia*	92
France	92	Slovenia*	92
Germany	92	Spain	92
Greece	92	Sweden	92
Hungary*	94	Switzerland	92
Iceland	110	Ukraine*	100
Ireland	92	United Kingdom of	92
Italy	92	Great Britain and	
Japan	94	Northern Ireland	
Latvia*	92	United States of America**	93

* Countries that are undergoing the process of transition to a market economy.
** The USA later declared its intention not to ratify the protocol and not to decide any target of emission reductions.

Thirty-nine countries are part of Annex B to the Kyoto Protocol. Even though Annex 1 and Annex B are often used as if they were the same, only countries from Annex B have some obligations of emission reductions in the frame of the Kyoto Protocol. Moreover, Bielorussia and Turkey are part of Annex 1 but not of Annex B. Croatia, Liechtenstein and Monaco are part of Annex B but not of Annex 1.

References

Aldy J., P. Orzag and J. Stiglitz. 2001. *Climate Change: An Agenda for Collective Action.* Centre on Global Climate Change.

Bernard, A. 2001. 'Vers une Nouvelle Architecture du Protocole de Kyoto: Quelques Simulations Préliminaires Effectuées Avec le Modèle Gemini E3'. Miméo, Conseil Général des Ponts et Chaussées.

Cournède, B. and S. Gastaldo. 2001. 'Comparaison d'Instruments Prix Quantités Dans le cas de L'effet de Serre'. Miméo, Ministère de l'Economie, des Finances et de l'Industrie.

Criqui, P., S. Mima and L. Viguier. 1999. 'Marginal Abatement Costs of CO_2 Emission Reductions, Geographical Flexibility and Concrete Ceilings: An Assessment Using the POLES Model', *Energy Policy*, 27: 585–601.

Freixas, X., R. Guesnerie and J. Tirole. 1985. 'Planning Under Incomplete Information and the Ratchet Effect', *Review of Economic Studies*, 52: 173–92.

Germain M. and E. Van Steenberghe. 2001. 'Constraining Acceptable Allocations of Tradable Greenhouse Gases Emissions Quotas by Acceptability'. Mimeo, Core , Louvain.

Guesnerie, R. 2003a. Les Enjeux Économiques de L'effet de Serre', *Kyoto et L'économie de L'effet de Serre*, 9–90.

———. 2003b. (sous la direction de) 'Kyoto et l'économie de l'effet de serre'. La Documentation Française, Paris.

Kopp, R., R. Morgenstern and W. Pizer. 1997. 'Something for Everyone: A Climate Policy that Both Environmentalists and Industry Can Live With'. Washington, DC: Resources for the Future.

Newell, D. and W. Pizer. 2000. 'Regulating Stock Externalities Under Uncertainties', *Resources for the Future*, DP 9910, Washington, DC.

Philibert, C. 2002. *Evolution of Mitigation Commitments.* Paris: Agence Internationale de l'Energie.

Victor, D. 2000. *Collapse of the Kyoto Protocol.* Princeton: Princeton University Press.

Weitzman, M. 1974. 'Prices versus Quantities', *Review of Economic Studies*, 41.

5

Estimating Environmentally Sustainable Industrial Development: A Study of Thermal Power Generation

M.N. Murty and S.C. Gulati

Introduction

The environment provides waste disposal services as productive inputs to industry. Given environmental regulation, producers place a value on these inputs the same way they value other conventional inputs like labour, man-made capital and materials. Environmental regulation meant for ensuring environmentally sustainable industrial development imposes a cost on the industry. The methodology for integrated environmental and economic accounting as laid down by the United Nations calls this maintenance cost or cost to industry for maintaining the quality of the environment at its natural regenerative level. Two alternative models in the theory of production are considered here for estimating maintenance cost.

The first considers pollution load as one of the inputs, and production function and material balance condition in power generation as simultaneous equations. The second model describes the technology of power generation as one of producing jointly good output, power and bad output, pollution load. In both models the processes of waste generation or material balance conditions are considered. In the first model material balance condition is explicitly incorporated, while in the second it is implicit in the production relation expressed in reduced form as output distance function. [1]

The producer demand price for waste disposal services from the environment could be defined as the value of marginal product in the case of the first model. Alternatively, it could be defined as the opportunity cost in terms of good output foregone to reduce bad output in the case of the second model. In any attempt to measure green GDP, estimates of these shadow prices are necessary to value changes in environmental quality brought about by developmental activities.

A Model Describing Production and Pollution Generating Processes Considering Pollution as a Productive Input

The technology of a polluting firm can be described as containing two parts: T_1, a standard technology set, showing the way in which inputs get transformed into outputs, and T_2, showing nature's residual generating mechanism.[2] Suppose a firm employs a vector of inputs $x \in \mathfrak{R}^N_+$ to produce a vector of outputs $y \in \mathfrak{R}^M_+$. $\mathfrak{R}^N_+$, $\mathfrak{R}^M_+$, are non-negative N- and M-dimensional Euclidean spaces respectively. Let $P(x)$ be the feasible output set for the given input vector x, and $L(y)$ is the input requirement set for a given output vector y. Let us say that the firm generates pollution z because it uses a certain input x_s (for instance suspended particulate matter generated because it uses coal). Now the technology sets are defined as:

$$T_1 = \{(y, x) \in \mathfrak{R}^{M+N} / y \in P(x)\}.$$

$$T_2 = \{(y, z, x) \in \mathfrak{R}^{M+N+1} / z = g(x_s)\}.$$

$$T = T_1 \cap T_2. \tag{5.1}$$

[1] Murty and Russell (2002) have shown that there could be problems in defining the shadow prices of pollution and finding the trade-off between pollution and output along the production frontier in both these models. However, they have shown that modelling abatement as an intermediary input does yield positive trade-off and facilitates the definition of shadow prices of pollution.

[2] See Murty and Russell (2002) for a lucid description of technologies of a polluting firm with material balance condition and pollution abatement.

Now assume that the firm is involved in pollution abatement and produces abatement output y_a, in addition to conventional output represented by the output vector y, and uses this abatement output to reduce pollution z. The technology sets in this case are defined as:

$$T_1 = \{(y, y_a, x) \in \Re^{M+N+1}/y \in P(x)\}.$$
$$T_2 = \{(y, y_a, z, x) \in \Re^{M+N+2}/z = g(y_a, x_s)\}.$$
$$T = T_1 \cap T_2. \tag{5.2}$$

The model with abatement output and material balance condition as described in (5.2) is estimated using data for thermal power generation in the state of Andhra Pradesh. The model for estimation is given as follows:

$$\ln y_i = a_1 + a_2 \ln x_{1i} + a_3 \ln x_{2i} + a_4 \ln x_{3i} + a_5 \ln x_{4i}$$
$$+ a_6 d_{1i} + a_7 d_{2i} + a_8 d_{3i} + a_9 d_{4i} + u_i \tag{5.3}$$
$$\ln z_i = b_1 + b_2 \ln x_{4i} + b_3 \ln y_i + v_i \tag{5.4}$$

where x_1, x_2, x_3 and x_4 are respectively capital, labour, energy and reduction in pollution load (abatement effort), and d_1, d_2, d_3 and d_4 are dummy variables representing power plants, y and z are output (electricity generated) and actual pollution load, and u and v are disturbance terms. The inputs capital, labour and energy are respectively measured as the value of capital services, wage bill and expenditures on energy inputs. The values of all these variables are expressed at constant prices. The abatement effort (x_4) of the plant is measured as the pollution reduction obtained (difference between influent and effluent flows). Influent flows of each plant are estimated using engineering norms (x_7) or emission coefficients, while the effluent flows (z) are the actual emissions by the plants after their abatement efforts. The analysis is done considering emissions of suspended particulate matter (SPM) as pollution loads. Equation (5.3) is a simple Cob-Douglas production function, while the equation (5.4) represents material balance condition with a plant having both production processes of electricity generation and pollution abatement.

Appendix 5.1 provides data on production details of thermal power plants of the Andhra Pradesh Power Generating Company (APGENCO) over a period of eight years between 1996 and 2003. There are five thermal plants of APGENCO, resulting in 40 observations on each variable for estimating the model. Appendix A2 provides estimated pollution loads of SPM, nitrous oxides and sulphur dioxide. The descriptive statistics of variables used in estimating equations (5.3) and (5.4) are given in Table 5.1. The model consisting of a system of two simultaneous equations is estimated using the method of three stage least squares. Table 5.2 provides the estimates of the parameters of the model. The estimates of coefficients of all the variables in the model have the relevant signs and most of them are significant at 5 per cent level. In the equation explaining the material balance condition, the pollution load (z) of a plant is negatively related to the pollution abatement effort (x_4) and positively related to output (y) as expected.

Taking the values of all other variables in the production function at their sample mean values, the marginal productivity function of abatement effort (SPMEF) could be derived from the estimated production function as:

$$\partial Output \Big/ \partial SPME = 149.6559 \times SPME^{-0.90347}$$

Figure 5.1 depicts the marginal productivity curve of abatement effort. The current electricity tariff (tariff during the year 2002–04) charged by APTRANSCO (Andhra Pradesh Transmission Corporation) is, on average, Rs. 3.68 per unit. The value of marginal product of SPMEF at its sample mean is computed as Rs. 1,117 per tonne while it is Rs. 1,029 per tonne at the level of pollution abatement required as per the safety standards specified for thermal power generation in India.

A Model Describing Production Processes of Firms with Joint Production of Good Output and Pollution

Suppose that a firm employs a vector of inputs $x \in \mathfrak{R}^N_+$ to produce a vector of outputs $y \in \mathfrak{R}^M_{++}$, $\mathfrak{R}^N_+$, $\mathfrak{R}^M_{++}$ are non-negative N- and M-dimensional Euclidean spaces respectively. Let $P(x)$ be the feasible output set for the given input vector x, and $L(y)$ is the input requirement set for a given output vector y. Now the technology set is defined as:

$$T = \{(y, x) \in \mathfrak{R}^{M+N}_+, y \in P(x)\} \tag{5.5}$$

Table 5.1

Descriptive Statistics of Variables Used in Estimation of Equations

	Output (Million Units) (y)	Capital (Million) (x_1)	Wage (Million) (x_2)	Fuel (Million) (x_3)	SPM (100 Tonnes) (z)	SPMEN (100 Tonnes) (x_7)	SO_2 (100 Tonnes) (x_5)	NO_x (100 Tonnes) (x_6)
Mean	3984.666	2141.390	287.6656	3976.046	91.9737	1049.108	126.1028	19.873
Standard Deviation	3938.285	2147.295	260.8882	3590.769	97.0023	1096.374	152.4888	39.049

Source: Andhra Pradesh Power Generating Corporation (AP-GENCO).

Table 5.2
Three Stage Least Squares Estimates of Parameters of the Model

Dependent Variable Electricity Output		
Parameter	Variables	Coefficients(t Stat)
a_1	Constant	0.571835 (0.904)
a_2	Capital	0.123319* (4.642)
a_3	Wage	0.098759* (2.042)
a_4	SPME	0.09653* (5.033)
a_5	Fuel	0.454351* (5.613)
a_6	d_1	0.278941* (4.274)
a_7	d_2	0.568066* (8.644)
a_8	d_3	−0.246717 (−1.583)
a_9	d_4	−0.868909* (−4.977)
Adjusted R^2	0.997695	

Dependent Variable SPM (Actual Load)		
2nd Equation	Variables	Coefficients
b_1	Constant	−3.618222* (−3.103)
b_2	SPME	−1.076761* (−3.283)
b_3	Output	1.845845* (4.788)
Adjusted R^2	0.477009	

Note: Figures in brackets are *t* values; * shows 1 per cent significance level.

Figure 5.1
The Marginal Productivity Curve of Abatement Effort

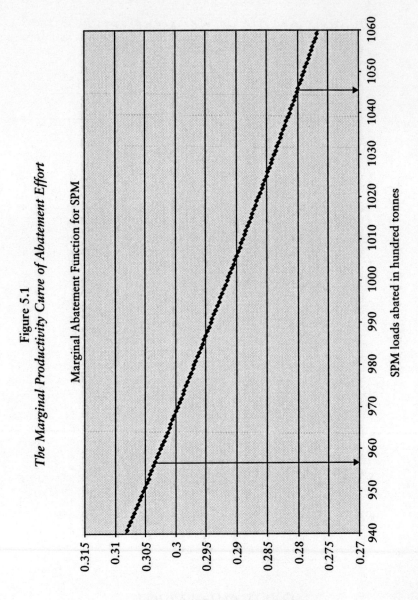

Marginal Abatement Function for SPM

The output distance function is defined as:

$$D_0(x, y) = \min\{\lambda > 0 : (y/\lambda) \in P(x)\} \ \forall x \in \mathfrak{R}^N_+ \qquad (5.6)$$

Equation (5.6) characterises the output possibility set by the maximum equi-proportional expansion of all outputs consistent with the technology set (5.5).

The assumptions about the disposability of outputs become very important in the context of a firm producing both good and bad outputs. The normal assumption of strong or free disposability about the technology implies that:

$$\text{if } (y_1, y_2) \in P(x) \text{ and } 0 \leq y_1^* \leq y_1, 0 \leq y_2^* \leq y_2 \Rightarrow (y_1^*, y_2^*) \in P(x).$$

That means we can reduce some outputs given the other outputs or without reducing them. This assumption may exclude important production processes such as undesirable outputs like pollution. The assumption of weak disposability is relevant in describing such production processes. The assumption of weak disposability implies that:

$$\text{if } y \in P(x) \text{ and } 0 \leq \lambda \leq 1 \Rightarrow \lambda y \in P(x).$$

That is, a firm can reduce bad output only by simultaneously decreasing the output of desirable produce.

The idea of deriving shadow prices using output and input distance functions and duality results is originally from Shepard (1970). A study by Fare et al. (1990) was the first to compute shadow prices using the distance function and non-parametric linear programming methods.

The derivation of absolute shadow prices for bad outputs using distance function requires the assumption that one observed output price is shadow price. Let y_1 denote good output and assume that the observed good output price (r_1^0) equals its absolute shadow price (r_1^s) (that is, for $m = 1$, $r_1^0 = r_1^s$). Fare et al. (1993) have shown that the absolute shadow prices for each observation of undesirable output $(m = 2, \ldots, M)$ can be derived as:[3]

$$(r_m^s) = (r_1^0) \bullet \frac{\partial D_0(x, y)/\partial y_m}{\partial D_0(x, y)/\partial y_1}. \qquad (5.7)$$

[3] See Fare (1988) for derivation.

The shadow prices reflect the trade-off between desirable and undesirable outputs at the actual mix of outputs, which may or may not be consistent with the maximum that is allowed under regulation (ibid.: 376). Further, the shadow prices do not require that the plants operate on the production frontier.

Estimation Procedure and Data

In order to estimate the shadow prices of pollutants (bad outputs) for thermal power generation in Andhra Pradesh using equation (5.7), the parameters of output distance function has to be estimated. The translog functional form[4] used for estimating these functions is given as follows:

$$\ln D_0(x, y) = \alpha_0 + \Sigma\beta_n \ln x_n + \Sigma\ \alpha_m \ln y_m + 1/2\Sigma\ \Sigma\beta_m (\ln x_n)(\ln x_n') + 1/2\ \Sigma\ \Sigma\alpha_{mm} (\ln y_m)(\ln_m') + \Sigma\Sigma\gamma_{nm}(\ln x_n)(\ln y_m) + \iota_1 d_1 + \iota_2 d_2 + \iota_3 d_3 + \iota_{d4} \tag{5.8}$$

where x and y are respectively $Nx1$ and $Mx1$ vectors of inputs and outputs. There are three inputs: capital, labour and energy; and three outputs: good output like electricity, bad outputs like SPM, nitrous oxides and sulphur dioxide. And, d_i is the dummy variable representing the plant. A linear programming technique is used to estimate the parameters of a deterministic translog output distance function (Aigner and Chu 1968). This is accomplished by solving the problem:

$$\max \Sigma[\ln D_0 (x, y) - \ln 1], \tag{5.9}$$

subject to:

(i) $\ln D_0 (x, y) \leq 0$
(ii) $(\partial \ln D_0 (x, y))/(\partial \ln y_1) \geq 0$
(iii) $(\partial \ln D_0 (x, y))/(\partial \ln y_i) \leq 0$
(iv) $(\partial \ln D_0 (x, y))/(\partial \ln x_i) \leq 0$

[4] Many earlier studies for estimating shadow prices of pollutants have used the translog functional form for estimating output distance function. These include Pittman (1983), Fare et al. (1990), and Coggins and Swinton (1996).

(v) $\sum \alpha_m = 1$

$\sum \alpha_{mm} = \sum \gamma_{nm} = 0$

(vi) $\alpha_{mm} = \alpha_{mm}$

$\beta_{nn} = \beta_{nn}$

Here the first output is desirable and the remaining $(M-1)$ outputs are undesirable. The objective function minimises the sum of the deviations of individual observations from the frontier of technology. Since the distance function takes a value of less than or equal to one, the natural logarithm of the distance function is less than or equal to zero, and the deviation from the frontier is less than or equal to zero. Hence, the maximisation of the objective function [is done implying] the minimisation of sum of deviations of individual observations from the frontier. The constraints in (i) restrict the individual observations to be on or below the frontier of technology. The constraints in (ii) ensure that the desirable output has a non-negative shadow price. The constraints in (iv) restrict the shadow prices of bad outputs as non-positive, that is, weak disposability of bad outputs, whereas the restrictions in (v) are the derivative property of output distance function with respect to inputs, that is the derivatives of output distance function with respect to inputs is non-increasing. The constraints in (v) impose homogeneity of degree +1 in outputs (which also ensures that technology satisfies weak disposability of outputs). Finally, constraints in (vi) impose symmetry. There is no constraint imposed to ensure non-negative values to the shadow prices of undesirable outputs.

Output distance function described earlier is estimated by considering electricity as good output and pollution loads of SPM, nitrous oxides and sulphur dioxide as bad outputs using data about thermal power generation by APGENCO in AP. The data set used is given in the appendices. Table 5.3 provides the descriptive statistic of variables used in the estimation of distance function. The estimates of parameters of distance function are reported in Table 5.4. Using the estimated distance function, the shadow price of a pollutant is estimated in terms of units of good output foregone for one unit reduction in pollution. The computed shadow prices for a representative plant of APGENCO

Table 5.3
Descriptive Statistics of Variables Used in the Estimation of Distance Function

	Electricity Generated (Million Units)	Coal (100 Tonnes)	SPMA (100 Tonnes)	SO_2A (100 Tonnes)	NO_xA (100 Tonnes)	CO_2EN (100 Tonnes)
Mean	3984.666	316.669	91.97375	126.1028	19.87342	6223.227
Std	3938.285	3058.713	97.00221	152.4888	39.04904	6005.38

	Capital (Rs Lakh)	Wage (Rs Lakh)	Fuel (Rs Lakh)	Other Inputs (Rs Lakh)
Mean	21413.9	2876.656	39760.46	914.4735
Std	21472.95	2608.882	35907.69	1213.855

Source: APGENCO.
Note: A: actual load; EN: load as per engineering norms.

Table 5.4
Estimates of Parameters of Output Distance Function

		Coefficients of the Output Distance Function Model						
Variables	Description	Coefficients	Variables	Coefficients	Variables	Coefficients	Variables	Coefficients
y_1	Electricity	1.294	y_{11}	0.059	y_1x_3	−0.405	y_4x_1	−0.002
y_2	SPM	−0.151	y_{22}	3.04E-04	y_1x_4	0.039	y_4x_2	−0.005
y_3	SO_2	−0.169	y_{33}	−0.004	y_{23}	8.05E-04	y_4x_3	−7.90E-04
y_4	NO_x	0.025	y_{44}	−2.47E-04	y_{24}	−1.61E-04	y_4x_4	0
x_1	Capital	1.006	x_{11}	0.05	y_2x_1	−9.94E-04	x_{12}	−0.221
x_2	Wage	0.149	x_{22}	−0.03	y_2x_2	0.015	x_{13}	−0.106
x_3	Fuel	−2.899	x_{33}	0.578	y_2x_3	0.029	x_{14}	−0.02
x_4	Other Costs	0.138	x_{44}	0.015	y_2x_4	−0.006	x_{23}	0.12
x_5	Time	0.002	y_{12}	−0.031	y_{34}	0.002	x_{24}	−0.006
d_1	Plant Dummy	0.092	y_{13}	−0.03	y_3x_1	−0.008	x_{34}	−0.024
d_2	Plant Dummy	−0.066	y_{14}	0.003	y_3x_2	0.009	Intercept	4.078
d_3	Plant Dummy	0.267	y_1x_1	0.197	y_3x_3	0.04		
d_4	Plant Dummy	0.569	y_1x_2	0.101	y_3x_4	−0.002		

(Table 5.4 continued)

(Table 5.4 continued)

Description of Variables in the Estimated Distance Function:

Names of Variables and Their Identification

Output	Y_1	$Output_2$	y_{11}	Outfuel	y_1x_3	Sofuel	y_3x_3
SPM	Y_2	Spm_2	y_{22}	Outother	y_1x_4	Soother	y_3x_4
SO_2	Y_3	So_2	y_{33}	Spmso	y_{23}	Nocap	y_4x_1
NO_x	Y_4	No_2	y_{44}	Spmno	y_{24}	Nowage	y_4x_2
Capital	X_1	Cap_2	x_{11}	Spmcap	y_2x_1	Nofuel	y_4x_3
Wage	X_2	$Wage_2$	x_{22}	Spmwage	y_2x_2	Noother	y_4x_4
Fuel	X_3	$Fuel_2$	x_{33}	Spmfuel	y_2x_3	Capwage	x_{12}
Others	X_4	$Other_2$	x_{44}	Spmother	y_2x_4	Capfuel	x_{13}
Time	X_5	Outspm	y_{12}	Sono	y_{34}	Capother	x_{14}
Dummy 1	d_1	Outso	y_{13}	Socap	y_3x_1	Wagefuel	x_{23}
Dummy 2	d_2	Outno	y_{14}	Sowage	y_3x_2	Wageother	x_{24}
Dummy 3	d_3	Outcap	y_1x_1			Fuelother	x_{34}
Dummy 4	d_4	Outwage	y_1x_2				

are 11.835, 2.975 and 14.204 thousand units of electricity, re-spectively, per tonne reduction of SPM, nitrous oxides and sulphur dioxide. The current electricity tariff for industries in AP is on average Rs. 3.68 per unit. Using this, the shadow prices of pollutants could be expressed in rupees as shown in Table 5.5.

Shadow Prices of Pollutants and Pollution Taxes

Estimation of pollution taxes using the taxes standards method requires the estimates of marginal cost of pollution abatement and data on pollution standards. The shadow prices of pollutants estimated in the previous section could be also interpreted as marginal costs of pollution abatement. Plant-specific shadow prices may be calculated using the estimated distance function for thermal power generation in our example. The marginal cost of pollution abatement for each pollutant can be obtained by finding a relationship between the shadow price of pollutants and pollution load. The marginal cost of pollution abatement of a plant could depend on output, pollution load and plant-specific characteristics among others. Specifying this relationship as the stochastic, marginal cost of pollution abatement function for APGENCO is estimated each for SPM as given in equations (5.10). In this equation the dependent variables are shadow prices of pollutants (*SPMS*) and independent variables are pollution concentrations (*SPMC*), plant-specific dummy variables (D_i, $i = 1....4$) and time. As expected, there is a rising marginal cost with respect to pollution reduction.

SPM

$$\ln SPMS = -1.099^* \ln (OUT) - 1.1864^* \ln (SPMC)$$
$$(-1.48) \qquad\qquad (-4.80)$$
$$+ 0.955^*D_1 + 2.326^*D_2 - 2.463^*D_3$$
$$(1.28) \qquad (2.51) \qquad (-1.45)$$
$$- 6.121^*D_4 - 0.141^*TIME + 19.300$$
$$(-2.81) \qquad (-2.04) \qquad\qquad (2.97) \qquad\qquad (5.10)$$

Adjusted $R^2 = 0.82$

Figure 5.2 depicts the marginal pollution abatement cost function for SPM. On the y-axis is the marginal cost of abatement and on the x-axis SPM concentration is measured.

Table 5.5
Shadow Prices of Pollutants

(*Rs thousand per tonne*)

Industrial Pollutants	Mean	Standard Deviation
SPM	40.29	73.22
SO$_2$	10.13	17.57
NO$_2$	48.35	103.80

Using the abatement cost of function of SPM in equation (5.10) and using MINAS Stack Emission Standard of 115 milligrams per Nm^3, the pollution tax of Rs. 7,200 per tonne of SPM is calculated. The tax rates for other pollutants could be calculated given their emission standards.

Cost of Environmentally Sustainable Industrial Development and Measurement of Green GDP

There is a cost associated with environmentally sustainable development. The Integrated Environmental and Economic Accounting Methodology calls it the maintenance cost or the cost of maintaining environmental quality at its natural regenerative level. Scientifically, the environmental standards (Minimum National Standards [MINAS] in India or WHO standards) are supposed to be designed taking into account the natural regenerative capacity of environment media. Therefore, the cost of complying with these standards may be interpreted by the industry as cost of environmentally sustainable industrial development. This cost has to be accounted in the measurement of green GDP or environmentally corrected net national product (ENNP). The ENNP could be defined as (see Dasgupta and Maler (1998); Murty and Kumar 2004; Weitzman 1974):

$$ENNP = C + P_k \Delta K + P_n \Delta N \qquad (5.11)$$

where C, ΔK and ΔN represent, respectively, consumption, changes in man-made capital, and natural capital, and P_k and P_n are prices of man-made and natural capital.

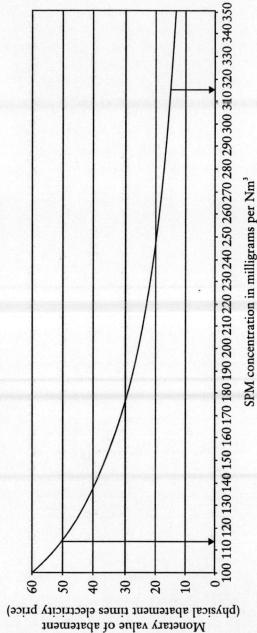

Figure 5.2
Abatement Function for SPM Concentration

The first two terms in equation (5.11) constitute conventional NNP, while the last term accounts for the value of change in natural resource stock (change in environmental quality) due to economic activities during the year. The UN methodology suggests the development of physical and monetary accounts of natural capital as satellite accounts to conventional national accounts for estimating $P_n \Delta N$. Time-series of physical accounts of the ambient quality of the atmosphere, water resources and forest cover has to be developed to estimate ΔN. For example, in the case of air pollution, ΔN could be measured as the excess of pollution load of SPM over the pollution load corresponding to safe ambient standards. In the case of carbon dioxide, ΔN could simply be pollution load generated because it adds to the stock of carbon dioxide already present in the atmosphere.

Different concepts of environmental values and methods of valuation are discussed in the literature. The price of natural capital (P_k) has to be estimated using one of these methods. The UN methodology discusses two concepts: producer values and household values (Murty and Kumar 2004). The producer value is also called maintenance cost or cost of sustainable use of environment for the producer/polluter. The methodology for its estimation is described in previous sections. Table 5.5 provides estimates of shadow prices of pollutants for thermal power generation in Andhra Pradesh.

Table 5.6 provides physical and monetary accounts of pollution for APGENCO during the year 2003. The cost of reducing

Table 5.6
Physical and Monetary Accounts of Air Pollution for
APGENCO (2003)

	SPM	SO_2	NO_X	CO_2
Load (TT)	372.75	735.66	213.88	35145.36
Shadow Price (Rs Thousand)	40.29	10.13	48.35	3.381
Cost of Abatement (Rs Million)	15018.09	7452.30	10341.12	118812.07

Note: Row 2 shows the data of observed emissions of SPM, NO_X and SO_2, and emissions estimated using the engineering norms of CO_2.

the pollution levels of SPM, sulphur dioxide and nitrous oxides from the current levels to zero is estimated at Rs 32,811.5 million. The estimated green gross state domestic product (GGSDP) for AP is Rs 1,468,148.5 million after correcting for this cost. The cost of abatement constitutes 2.18 per cent of the GSDP.

Conclusion

There is a cost associated with environmentally sustainable industrial development that is described by the UN methodology of Integrated Environmental and Economic Accounting as maintenance cost. This can be considered as the cost to the industry of complying with fixed environmental standards, taking into account the natural regenerative capacity of environmental media. Some methods in the theory of production can be used to estimate maintenance cost.

Two models of describing the technology of polluting firms are presented, one which looks at pollution as an input in production, and the other which regards pollution as a bad output jointly produced with good output. Both these models are estimated using data for thermal power generation in AP.

The shadow prices of pollutants and cost of pollution abatement are estimated for APGENCO. The maintenance cost or cost of pollution abatement in thermal power generation constitute 2.18 per cent of the GSDP of Andhra Pradesh. This cost does not account for the cost of carbon dioxide reductions in thermal power generation, which could be very high.

Appendix 5.1
Plant-wise Production Details of APGENCO (Rs million)

Unit	Year	Electricity Generated MU	Capital	Wage	Fuel	Other Inputs
KTPS	1996	341.4	520.8385	392.7207	3598.544	98.35302
	1997	352.0	706.3285	390.0065	3980.35	203.1511
	1998	516.281	2091.366	454.4283	5420.716	301.4923
	1999	616.315	4903.302	624.0229	6928.048	73.13237
	2000	782.037	5301.15	775.3307	7971.848	73.48843
	2001	764.763	5633.724	841.7165	7359.555	10.57257
	2002	803.454	6452.283	817.3769	7405.717	260.8398
	2003	872.553	6223.225	933.204	6736.444	99.795
VTPS	1996	985.8	3974.531	282.9839	8690.966	95.11441
	1997	1027.4	3264.57	290.8693	9514.525	414.1977
	1998	1035.748	2857.289	322.0471	9899.48	448.5739
	1999	982.793	3655.848	462.5683	9096.71	233.3007
	2000	962.153	4569.552	608.7684	9374.362	94.91069
	2001	1019.821	4884.831	557.1023	9366.447	116.5993
	2002	1022.805	4551.6	521.6052	9311.96	305.7952
	2003	1028.363	4534.705	614.607	8768.296	89.429
RTS	1996	37.4	81.06809	60.62961	287.0153	1.181043
	1997	37.8	56.20845	68.73419	347.3033	32.52862

	Year					
	1998	40.019	67.96723	89.93132	326.4721	8.647726
	1999	38.037	60.26021	74.43287	440.4694	16.0991
	2000	42.87	17.05768	122.6411	424.9887	2.243133
	2001	44.37	62.84514	120.1721	474.3044	6.561657
	2002	42.54	78.70002	101.0138	405.0034	7.396902
	2003	38.867	121.389	100.539	336.21	9.497
NTS	1996	12.9	34.29276	47.46118	174.8478	1.82849
	1997	11.1	31.76674	46.25684	206.8884	19.13873
	1998	11.623	39.01964	43.22733	166.3616	7.779813
	1999	9.712	56.24254	52.22251	205.0941	2.744435
	2000	12.794	35.20249	64.55493	254.5542	3.927205
	2001	16.932	63.90464	64.03427	311.0354	1.847977
	2002	15.609	77.70212	58.20524	243.527	4.434212
	2003	14.59	79.23	64.534	250.598	3.884
RTPP	1996	132.8	1144.555	78.46184	1884.78	0.4993026
	1997	243.7	1693.822	95.41826	3603.15	276.2625
	1998	298.275	1703.572	102.9864	4174.042	30.92959
	1999	336.505	2230.705	153.8045	4394.299	5.771019
	2000	350.035	3354.313	262.6957	4092.261	135.2182
	2001	347.537	3233.651	255.0101	4707.421	3.303861
	2002	340.08	3447.845	237.1642	4083.548	141.993
	2003	348.883	3759.155	253.135	3823.701	15.431

Appendix 5.2
Plant-specific Estimates of Pollution Loads (thousand tonnes)

Unit	Year	Coal	SPMA	SO_2A	NO_xA	CO_2EN
KTPS	1996	3687.12	134.31	33.59624	2.585589	7239.173
	1997	3344	207.67	245.5119	5.785184	6565.503
	1998	5111.18	355.51	216.3872	13.18501	10035.13
	1999	5731.73	304.18	191.5872	20.30537	11253.5
	2000	7272.94	224.49	170.3936	31.36158	14279.46
	2001	7112.3	108.18	171.5412	129.0677	13964.06
	2002	7873.85	139.25	116.1393	167.2025	15459.27
	2003	8551.02	57.91	143.0931	140.1254	16788.8
VTPS	1996	7196.34	208.37	329.89	5.579009	14129.06
	1997	7191.8	208.4	404.5654	6.071154	14120.15
	1998	7146.66	235.84	292.3674	6.740556	14031.52
	1999	6879.55	185.88	144.4494	5.974439	13507.09
	2000	6735.07	156.38	405.902	10.66144	13223.42
	2001	7138.75	164.25	462.1217	12.9733	14015.99
	2002	7159.64	182.44	484.6852	12.69603	14057.01
	2003	7198.54	105.68	523.9432	60.34528	14133.38
RTS	1996	273.02	7.45	2.171993	0.891	536.0387
	1997	260.82	5.48	10.51516	0.749709	512.0856
	1998	292.14	8	10.51516	0.749709	573.5783
	1999	289.08	3.07	19.20409	6.084177	567.5704

	Year					
NTS	2000	351.53	2.96	17.01263	5.651653	690.1828
	2001	328.34	0.25	13.52622	1.54136	644.6522
	2002	314.8	4.98	23.68952	11.29369	618.0682
	2003	287.62	4.89	22.51187	10.0586	564.7039
	1996	150.93	38.2	14.27074	0.398	296.3311
	1997	128.76	43.29	15.37624	0.397998	252.8033
	1998	142.96	51.74	17.13027	0.591121	280.6831
	1999	101.98	48.07	6.41343	0.419385	200.2243
	2000	139.45	33.96	24.08714	0.67472	273.7917
	2001	186.25	0.34	35.32626	0.867665	365.6773
	2002	171.7	27.94	34.78036	0.859322	337.1103
	2003	160.49	25.21	32.47018	4.580414	315.1009
RTPP	1996	1049.12	227.66	102.2584	5.339009	2059.809
	1997	1803.38	43.32	27.28485	5.501822	3540.699
	1998	2237.06	31.71	24.02527	6.163619	4392.172
	1999	2523.79	20.02	9.548293	5.727009	4955.129
	2000	2625.26	18.52	24.79577	4.141103	5154.351
	2001	2815.05	16.28	32.30186	4.969152	5526.979
	2002	2380.56	18.14	76.37216	21.82907	4673.915
	2003	2442.18	18.73	112.3512	64.79794	4794.898

114 *M.N. Murty and S.C. Gulati*

References

Aigner, D.J. and S.F. Chu. 1968. 'Estimating the Industry Production Function', *American Economic Review*, 58: 826–39.
Aigner, D.J. et al. 1977. 'Formulation and Estimation of Stochastic Frontier Production Function Models', *Journal of Econometrics*, 6: 21–37.
Coggins, J.S. and J.R. Swinton. 1996. 'The Price of Pollution: A Dual Approach to Valuing SO_2 Allowances', *Journal of Environmental Economics and Management*, 30: 58–72.
Dasgupta, P. and K.G. Maler. 1998. 'Decentralization Schemes, Cost–Benefit Analysis and Net National Product as a Measure of Social Well-being', Development Economics Discussion Paper Series No.12. London: London School of Economics, STICERD.
Fare, R. 1988. *Fundamentals of Production Theory*. Berlin: Springer-Verlag.
Fare, R. and S. Grosskopf. 1998. 'Shadow Pricing of Good and Bad Commodities', *American Journal of Agricultural Economics*, 80: 584–90.
Fare, R., S. Grosskopf, C.A.K. Lovell and S. Yaisawarng. 1993. 'Derivation of Shadow Prices for Undesirable Outputs: A Distance Function Approach', *Review of Economics and Statistics*, 75: 375–80.
Fare, R., S. Grosskopf and C.A.K. Lovell. 1994. *Production Frontiers*. Cambridge: Cambridge University Press.
Fare, R., S. Grosskopf and J. Nelson. 1990. 'On Price Efficiency', *International Economic Review*, 31: 709–20.
Fare, R. and D. Primont. 1995. *Multi-output Production and Duality: Theory and Applications*. Dordrecht: Kluwer Academic Publishers.
Frisch, R. 1965. *Theory of Production*. Dordrecht: D. Reidel Publishing Company/Holland.
Murty, M.N. 2003. 'Measuring Environmentally Corrected Net National Product: Case Studies of Industrial Water Pollution and Urban Air Pollution in India'. Proceedings of the Fourth National Workshop on Environmental Statistics, Central Statistical Organization, Government of India.
Murty, M.N., S.C. Gulati and Pitamber Chettri. 2003. 'Valuation and Accounting of Urban Air Pollution in the Indian Subcontinent, 2001–2003'. Monograph, South Asian Network of Economic Institutions (SANEI).
Murty, M.N., A.J. James and Smita Mishra. 1999. *Economics of Industrial Pollution: Indian Experience*. New Delhi: Oxford University Press.

Murty, M.N. and Surendar Kumar. 2004. 'Win–Win Opportunities and Environmental Regulation: Testing of Porter Hypothesis for Indian Manufacturing Industries', *Journal of Environmental Management*, 67: 139–44.

Murty, Sushama and R.R. Russell. 2002. 'On Modeling Pollution', Mimeograph, Department of Economics, University of California, Riverside, CA, USA.

Pittman, R.W. 1983. 'Multilateral Productivity Comparisons with Undesirable Outputs', *Economic Journal*, 93: 883–91.

Shepard, R. 1970. *Theory of Cost and Production Functions*. Princeton: Princeton University Press.

UN. 1993. 'Integrated Environmental and Economic Accounting' (*Interim version*, Sales No. E93 XVII. 12). New York: United Nations.

Weitzman, M. 1974. 'On the Welfare Significance of National Product in a Dynamic Economy', *Quarterly Journal of Economics*, 90: 156–62.

6

Sustainable Development with Inter-generational and International Cooperation

Ngo Van Long

Introduction

Each one of us is made up of at least two individuals. The first is a selfish one who seeks to maximise personal satisfaction. The second is an ethical one who values 'social justice'—including 'inter-generational justice'—and is willing to cooperate with others to develop institutions that ensure a just society.[1] That is why many people, including individuals who have no offspring, are committed to the idea of sustainable development, which is inherently linked to the concept of inter-generational justice.

In this chapter, sustainable development roughly means that (*a*) future generations have a sufficiently high level of well-being, without (*b*) present generations having to sacrifice too much. Utilitarian welfare criteria often fail to achieve (*a*) and/or (*b*). For example, as shown by Dasgupta and Heal (1980), under the

[1] That individual might not have a well formulated view of what constitutes a just society. That is something one has to develop, possibly with the help of philosophers. Recommended readings include, among others, Anderson (1999), Arneson (2002), Frankfurt (1987), Rawls (1958, 1963, 1972, 1999); Reiss (1970), Roemer and Suzumura (2006), Waltzer (1983).

discounted utility criterion, an economy with a man-made capital stock and an essential exhaustible resource will follow a path where consumption at first rises but eventually falls to zero (even though it is technically feasible to maintain a constant and positive level of consumption for ever). Chichilnisky (1996) has argued convincingly that the discounted utility criterion is incompatible with sustainable development: using any positive rate of discount in the objective function would imply 'dictatorship of the present'. A quote from Chichilnisky (ibid.: 235) is most striking:

> Discounting future utility is generally inconsistent with sustainable development. It can produce outcomes which seem patently unjust to later generations. Indeed, under any positive discount rate, the long-run future is deemed irrelevant. For example, at a standard 5% discount rate, the present value of the earth's aggregate output discounted 200 years from now, is a few hundred thousand dollars. A simple computation shows that if one tried to decide how much it is worth investing in preventing the destruction of the earth 200 years from now [on the basis of measuring the value of forgone present consumption], the answer would be no more than one is willing to invest in an apartment.

A criterion that is perhaps more acceptable than the discounted utility criterion—at least from the point of view of sustainable development—is to maximise the welfare level of the worse-off generation. This is often called the maximin criterion.[2] This criterion, however has a drawback: it would rank as equal to any two paths of consumption that have the same maximin welfare level, even if one path is a Pareto improvement (in terms of individual welfare) over the other path. For this reason, Sen (1976)

---

[2] Note that many people refer to the 'maximin criterion' as the 'Rawlsian criterion', named after John Rawls, author of the influential work, *A Theory of Justice* (1972, 1999). I have argued elsewhere (Long 2006) that, in the context of welfare comparison of infinite utility streams, it is unfair to attribute the maximin criterion to Rawls, because he has clearly argued that such a criterion is not acceptable for justice among generations.

and Rawls (1999) have suggested a refinement called the lexical maximin criterion, which permits a more refined ranking.[3] Under this refinement, in any discrete-time finite horizon model, if two paths have the same maximin welfare level, then they should be ranked by comparing the welfare level of the second worse-off generation in one path with that of the other path.[4] When there are infinitely many generations, the concept of the 'second worse-off generation' is not well defined.[5] In this case, we use the concept of 'sequential maximin': if two paths that start at time τ have the same maximin welfare level, they can be ranked by comparing their maximin welfare levels starting at time $\tau + 1$. A more formal definition is given in the following section.

This chapter applies the concept of sequential maximin to the problem of managing an international and inter-generational common property resource which provides both an intermediate input (in the production of consumption goods) and a flow of amenity services. The enjoyment of the latter by any individual does not preclude the enjoyment by other individuals at other locations or other times. Therefore, we may say that the resource contains elements of international and inter-generational public goods. However, the harvesting of the intermediate input in any period reduces the flow of amenity services in that period and in subsequent periods.

The theory of public goods, in its purest form, is usually set in the context of interaction among contemporaneous individuals. In the real world, however, many public goods (or 'bads') are passed down to future generations. Present and future generations cannot negotiate binding contracts that would allow future

---

[3] It should be noted that although Rawls (1999) did mention the lexical maximin criterion, he did not believe that this criterion, nor the standard maximin criterion, can be justifiably used without modification for making a judgement about inter-generational justice.

[4] If the utility level of the second worse-off generation in one path is the same as that in the other, then we must compare the utility levels of the third worse-off generation, and so on.

[5] Consider two utility sequences {1, 1/2, 1/4, 1/8, 1/16, ...} and {1, 1/2, 1/3, 1/4, ...}. The infimum of each is zero. Who is the second worse-off individual in each sequence?

generations to compensate the present generation for their investment in public goods (which, unlike private capital stocks, cannot be bought or sold in the marketplace). Imperfect parental altruism implies that a family line cannot be treated as an infinitely lived individual. (For empirical evidence of imperfect parental altruism, see Altonji et al. 1992, 1997.)

Some questions arise: under what conditions is the unrestrained exploitation of the resource by the current generation compatible with sustainable development? If these conditions are not met, what can be done by a government to restore sustainability? What will happen if governments of different countries do not cooperate while they seek to achieve sustainable development for their own country?

One important result of our model is that even if governments do not cooperate, there exists a symmetric Nash equilibrium that achieves the sustainable development path that a (fictitious) benevolent international dictator would choose. This is in sharp contrast to the standard result that non-cooperation under a discounted utilitarian objective function typically leads to an inefficient outcome.

Another interesting result is that if only one government is active, it can still achieve positive utility for both countries by acting as a Stackelberg leader with a sequential maximin objective for its country, but the other country will have a higher welfare level in this equilibrium.

Before proceeding, a few words about related literature are in order. Several recent papers deal with some aspects of intergenerational goods. Rangel (2003) considers an infinite horizon model with overlapping generations. He shows that backward inter-generational goods (BIGs) such as social security can play a crucial role in sustaining forward inter-generational goods (FIGs). In Rangel (2005), in a simple two-period model, it is shown that tax-based restrictions on categories of government expenditures can help protect future generations against overexploitation (by the present generation) of FIGs. Other related papers include Kolikoff et al. (1988), Sandler and Smith (1976), Sandler (1978, 1982), Silvestre (1994, 1995), all cited in Rangel (2003). Roemer (2006) considers the issue of sustainability in a model with a renewable resource with linear dynamics similar to ours. Roemer and Veneziani (2006) consider a game between two countries with the leximin objective, but they focus on open-loop Nash equilibria.

Sequential Maximin

Some Preliminary Definitions

Let N be the set of positive integers

$$N = \{1, 2, ..., ..., ...\}$$

We may think that these numbers represent a sequence of non-overlapping generations. For simplicity, suppose each generation consists of n identical individuals.

Let us represent an infinite utility sequence by:

$$u = \{u_t\}_{t \in N}$$

Think of u_t as the utility level of generation t. Here we assume utility levels can be compared.

A sequence is said to have a constant tail $\bar{u}$ from time T if $u_t = \bar{u}$ for all $t \geq T$ and $u_{T-1} \neq \bar{u}$. In such a case, we write the sequence as:

$$u = \{u_1, u_2, .., u_{T-1}, {}_T\bar{u}\}$$

or, alternatively, as:

$$u = \{u_1, u_2, .., u_{T-1}, \bar{u}^{(\infty)}\}$$

where the superscript (∞) means that $\bar{u}$ is repeated forever. A sequence such as:

$$\{7, 7, 7, 8, 4, 4, {}_{,6}\bar{u}\}$$

is also written as:

$$\{7^{(3)}, 8^{(1)}, 4^{(2)}, {}_{,6}\bar{u}\}$$

A sequence u^A is said to Pareto-dominate u^B if:

$u_t^A \geq u_t^B$ for all $t \in N$ with $u_t^A > u_t^B$ for some $t \in N$

Given a set S of feasible utility sequences, a sequence $u^A \in S$ is said to be Pareto efficient in S if there is no $u^B \in S$ such that u^B Pareto-dominates u^A.

Consider a pair of sequences (u^A, u^B). We say u^A *is not inferior to u^B in the maximin sense* if:

$$\text{inf. } u^A \equiv \text{inf. } \{u_t^A : t \in N\} \geq \text{inf. } u^B \equiv \text{inf. } \{u_t^B : t \in N\}$$

We say u^A *dominates u^B in the maximin sense* if:

$$\text{inf. } u^A \equiv \text{inf. } \{u_t^A : t \in N\} > \text{inf. } u^B \equiv \text{inf. } \{u_t^B : t \in N\}$$

We say u^A *is ranked equal to u^B in the maximin sense* if:

$$\text{inf. } u^A \equiv \text{inf. } \{u_t^A : t \in N\} = \text{inf. } u^B \equiv \text{inf. } \{u_t^B : t \in N\}$$

Consider for example:

$u^A = \{1, 3, 6, 7^{(\infty)}\}$
$u^B = \{1, 5, 4, 7^{(\infty)}\}$

Then u^A is ranked equal to u^B in the maximin sense. However, there are good reasons to argue that u^B is 'better' than u^A because the second worse-off generation in u^A has a lower level of utility than the second worse-off generation in u^B (that is, $3 < 4$). Clearly, some refinement of the maximin criterion is called for. One such refinement uses the concept of 'sequential maximin', which we shall define in the following subsection. For this purpose, it is useful to describe a generic dynamic system where optimisation takes place over time.

A Dynamic System

Consider a dynamic system consisting of a state variable x, a control variable h, and a transition equation:

$$x_{t+1} = f(x_t, h_t, t)$$

At any time t, given x_t, we assume that h_t must belong to some feasible set $S(x_t, t)$. Often we represent such sets by:

$$S(x_t, t) \equiv \{h_t : g(x_t, h_t, t) \geq 0\} \tag{6.1}$$

For example, x_t may represent a stock of natural capital (say, environmental quality), and h_t is the output of a final good, the production of which may have an upper bound, which depends on the current environmental quality. The output h_t may generate pollutants that harm the environment.

The utility function of the representative individual of generation t is:

$$u_t = u(x_t, h_t, t)$$

This may be interpreted as follows. At the beginning of period t, the representative individual of generation t is endowed with a stock x_t. He makes a decision h_t, and enjoys the utility u_t, which depends on both x_t and h_t (and also on t). The stock x_{t+1} is passed on to the next generation, without any charge.

An entire time path of the control variable is denoted by:

$$_1h = \{h_1, h_2, ..., h_\tau, h_{\tau+1}, h_{\tau+2}, ..., ...\}$$

We define the τ-truncated subsequence of $_1h$ by:

$$_\tau h = \{h_\tau, h_{\tau+1}, h_{\tau+2}, ..., ...\}$$

At a given time τ, with x_τ given, consider the problem of choosing a time path $_\tau h$ of the control variable to solve:

$$\max. \left[\inf_{t \geq \tau} u(x_t, h_t, t) \right] \tag{6.2}$$

subject to:

$$h_t \in S(x_t, t) \text{ for all } t \geq \tau \tag{6.3}$$
$$x_{t+1} = f(x_t, h_t, t) \text{ where } t \geq \tau \text{ and } x_\tau \text{ given} \tag{6.4}$$
$$x_t \geq 0 \text{ for all } t \geq \tau \tag{6.5}$$

If the problem has a solution $_\tau h^*$, we say that $_\tau h^*$ is the *maximin solution of the problem (6.2) at stage τ given x_τ*. The path $_\tau h^*$ has a corresponding path $_\tau x^*$ of the state variable.

For given x_1, let $Q_1(x_1)$ be the set of all solutions $_1 h$ to problem (6.2), where $\tau = 1$. That is:

$$Q_1(x_1) = \left\{ \text{arg. max.} \left[\inf_{t \geq 1}. u(x_t, h_t) \text{ subject to (6.3),(6.4) and (6.5)} \right] \right\}$$

Given any sequence $_1\hat{h} \in Q_1(x_1)$, and the associated time path $_1\dot{x}$, we say that $_1\hat{h}$ *survives stage τ elimination*, if $_\tau\hat{h}$ is a solution of problem (6.2) where the initial condition is

$$x_\tau = \hat{x}_\tau$$

If $_1\hat{h}$ survives all stage τ eliminations (where $\tau = 2, 3, \ldots$) then we say $_1 h$ is a *sequential maximin solution* of problem (6.2) (with $\tau = 1$) given x_1.

Example 1: Let $u(x_t, h_t, t) = h_t - x_t$, with $x_{t+1} = x_t - \min. \{h_t, 0\}$, $t - h_t \geq 0$, $x_1 = 0$. (A possible interpretation is: utility is an increasing function of performance, h_t, and negative performance gives rise to accumulation of bad points, x_t, which reduces utility. At any time t, h_t is bound above by t, which may represent exogenous technical progress.) Following are a few maximin solutions at Stage 1:

$_1 h^A = \{1, 1, 1, 1, 1^{(\infty)}\} = u^A$
$_1 h^B - \{1, 2, 2, 3, 5, \ldots\} = u^B$
$_1 h^C = \{1, 2, 3, 3, 5\ldots\} = u^C$
$_1 h^D = \{1, 2, 3, 4, 5, \ldots\} = u^D$

At Stage 2, path $_1 h^A$ is eliminated. At Stage 3, path $_1 h^B$ is eliminated. At Stage 4, path $_1 h^C$ is eliminated. In fact it is easy to see that path $_1 h^D$ is the sequential maximin solution.

Remark: As Example 2 illustrates a sequentially maximin solution is not the same as lexical maximin in the sense of Sen and Rawls.

Example 2: Let $u(x_t, h_t, t) = h_t - x_t$, with $x_{t+1} = x_t - \min. \{h_t, 0\}$, $S(x_1, 1) = \{5, 6\}$ and $S(x_t, t) = \{0, 1\}$ for all $t \geq 2$. Then the following paths are sequential maximin paths:

$$u^A = \{6, 1^{(\infty)}\}$$
$$u^B = \{5, 1^{(\infty)}\}$$

However, only u^A is the lexical maximin path.

Remarks on the value function and the modified Bellman Equation: Let $V(x_{t+1}, t+1)$ be the value function at stage $t + 1$. Then, under the sequential maximin criterion, the value function at stage t is:

$$V(x_t, t) = \max_{h_t} . \min. \{u(x_t, h_t, t), V(f(x_t, h_t, t), t)\} \qquad (6.6)$$

We call the equation (6.6) the Modified Bellman Equation. If a path is optimal in the sequential maximin sense, it must satisfy the modified Bellman equation. Along such a path, it is clear that value cannot be decreasing:

$$V(x_t, t) \leq V(f(x_t, h_t, t), t) \qquad (6.7)$$

A sequential maximin path is said to be 'tight' if $V(f(x_t, h_t, t), t) - V(x_t, t) = 0$ for all t. If, in addition, $V(x_t, t)$ is a convex function, then along a tight path:

$$0 = V(f(x_t, h_t, t), t) - V(x_t, t), \leq V_x(x_{t+1}, t) [x_{t+1} - x_t] + V_t(x_{t+1}, t) \qquad (6.8)$$

If V is time-independent (which is true for autonomous problems), then a strictly convex value function (in x) implies that along a constant utility path net investment is strictly positive. This result indicates that Hartwick's rule (which states that zero net saving implies constant utility) holds only in continuous time.[6]

---

[6] Dasgupta and Mitra (1985) obtained the same result.

The Basic Model

We now look at the basic version of our model. In this simple version there is only one country, and in any period t the country is populated by a single household consisting of an adult and a child. The adult in period t is endowed with a stock of resource (for example, a forest) of size x_t, which is available at the beginning of period t. He can harvest any amount $h_t \in [0, x_t]$. The amount harvested is transformed into a consumption good under the technology:

$$c_t = \mu_t h_t$$

where $\mu_t > 0$ represents the level of technological know-how in period t. We assume $\mu_{t+1} \geq \mu_t$ for all t. The amount c_t is directly consumed by the household. The unharvested quantity, $x_t - h_t$, grows into a stock x_{t+1}, which is determined by the following transition equation:

$$x_{t+1} = A(x_t - h_t)^\alpha$$

where $A > 0$ and $\alpha \in (0, 1)$. The stock x_{t+1} provides, towards the end of period t, a flow of amenity services denoted by $s_t = \kappa x_{t+1}$, which the adult in period t enjoys. We choose units so that $\kappa = 1$. The utility of the adult in period t is:

$$u_t = c_t s_t^\beta$$

where $\beta > 0$ is an indicator of the strength of his enjoyment of amenity services. He maximises u_t by his choice of h_t. He dies at the beginning of period $t + 1$, when his offspring has grown into an (period $t + 1$) adult. The latter inherits the stock x_{t+1}, and chooses $h_{t+1} \in [0, x_{t+1}]$ to maximise

$$u_{t+1} = c_{t+1} s_{t+1}^\beta$$

In this model, the adult has no interest in the utility of his offspring. The central questions we pose are: under what conditions does the pursuit of happiness of self-interested adults (without regard for the utility of their offspring) result in a sustainable flow of strictly positive utility levels for all generations? If these conditions are not met, what can a benevolent dictator do to ensure that all generations have strictly positive utility? If the benevolent dictator wants to maximise the utility level of the worse-off generation, what form of intervention must take place?

Before answering these questions, it is worth pausing to ask who this benevolent dictator in our model is. A possible answer is that an individual may wear two hats. In his private sphere he maximises private utility, while in his social sphere he designs (or at least votes on) institutions that provide for the well-being of future generations.

State Dynamics with Selfish Adults

The adult in period t, facing a given $x_t > 0$, chooses h_t and hence x_{t+1} to maximise u_t subject to the constraint:

$$x_{t+1} = A(x_t - h_t)^\alpha$$

and $0 \le h_t \le x_t$.

Let us define:

$$q_t = (x_{t+1})^{1/\alpha}$$

Then the utility maximisation problem is equivalent to a simple problem:

$$\max_{h_t, q_t} \ln(\mu_t h_t) + \alpha\beta \ln q_t$$

subject to:

$$q_t + A h_t = A x_t$$

with the familiar solution:

$$q_t^* = \left(\frac{\alpha\beta}{1 + \alpha\beta}\right) A x_t$$

$$A h_t^* = \left(\frac{1}{1 + \alpha\beta}\right) A x_t$$

Thus, the time path of the resource stock follows the dynamic process

$$x_{t+1} \equiv (q_t^*)^\alpha = \left(\frac{\alpha\beta A x_t}{1+\alpha\beta} \right)^\alpha \tag{6.9}$$

The time path of utility is:

$$u_t = (\mu_t h_t^*)(q_t^\alpha)^\beta = \mu_t \left(\frac{1}{1+\alpha\beta} \right) \left(\frac{\alpha\beta}{1+\alpha\beta} \right)^{\alpha\beta} (Ax_t)^{1+\alpha\beta} \tag{6.10}$$

We consider two cases. Case I is that of linear growth, that is, $\alpha = 1$. Case II is the case where $0 < \alpha < 1$.

Case I: Linear Transition Equation

With $\alpha = 1$, the dynamic process (6.9) reduces to:

$$x_{t+1} = \left(\frac{\beta}{1+\beta} \right) A x_t$$

Note that we can interpret $\beta / (1 + \beta)$ as the 'budget share' of the amenities. Its inverse, $(1 + \beta) / \beta = 1 + \frac{1}{\beta}$ is thus a measure of the **strength of his love of consumption.**

There are three sub-cases:

Case I(a): High biological rate of interest, $A > 1 + \frac{1}{\beta}$

In this case the natural growth rate of the resource (which is also called the **biological rate of interest**)[7] exceeds the strength of consumption demand. As a result, the stock x_t tends to infinity as $t \to \infty$.

Case I(b): Low biological rate of interest, $A < 1 + \frac{1}{\beta}$

In this case, x_t tends to zero as $t \to \infty$.

---

[7] Strictly speaking, A is the biological interest factor, and $A - 1$ is the biological rate of interest.

Case I(c): $A = 1 + \frac{1}{\beta}$

In this (razor-edge) case, the stock remains unchanged over time ($x_t = x_1$ for all $t > 1$).

Case II: Non-linear Transition Equation

With $\alpha \in (0, 1)$, starting from any $x_1 > 0$, the stock will converge monotonely to a unique steady state $\bar{x}$ where:

$$\bar{x} = \left(\frac{\alpha \beta A}{1 + \alpha \beta} \right)^{\alpha /(1 - \alpha)}$$

Suppose μ_t converges to some $\bar{u} > 0$. Then utility will converge to:

$$\bar{u} = \bar{\mu} \left(\frac{1}{1 + \alpha \beta} \right) \left(\frac{\acute{a}\hat{a}}{1 + \acute{a}\hat{a}} \right)^{\acute{a}\hat{a}} (A\bar{x})^{1 + \acute{a}\hat{a}} > 0$$

Utility Path under Case I(a)

With $\alpha = 1$:

$$u_t = \mu_t \left(\frac{1}{1 + \beta} \right) \left(\frac{\hat{a}}{1 + \hat{a}} \right)^{\hat{a}} (A)^{1 + \hat{a}} x_t^{1 + \hat{a}}$$

Since μ_t is non-decreasing in t, and x_t is increasing, the sequence of utility is increasing. There is thus no need for government intervention. The worse-off generation is the first generation. Since each generation is already maximising its utility, and since future resources cannot be brought to the present, it is not feasible to increase the utility of the first generation. (Note, if this is an open economy facing a given rate of interest, then future resources can be brought to the present by means of international borrowing.)

Proposition 1: With $\alpha = 1$ and $A > 1 + \frac{1}{\beta}$, unrestrained exploitation is consistent with sustainable development, regardless of whether technical progress is positive on zero.

Utility Path under Case I(b)

In this case, under laissez-faire the stock x_t converges to zero. To determine whether utility is falling or rising over time, we compute the ratio u_{t+1}/u_t under laissez-faire:

$$\frac{u_{t+1}}{u_t} = \frac{\mu_{t+1}}{\mu_t}\left(\frac{x_{t+1}}{x_t}\right)^{1+\beta} = \frac{\mu_{t+1}}{\mu_t}\left(\frac{\beta A}{1+\beta}\right)^{1+\beta}$$

Suppose that the rate of technical progress is constant, that is:

$$\frac{\mu_{t+1}}{\mu_t} = \pi > 0$$

We call π the technical progress factor and $\pi - 1$ the rate of technical progress. (Our model admits the case of technical regress, that is, $\pi \in (0, 1)$, but we will focus on the case $\pi \geq 1$.) Then utility is increasing over time if and only if:

$$\pi > \left(\frac{1+\beta}{A\beta}\right)^{1+\beta}$$

where the right hand side exceeds 1 because $A < (1 + \beta)/\beta$ under case I(b).

Proposition 2: Assume $\alpha = 1$ (that is, the natural growth function is linear) and $A < (1 + \beta)/\beta$ (that is, a low rate of natural reproduction). Then in the absence of social intervention, the time path of utility will be declining, with $u_t \to 0$ as $t \to \infty$, if and only if:

$$\pi < \left(\frac{1+\beta}{A\beta}\right)^{1+\beta} \equiv \sigma$$

Corollary 1: If $\alpha = 1$ and $A < (1 + \beta)\beta$, then the unrestrained exploitation of the resource is consistent with sustainable development if $\pi \geq \sigma$.

In what follows, we will focus on the Case I(b) with low-rate technical progress ($\pi < \sigma$). We wish to find a sufficient condition under which a benevolent dictator can intervene to achieve a maximin utility level that exceeds the utility level of the worse-off generation under laissez-faire.

Achieving Maximin Welfare by Setting Quota on Harvesting

We adopt the following assumptions:

Assumption 1: Linear transition and low biological rate of interest:

$$\alpha = 1 \text{ and } A < 1 + \frac{1}{\beta}$$

Assumption 2: Low rate of technical progress:

$$\pi < \left(\frac{1+\beta}{A\beta}\right)^{1+\beta} \equiv \left(1+\frac{1}{\beta}\right)^{1+\beta}\left(\frac{1}{A}\right)^{1+\beta} \equiv \sigma$$

(This assumption admits the case of technical regress, though we will not focus on that case.)

Recall that under laissez-faire, the harvesting rule is:

$$h_t = \left(\frac{1}{1+\beta}\right)x_t$$

As we have seen, with $\alpha = 1$, $A < (1 + \beta)/\beta$ and $\pi < \sigma$, laissez-faire utility will converge to zero (with zero consumption and zero amenity services). Let us find a restraint factor $r \in (0, 1)$ such that if the dictator imposes the following constraint on harvest:

$$h_t \leq (1-r)\left(\frac{1}{1+\beta}\right)x_t \equiv \kappa\left(\frac{1}{1+\beta}\right)x_t \tag{6.11}$$

where $\kappa \equiv 1 - r < 1$, then a constant and positive level of utility can be achieved for all generations, provided π is not too low.

The individual utility maximisation problem under restraint on harvesting is:

$$\max_{h_t, x_{t+1}} (\mu_t h_t)(x_{t+1})^\beta$$

subject to (6.11) and $x_{t+1} = A(x_t - h_t)$. It is easy to verify that the constraint (6.11) binds. Thus:

$$h_t = (1-r)\left(\frac{1}{1+\beta}\right)x_t$$

and:

$$x_{t+1} = \left(1 - \frac{\kappa}{1+\beta}\right)Ax_t$$

Then:

$$\frac{x_{t+1}}{x_t} = \frac{A(\beta + 1 - \kappa)}{1+\beta} \tag{6.12}$$

and:

$$u_t = \mu_t \kappa \left(\frac{1}{1+\beta}\right)\left(\frac{\beta + 1 - \kappa}{1+\beta}\right)^\beta A^\beta (x_t)^{1+\beta} \tag{6.13}$$

Proposition 3: Under Assumptions 1 and 2, if π is not too low, in the sense that:

$$\left(\frac{1}{A}\right)^{1+\beta} < \pi \tag{6.14}$$

then the planner can achieve a constant utility stream $u_t = \bar{u} > 0$ by setting a restraint rate r such that:

$$r = \bar{r} \equiv (1+\beta)\left[\left(\frac{1}{\pi}\right)^{1/(1+\beta)} - \frac{A\beta}{1+\beta}\right] \tag{6.15}$$

The optimal harvest is:

$$h_t = x_t\left[1 - \frac{1}{A}\left(\frac{1}{\pi}\right)^{1/(1+\beta)}\right] > 0$$

and the constant utility is:

$$u_t = \mu_t(1-z)\,z^\beta A^\beta(x_t)^{1+\beta} \tag{6.16}$$

where z is defined by:

$$z \equiv \frac{1}{A}\left(\frac{1}{\pi}\right)^{1/(1+\beta)} \tag{6.17}$$

Proof:
From (6.13):

$$\frac{u_{t+1}}{u_t} = \pi\left(\frac{x_{t+1}}{x_t}\right)^{1+\beta} = \pi\left[\frac{A(\beta+1-\kappa)}{1+\beta}\right]^{1+\beta} = 1$$

if and only if:

$$\kappa = (1+\beta)\left[1 - \frac{1}{A}\left(\frac{1}{\pi}\right)^{1/(1+\beta)}\right] \tag{6.18}$$

which is equivalent to $1 - \kappa = \bar{r}$. Note that $\kappa > 0$ if and only if condition (6.14) holds. Assumption 2 implies that $\kappa < 1$, that is, restraint is required for a constant flow of positive utility. QED.

Remark 1: If condition (6.14) is satisfied but the planner sets $r > \bar{r}$, then utility will be rising over time, but the utility level of the first generation will be lower than the constant utility with $r = \bar{r}$.

Remark 2: With constant utility, what happens to the time path of the resource stock? Substituting (6.18) for (6.12) we get:

$$\frac{x_{t+1}}{x_t} = \left(\frac{1}{\pi}\right)^{1/(1+\beta)}$$

so the stock converges to zero if and only if $\pi > 1$. The reason is that if the rate of technical progress is positive, then the benevolent dictator can afford to allow the stock to decline and can still maintain a constant flow of positive utility. If $\pi = 1$, then the stock will be stationary. This is possible if A is great enough so that condition (6.14) is satisfied. (In the case of technical *regress*, the dictator with the sequential maximin objective must make sure that the stock rises over time to ensure constant utility, which is possible given [6.14] is satisfied.)

Remark on the modified Bellman equation: We can show that the modified Bellman equation, equation (6.6), holds for the following value function:

$$V(x_t, t) = \mu_t(1 - z)z^\beta A^\beta(x_t)^{1+\beta}$$

where z is defined by (6.17). One must verify that:

$$\mu_t(1 - z)z^\beta A^\beta(x_t)^{1+\beta} = \max_{h_t} \min \{\mu_t h_t(A(x_t - h_t))^\beta,$$

$$\mu_{t+1}(1 - z)z^\beta A^\beta (A(x_t - h_t))^{1+\beta}\} \tag{6.19}$$

where the maximisation of the right hand side of (6.19) with respect to h_t gives:

$$h_t^* = (1 - z)x_t \tag{6.20}$$

To see (6.20), note that the maximisation of the right hand side of (6.19) is equivalent to:

$$\max_{ht} . \min . \{\mu_t h_t, \mu_{t+1}(1-z)z^\beta A^\beta (A(x_t - h_t))\}$$

Now, the curve $\mu_t h_t$ is increasing in h_t and the curve μ_{t+1} $(1-z)z^\beta A^\beta (A(x_t - h_t))$ is decreasing in h_t for given x_t. The maximin solution is where the two curves intersect (the tip of the tent), where (6.20) holds.

A Multi-country Model with an International Public Good

We now modify the basic model by assuming that there are n identical countries that share a common resource stock x_t. In each country in period t there is a household consisting of an adult (who is the decision maker) and a child. The amenity service flow $s_t = \kappa x_{t+1}$ is enjoyed by all contemporaneous adults in period t. It is thus an international public good.

We will look at two scenarios. In the non-cooperative scenario the n contemporaneous adults do not coordinate their harvesting plans. In the cooperative scenario they fully coordinate. (In both scenarios individuals do not care about future generations.) For simplicity we assume the linear growth function:

$$x_{t+1} = A\left(x_t - \sum_i h_{it}\right)$$

where $\Sigma_i h_{it} \leq x_t$.

Outcome Under Cooperation among Contemporaneous Adults

Under cooperation among contemporaneous adults, their objective function is:

$$\max . \; c_t s_t^\beta$$

This is equivalent to:

max. $\ln(\mu_t h_t) + \beta \ln [A(x_t - nh_t)]$

Then:

$$h_t = \frac{x_t}{n(1+\beta)} \tag{6.21}$$

$$x_{t+1} = \left(1 - \frac{n}{n(1+\beta)}\right) Ax_t = \left[\frac{A\beta}{1+\beta}\right] x_t \tag{6.22}$$

The time path of the stock in the n country case with cooperation among contemporaneous adults is thus identical to that in the case of a single country. We will assume that:

$$\frac{A\beta}{1+\beta} < 1 \tag{6.23}$$

so that, even though contemporaneous adults cooperate, it is still true that $x_t \to 0$ as $t \to \infty$. Inequality (6.23) is identical to the inequality in Assumption 1 of the previous section.

The utility path is given by:

$$u_t = \mu_t \left(\frac{1}{n(1+\beta)}\right)\left(\frac{\beta}{1+\beta}\right)^\beta A^\beta (x_t)^{1+\beta} \tag{6.24}$$

Thus:

$$\frac{u_{t+1}}{u_t} = \left(\frac{\mu_{t+1}}{\mu_t}\right)\left(\frac{x_{t+1}}{x_t}\right)^{1+\beta} = \pi\left[\frac{A\beta}{1+\beta}\right]^{1+\beta}$$

Proposition 4: Under cooperation among contemporaneous individuals, utility will be falling over time, and converging to zero, if and only if:

$$\pi < \left[\frac{1+\beta}{A\beta}\right]^{1+\beta} \tag{6.25}$$

Proposition 5: If there is a world benevolent dictator with the maximin objective, to remedy the situation depicted in Proposition 4, a restraint rate $r \in (0, 1)$ can be found to achieve a constant positive utility stream, provided that:

$$\left(\frac{1}{A}\right)^{1+\beta} < \pi \tag{6.26}$$

Along the optimal path the stock evolves according to the rule:

$$\frac{x_{t+1}}{x_t} = \left(\frac{1}{\pi}\right)^{1/(1+\beta)} \tag{6.27}$$

Proof: This is similar to the proof of Proposition 3.

Remark 3: With the restraint, the stock x_t still converges to zero if and only if the rate of technical progress, $\pi - 1$, is positive. The intuition is that with positive technical progress, one has incentive to deplete the stock asymptotically, relying on an ever-increasing consumption of the final good to compensate for an ever-declining flow of amenity services.

Remark 4: The intervention described in Proposition 5 achieves sustainability, but it does reduce the utility level of the first generation below the laissez-faire level.

Outcome under Non-cooperation among Contemporaneous Adults

When there is lack of cooperation, it is still the case that the sum of harvests of generation t adults cannot exceed the available stock:

$$\sum_{i=1}^{n} h_{it} \le x_t$$

Since contemporaneous adults do not cooperate, we must make a distinction between an individual's intended harvest, denoted by E_{it}, and his realised harvest, denoted by h_{it}. Each individual i

must choose E_{it} in $[0, x_t]$. We postulate that realised harvests are given by:

$$h_{it} = E_{it} \text{ if } \sum_{j=1}^{n} E_{jt} \leq x_t$$

$$h_{it} = \left(\frac{E_{it}}{\sum_{j=1}^{n} E_{it}} \right) x_t \text{ if } \sum_{j=1}^{n} E_{jt} > x_t$$

It follows that if $\sum_{j=1}^{n} E_{jt} \geq x_t$, then $\sum_{j=1}^{n} h_{jt} = x_t$, implying that $x_{t+1} = 0$.

Consider the case $n = 2$. Let us find the best reply correspondence for player 2, given E_{1t}. Clearly, if $E_{1t} = x_t$, then $s_t = 0$, and both individuals have the lowest possible utility ($u_{jt} = 0$ for $j = 1, 2$). Thus, any E_{2t} in $[0, x_t]$ is a best reply to $E_{1t} = x_t$. It follows that there are infinitely many Nash equilibria where at least one player chooses the corner strategy $E_{it} = x_t$. Such 'corner Nash equilibria' yield zero utility to each player.

If $E_{1t} < x_t$, then the best reply E_{2t} must satisfy:

$$\frac{1}{E_{2t}} = \frac{\beta}{x_t - E_{1t} - E_{2t}}$$

which yields the reaction function:

$$(1+\beta) E_{2t} = x_t - E_{1t} \tag{6.28}$$

It follows that there is a unique interior Nash equilibrium strategy profile:

$$\left(E_{1t}^N, E_{2t}^N \right) = \left(\frac{x_t}{2 + \beta}, \frac{x_t}{2 + \beta} \right)$$

Clearly, for given $x_t > 0$, the unique interior Nash equilibrium strategy profile Pareto dominates the 'corner Nash equilibria'. In what follows we assume that the Pareto-dominant Nash equilibrium will be chosen.

Generalising to the case of n players, in the unique interior Nash equilibrium, each player chooses:

$$E_{it}^N = \frac{x_t}{n + \beta} \tag{6.29}$$

and thus the total harvest in period t is:

$$nh_{it} = \frac{nx_t}{n + \beta}$$

which is greater than under cooperation. (See equation [6.21].)

The evolution of the stock is then given by:

$$x_{t+1} = A\left(1 - \frac{n}{n + \beta}\right)x_t = \left(\frac{\beta}{n + \beta}\right)Ax_t$$

Thus:

$$\frac{x_{t+1}}{x_t} = \frac{A\beta}{n + \beta}$$

It follows that, under non-cooperation by contemporaneous adults, the stock x_t will converge to zero if and only if:

$$A < 1 + \frac{n}{\beta}$$

The resulting time path of utility is:

$$u_t = \mu_t\left(\frac{1}{n + \beta}\right)\left(\frac{\beta}{n + \beta}\right)^{\beta} A^{\beta}(x_t)^{1 + \beta} \tag{6.30}$$

$$\frac{u_{t+1}}{u_t} = \pi\left(\frac{A\beta}{n + \beta}\right)^{1 + \beta}$$

Thus, utility is decreasing over time if and only if:

$$\pi < \left(\frac{n + \beta}{A\beta} \right)^{1 + \beta}$$

It follows that under non-cooperation it is more likely that unsustainable development will occur.

Proposition 6: Under non-cooperation among contemporaneous individuals, utility will be falling over time, and converging to zero, if and only if:

$$\pi < \left(\frac{n + \beta}{A\beta} \right)^{1 + \beta} \tag{6.31}$$

Remark 5: The utility level of the first generation under the non-cooperative scenario is lower than under the cooperative one. The ratio of (6.24) to (6.30) is:

$$\frac{u_1^{COOP}}{u_1^{NON\ COOP}} = \frac{(n + \beta)^{1 + \beta} n^{-1}}{(1 + \beta)^{1 + \beta}} > 1 \text{ for } n > 1.$$

If all the adults in the first generation agree to cooperate, not only will they be better off, but future generations will also benefit from having a greater stock x_2.

Games between Governments with Sequential Maximin Objective

The situation depicted in Proposition 6 involves two sources of failures: (*a*) in any given period, contemporaneous adults do not cooperate, resulting in excessive harvesting; and (*b*) unsustainable development. Now suppose each country has a government that plans over an infinite horizon and wishes to achieve a stream of constant and positive consumption for its citizens. Suppose the governments do not cooperate. What will be the outcome?

For simplicity, we restrict attention to the situation with low natural growth and low technical progress, that is:

$$A < 1 + \frac{1}{\beta} \tag{6.32}$$

$$\left(\frac{1}{A}\right)^{1+\beta} < \pi < \left(\frac{n+\beta}{A\beta}\right)^{1+\beta} \tag{6.33}$$

where the right hand inequality in (6.33) comes from Proposition 6.

Consider the two-country case ($n = 2$). Suppose the government of country 1, denoted by G_1, believes that G_2 sets a harvest quota policy so that the citizens of country 2 follow the harvesting rule:

$$E_{2t} = \omega_2 x_t \tag{6.34}$$

where $0 \leq \omega_2 \leq 1$. (Technically, this means G_2 is using a feedback strategy: the intended harvest is a function of the currently observed stock level.) Then G_1 must choose a harvesting path E_{1t} that achieves:

$$\max. \left[\inf_t. \ u(\mu_t, h_{1t}, s_t)\right]$$

where:

$$s_t = x_{t+1} = A(x_t - h_{1t} - h_{2t})$$

with:

$$h_{it} = E_{it} \text{ if } E_{1t} + E_{2t} \leq x_t$$

$$h_{it} = \left(\frac{E_{it}}{E_{1t} + E_{2t}}\right) x_t \text{ if } E_{1t} + E_{2t} \geq x_t$$

Note that if $E_{1t} + E_{2t} \geq x_t$, then $\Sigma_{i=1}^2 h_{it} = x_t$, and $x_{t+1} = 0$.

Clearly, if $\omega_2 = 1$, then whatever G_1 does, the utility levels of its citizens will be zero for all t (because $x_{t+1} = 0$). But so will be the utility levels of all citizens of country 2. Obviously, these Nash equilibria (where $\omega_i = 1$ for at least one i) are Pareto-dominated by interior Nash equilibria where $\omega_i \in (0, 1)$ for both $i = 1, 2$. Henceforth, we will focus on interior Nash equilibria.

Take any $\omega_2 \in (0, 1)$. Then for any given $x_t > 0$, in order to ensure that $x_{t+1} > 0$, G_1 must choose E_{1t} such that:

$$E_{1t} < x_t - \omega_2 x_t$$

This implies that:

$$h_{1t} = E_{1t} < (1 - \omega_2)x_t$$

It follows that, given G_2's strategy (6.34) with $\omega_2 \in (0,1)$ the optimisation problem of G_1 can be written as:

$$\max \left[\inf_t u \left(\mu_t h_{1t}, A(x_t(1-\omega_2) - h_{1t}) \right) \right]$$

Consider the policy:

$$h_{1t} = \omega_1 x_t$$

where:

$$0 < \omega_1 < 1 - \omega_2$$

Then:

$$x_{t+1} = A(1 - \omega_1 - \omega_2)x_t$$
$$u_{1t} = \mu_t \omega_1 A^\beta (1 - \omega_1 - \omega_2)^\beta x_t^{1+\beta} \tag{6.35}$$
$$\frac{u_{1t+1}}{u_{1t}} = \pi A^{1+\beta}(1 - \omega_1 - \omega_2)^{1+\beta}$$

Let us assume for the moment that:

$$\pi A^{1+\beta} > \left(\frac{1}{1-\omega_2} \right)^{1+\beta} \tag{6.36}$$

Then there exists a unique $\bar{\omega}_1(\pi, \omega_2) \in (0, 1 - \omega_2)$ that satisfies:

$$\pi A^{1+\beta} = \left(\frac{1}{1 - \bar{\omega}_1(\pi, \omega_2) - \omega_2} \right)^{1+\beta}$$

Then, by setting $\omega_1 = \bar{\omega}_1(\pi, \omega_2)$, G_1 obtains a path of constant utility with:

$$u_{1t} = u_{11} = \mu_t \bar{\omega}_1(\pi, \omega_2) A^{\beta}(1 - \bar{\omega}_1(\pi, \omega_2) - \omega_2)^{\beta} x_1^{1+\beta}$$

On the other hand, by choosing $\omega_1 < \bar{\omega}_1(\pi, \omega_2)$, G_1 can obtain a path of ever-rising utility,[8] but then the first generation's utility is at:

$$u_{11} = \mu_1 \omega_1 A^{\beta}(1 - \omega_1 - \omega_2)^{\beta} x_1^{1+\beta} \tag{6.37}$$

which is lower than the utility level along the constant utility path.

It follows that if (6.36) holds, then the reaction function of G_1 is:

$$\omega_1 = \bar{\omega}_1(\pi, \omega_2) = 1 - \omega_2 - \left(\frac{1}{A}\right)\left(\frac{1}{\pi}\right)^{1/(1+\beta)}$$

By the same reasoning, the reaction function of G_2 is:

$$\omega_2 = \bar{\omega}_2(\pi, \omega_1) = 1 - \omega_1 - \left(\frac{1}{A}\right)\left(\frac{1}{\pi}\right)^{1/(1+\beta)}$$

Thus, the two reaction curves coincide, and we have a continuum of Nash equilibria.

Proposition 7: If governments optimise under the sequential maximin objective function, there is a continuum of Nash equilibrium strategy profiles. Each government uses a feedback strategy of the form:

$$E_{it} = \omega_i x_t$$

Each equilibrium profile satisfies:

$$1 - \omega_1 - \omega_2 = \left(\frac{1}{A}\right)\left(\frac{1}{\pi}\right)^{1/(1+\beta)}$$

[8] An ever-falling utility path would not satisfy the sequential maximin objective.

where $\omega_i \in (0, 1 - (\frac{1}{A})(\frac{1}{\pi})^{1/(1+\beta)})$. Along any equilibrium path:

$$\frac{x_{t+1}}{x_t} = \left(\frac{1}{\pi}\right)^{1/(1+\beta)} \tag{6.38}$$

Observe that each Nash equilibrium gives rise to the same time path of the stock as the one described in Proposition 5 under a benevolent international dictator. (Compare equation [6.38] and equation.) It follows that we can state:

Corollary 7: There exists a symmetric Nash equilibrium for the game between the two governments. This equilibrium achieves the optimum that would be chosen by a benevolent international dictator with a sequential maximin objective function. Each country will set:

$$E_{it} = \omega^* x_t$$

where

$$\omega^* = \frac{1}{2}\left[1 - \left(\frac{1}{A}\right)\left(\frac{1}{\pi}\right)^{1/(1+\beta)}\right] \equiv \frac{1-z}{2} \tag{6.39}$$

Stackelberg Equilibrium

Now suppose that there is no government in country 2. If the government of country 1 does not take any action, then the equilibrium described in Proposition will apply. Suppose π is in the range specified by the inequalities in (6.33), then this equilibrium implies a declining sequence of utility for both countries. What happens if G_1 takes action (for example, by setting harvesting quotas for its citizens)? Clearly, it must take into account the reaction function of adults in country 2 in period t, for all t. This reaction function is given by equation (6.28). Thus, the period t utility of the adult in country 1 is:

$$u_{1t} = \mu_t h_{1t}\left[A\left(x_t - h_{1t} - \frac{(x_t - h_{1t})}{1+\beta}\right)\right]^{\beta}$$

Write $h_{1t} = \phi x_t$, then:

$$x_{t+1} = A_{x_t}(1-\phi)\left(\frac{\beta}{1+\beta}\right)$$

$$u_{1t} = \mu_t\phi(1-\phi)^\beta A^\beta \left(\frac{\beta}{1+\beta}\right)^{1+\beta}(x_t)^{1+\beta}$$

and:

$$\frac{u_{1t+1}}{u_{1t}} = \pi\left(\frac{x_{t+1}}{x_t}\right)^{1+\beta} = \pi A^{1+\beta}(1-\phi)^{1+\beta}\left(\frac{\beta}{1+\beta}\right)^{1+\beta}$$

Thus, constant utility will occur if and only if ϕ is chosen such that:

$$A(1-\phi)\left(\frac{\beta}{1+\beta}\right) = \left(\frac{1}{\pi}\right)^{1/(1+\beta)}$$

With this choice, in response, the adult in country 2 will harvest:

$$E_{2t} = \frac{(1-\phi)x_t}{1+\beta}$$

and the resulting time path of stock satisfies:

$$\frac{x_{t+1}}{x_t} = \left(\frac{1}{\pi}\right)^{1/(1+\beta)}$$

which is the same as in Proposition 7. The total harvest is the same as in Proposition 7:

$$\frac{h_{1t} + h_{2t}}{x_t} = 1 - z$$

The division of harvest can be shown to be:

$$\frac{h_2}{x_t} = \frac{z}{\beta} > z$$

$$\frac{h_{1t}}{x_t} = 1 - z - \frac{z}{\beta}$$

which is positive provided that:

$$\frac{\beta}{1+\beta} > z \tag{6.40}$$

that is, provided that:

$$\left(\frac{1+\beta}{A\beta}\right)^{1+\beta} < \pi \tag{6.41}$$

Note that the harvest share of country 2 ($h_{2t} / \Sigma h_{it}$) is greater than half if (6.40) holds.

Proposition 8: If G_2 does not exist and G_1 acts as the leader while citizens of country 2 are followers, then a constant utility path can be sustained for each country provided $z < \beta / (1 + \beta)$. Citizens of country 2 (the followers) have a greater share of harvest.

Remark: The intuition behind Proposition 8 is as follows. Suppose the system starts at a Nash equilibrium without government intervention (depicted in Proposition 6), and π satisfies (6.31), so that utility is falling in both countries. If G_1 steps in with the aim of achieving constant consumption, it must reduce total harvest. It knows the reaction function of citizens of country 2: if E_{1t} is reduced by one unit, E_{2t} will increase by $1 + \beta$ units. So country 2 ends up having a greater harvest share. (Note that if π is so small that [6.41] fails to hold, then it is not possible for G_1 to sustain positive utility as a leader.)

Conclusion

We have explored the question of sustainable development in the context of inter-generational and international non-cooperation. The lack of concern for future generations and the lack of cooperation among countries can as seen, impoverish future generations and result in a path of declining welfare. However, if governments play a differential game with a sequential maximin objective, the symmetric non-cooperative Nash equilibrium can achieve sustainable development.

Here the attention is restricted to the problem of inter-generational equity, and, to facilitate the analysis, we have abstracted from intra-generational equity. It is important to mention that, when considering real world problems, we should not forget two crucial facts that offend our sense of equity. The first one is about intra-generational equity. Within any economy at the present time, there are shocking disparities of income levels, health and education standards. The second fact relates to international equity. In the next millennium, when future generations look back to our time, they will find it difficult to understand our complacency about the most glaring inequality in human history: the disparities of per capita income across nations. Why is it that even the most generous nations allocate only about 1 per cent of national income to foreign aid? Why is it that many political philosophers who advocate egalitarian policies concerning income distribution within a country fail to extend this ethic to the international community?

Acknowledgements

In writing this paper, I have benefited from discussions with Geir Asheim, Basant Kapur, Kim Long, Xiao Luo, Tapan Mitra, Yew-Kwang Ng, Gerhard Sorger and Antoine Soubeyran. The research was supported by Social Sciences and Humanities Research Council of Canada, and Fonds Quebecois pour les Recherches sur la Societe et la Culture. The usual disclaimer applies.

References

Altonji, J.G., F. Hayashi and L.W. Kotlikoff. 1992. 'Is the Extended Family Altruistically Linked? Direct Tests Using Micro Data', *American Economic Review*, 82 (5): 1177–98.

———. 1997. 'Parental Altruism and Inter-Vivos Transfers: Theory and Evidence', *Journal of Political Economy*, 105 (6): 1121–66.

Anderson, Elizabeth. 1999. 'What is the Point of Equality?' *Ethics*, 109 (2): 287–337.

Arneson, Richard J. 2002. 'Why Justice Requires Transfer to Offset Income and Wealth Inequalities', *Social Philosophy and Policy*, 19 (1): 172–200.

Chichilnisky, G. 1996. 'An Axiomatic Approach to Sustainable Development', *Social Choice and Welfare*, 13 (3): 231–57.

Dasgupta, P. and G. Heal. 1980. *Economic Theory and Exhaustible Resources*. Cambridge: Nesbit.

Dasgupta, S. and T. Mitra. 1985. 'Intergenerational Equity and the Efficient Allocation of Exhaustible Resources', *International Economic Review*, 24 (1): 133–53.

Frankfurt, H. 1987. 'Equality as a Moral Idea', *Ethics*, 98: 21–42.

Kotlikoff, L.J. and R.W. Rosenthal. 1993. 'Some Inefficiency Implications of Generational Politics and Exchange', *Economics and Politics*, 5 (1): 27–42.

Long, N.V. 2006. 'Toward a Theory of Just Savings', in J. Roemer and K. Suzumura (eds), *Intergenerational Equity and Sustainable Development*. Palgrave.

Rangel, A. 2003. 'Forward and Backward Intergenerational Goods: Why is Social Security Good for the Environment?' *American Economic Review*, 93 (3): 813–34.

———. 2005. 'How to Protect Future Generations Using Tax-based Restrictions', *American Economic Review*, 95 (1): 314–46.

Rawls, J. 1958. 'Justice as Fairness', *Philosophical Review*, 67 (3): 164–94.

———. 1963. 'The Sense of Justice', *Philosophical Review*, 72 (2): 281–305.

———. 1972. *A Theory of Justice*. Oxford: Clarendon Press.

———. 1999. *A Theory of Justice*. Cambridge, MA: The Belknap Press of the Harvard University Press.

Reiss, H. 1970. *Kant's Political Writings*. Cambridge: Cambridge University Press.

Roemer, J. 2006. 'Notes on Intergenerational Justice and Sustainability', J. Roemer and K. Suzumura (eds), *Intergenerational Equity and Sustainable Development*. Palgrave.

Roemer, J. and K. Suzumura. 2006. *Intergenerational Equity and Sustainable Development*. Palgrave.

Roemer, J. and R. Veneziani. 2006. 'Intergenerational Justice, International Relations, and Sustainability', J. Roemer and K. Suzumura (eds), *Intergenerational Equity and Sustainable Development*. Palgrave.

Sandler, Todd. 1978. 'Interregional and Intergenerational Spillovers Awareness', *Scottish Journal of Political Economy*, 25 (3): 273–84.

———. 1982. 'A Theory of Intergenerational Clubs', *Economic Inquiry*, 20 (2): 191–208.

Sandler, Todd and Kerry Smith. 1976. 'Intertemporal and Intergenerational Efficiency', *Journal of Environmental Economics and Management*, 2 (3): 151–59.

Sen, A.K. 1976. 'Rawls versus Bentham: An Axiomatic Examination of the Pure Distribution Problem', in N. Daniels (ed.), *Reading Rawls: Critical Studies on Rawls' A Theory of Justice*. New York: Basic Books.

Silvestre, J. 1994. 'An Efficiency Arguement for Sustainable Use', Working Paper 94-11, Department of Economics, University of California–Davis.

———. 1995. 'Qusilinear Overlapping Generations Economics', Working Paper 95-09, Department of Economics, University of California–Davis.

Waltzer, Michael. 1983. *Spheres of Justices: A Defense of Pluralism and Equality*. New York: Basic Books.

7

Environmental Consequences of Trade Liberalisation in a Small Open Economy

Arghya Ghosh and Partha Sen

Introduction

Does free trade (or, more accurately, freer trade) improve environmental quality or worsen it? Over the past twenty years or so, this question has spawned a very lively debate, both in the academic and policy-making circles.[1] Academic literature seems to suggest that without other distortions, freer trade will improve the environment by raising incomes and thereby raising the demand for a cleaner environment.[2] In the real world where other distortions are present, it is possible that freer trade could be detrimental for the environment.

Historically, there are examples of countries that pursued outward-looking policies (that is, trade as an engine of growth) only to witness dramatic deterioration of the environmental quality followed by a clean-up act over time. The examples of Japan and South Korea come to mind. On the other hand, there are countries like India which pursued inward-looking policies and

---

[1] The other widely debated issue in environmental literature is whether growth leads to an improvement or worsening of the environment. See Stokey (1998) and Smulders (2001).

[2] See, for example, Copeland (1994), Copeland and Taylor (1994, 2003), Lopez (1994) and Rauscher (1997).

did not see either a dramatic worsening of the environmental quality or a significant improvement as income rose. So is the answer to the question posed at the beginning yes or no?

We provide a model which, given a monopolistically competitive production sector,[3] predicts that in the short run trade liberalisation worsens the environment, but in the long run improves it. In this model there are two ways of producing a differentiated good—a dirty technology that requires a little overhead capital but a lot of capital as raw material, and a clean technology that requires a lot of capital as fixed cost. When the market size is small, production is primarily dirty. Trade liberalisation makes possible the entry of firms and cleaner methods. But entry takes time, and in the short run it is primarily the output using dirty production techniques that expand. So in the short term incomes rise but environmental quality deteriorates, while in the long term the rise in incomes sustains a cleaner environment. It is important to emphasise that the mechanism is independent of the demand for a better quality of environment with a rise in incomes—we shut this channel off on purpose.

Thanks to the empirical work of Grossman and Krueger (1995) and subsequent theoretical developments (see Copeland and Taylor 2003), there exists a useful decomposition of change in pollution levels caused by trade liberalisation. First is the scale effect, which suggests that trade increases pollution by increasing the scale of activities. Second is the composition effect, which refers to the change in pollution levels due to change in composition of the production bundle following trade. Finally, the increase in income due to trade increases the demand for clean goods, which in turn raises pollution tax and subsequently forces firms to switch to cleaner techniques. In competitive models the environment improves (becomes cleaner) mainly through the last channel—the 'technique effect'.[4] In contrast, in our model the

[3] See Ethier (1982) and Krugman (1979) for a basic general equilibrium model with monopolistic competition; Helpman and Krugman (1985) for detailed analysis of two-country models; and Venables (1982) and Sen et al. (1997) for a small open economy set-up.

[4] For the country exporting clean goods, in addition to the technique effect, the composition effect also works in favour of lower pollution.

switch from dirty to clean production methods works through entry and exit—a channel previously unexplored.[5]

Model

Consider a small tariff-ridden open economy, which takes all foreign variables as given. Domestic residents consume differentiated goods—consisting of domestic and foreign brands—and suffer disutility from the pollution emitted during the production of domestic brands.[6] Depending on pollution emitted per unit of output—details of which are described later—a domestic brand is labelled as 'clean' or 'dirty'. We assume the pollution to be local, and hence pollution emitted during the production of foreign brands does not affect a representative consumer's utility. Furthermore, to focus on the channel through which our story works—entry and exit—we also abstract away from the issue of polluting taxes or abatement technologies.[7] Following the standard practice in a small open economy setting (see, for example, Sen et al. 1997; Venables 1982) we assume that the number of foreign brands is fixed. In the short run the number of brands—clean or dirty—is also fixed, while in the long run there is free entry and exit in the domestic industry, and the number of each domestic brand is endogenously determined.

Consumers

The representative consumer maximises the following utility function:

$$U(X, E) = X - \frac{E^{\gamma}}{\gamma}, \gamma \geq 1 \tag{7.1}$$

[5] This channel is also missing in the other widely used set of models in the literature—partial equilibrium oligopolistic ones—which typically consider symmetric and fixed number of firms.

[6] A similar story could be told if the pollution were from consumption, though the details would have been significantly different.

[7] See Ulph (1996) for a discussion of tax versus emissions and also choice of technologies in a partial equilibrium framework, with government(s) acting strategically.

subject to the budget constraint:

$$PX = z$$

The utility function $U(X, E)$ is increasing in the differentiated good X and decreasing in total emission E. The price index is P, corresponding to X, and z denotes national income. The aggregate X of the differentiated good and the associated price index P are defined in below.

$$X = \left[\sum_{i=1}^{n} x_{1i}^{b} + \sum_{j=1}^{m} x_{2j}^{b} + \sum_{k=1}^{n^*} x_k^{*b} \right]^{\frac{1}{b}}, b \equiv \frac{\sigma-1}{\sigma}, \sigma > 1 \text{ and}$$

$$P = \left[\sum_{i=1}^{n} p_{1i}^{1-\sigma} + \sum_{j=1}^{m} p_{2j}^{1-\sigma} + \sum_{k=1}^{n^*} (p_k^*(1+t))^{1-\sigma} \right]^{\frac{1}{1-\sigma}}$$

where x_{1i}, x_{2j} and x_k^* denote the amount of domestic consumption of a dirty brand i, clean brand j and a foreign brand k, and p_{1i}, p_{2j} and p_k^* denote the prices of those brands respectively. In the presence of an advalorem tariff $t > 0$, the price of a foreign brand, faced by domestic consumer is $p_k^*(1+t)$.

From the utility maximisation exercise, we obtain the domestic demands for the dirty, clean and foreign brands of the differentiated good as follows:

$$x_{1i} = p_{1i}^{-\sigma} P^{\sigma-1} z, \qquad\qquad i = 1, ..., n$$
$$x_{2j} = p_{2j}^{-\sigma} P^{\sigma-1} z, \qquad\qquad j = 1, ..., m$$
$$x_k^* = [p_k^*(1+t)]^{-\sigma} P^{\sigma-1} z. \qquad k = 1, ..., n^*$$

Assuming a utility function similar (but not identical) to (7.1) for the representative foreign consumer, we find that the foreign demand for the domestic dirty and clean brands, denoted by $\overline{x_{1i}}$ and $\overline{x_{2j}}$ respectively, are:

$$\overline{x_{1i}} = u_1 p_{1i}^{-\sigma} P^{*\sigma-1} z^* \qquad\qquad i = 1, ..., n$$

and

$$\overline{x_{2j}} = u_2 p_{2j}^{-\sigma}\, P^{*\sigma-1} z^*. \qquad\qquad j = 1, ..., m$$

where z^* and P^* denote the foreign GDP and the foreign price index respectively. The parameters u_1 and u_2 capture the difference between home and foreign consumers over the differentiated brands. Since our interest lies in environmental consequences of trade liberalisation in developing countries, it is natural to assume that $u_1 < u_2$, which reflects that, unlike the small open economy where all brands are equally weighted in X, the relative weights for clean brands are higher in the foreign consumption basket (compared to the small open economy). For convenience, we assume that the foreign elasticity of demand is also σ, and in the tradition of small open economy analysis, we hereafter treat z^* and P^* as exogenous.[8]

We focus on the symmetric equilibrium, where all firms within each category—clean, dirty and foreign—are identical. Since the prices of brands within a category are the same in the symmetric equilibrium, hereafter we drop i and j from the subscripts, and we denote the price of a dirty, clean and foreign brand as p_1, p_2 and p^* respectively. A similar argument applies to outputs .

Firms

The production of each brand consists of two components—a variable cost and a fixed cost. Both components use a linear homogeneous technology employing labour (L) and capital (K). Labour is interpreted as unskilled labour, while capital is broadly defined to include raw materials, machines, etc.[9] Let s_1 (respectively s_2) denote the quantity produced of a dirty (respectively clean) brand in the equilibrium, and a_{ij} denote the amount of factor i (= L, K) used in production of one unit of $j(=1, 2)$.

---

[8] Implicitly we assume that there are brands in the foreign consumption basket that are not in X. This implicit assumption can be used to justify exogeneity of P^*.

[9] The broad interpretation helps us avoid using trade models of higher dimensions.

Assumption 1: For all $w, r > 0$, which entail positive production for each good, $\dfrac{a_{K1}}{a_{L1}} > \dfrac{a_{K2}}{a_{L2}}$.

Profit maximisation by the firms implies that in the symmetric equilibrium the price of a domestically produced brand is a mark-up $\sigma/(\sigma - 1)$ of marginal cost:

$$\frac{\sigma}{\sigma - 1}(a_{L1}w + a_{K1}r) = p_1 \tag{7.2}$$

$$\frac{\sigma}{\sigma - 1}(a_{L2}w + a_{K2}r) = p_2 \tag{7.3}$$

The fixed costs component of production in dirty and clean brands, denoted by F and f respectively, are given by $F = a_{LF}w + a_{KF}r$ and $f = a_{Lf}w + a_{Kf}r$, where a_{iF} and a_{if} denotes the use of factor i as an overhead in production of a dirty and clean brand respectively. We assume that substitution between inputs used in fixed cost component is possible in the long run.[10]

Assumption 2: For all $w, r > 0$, for which both clean and dirty brands are produced, $\dfrac{a_{KF}}{a_{LF}} < \dfrac{a_{Kf}}{a_{Lf}}$.

In the long run, entry and exit takes place and firms earn zero profits. From (7.2) and (7.3) it follows that for each firm the variable cost represents a proportion $(\sigma - 1)/\sigma$ of total revenue and the rest, a proportion $1/\sigma$ of revenue, goes to cover the fixed costs. This yields the following:

$$a_{LF}w + a_{KF}r = \frac{p_1 s_1}{\sigma} \tag{7.4}$$

$$a_{Lf}w + a_{Kf}r = \frac{p_2 s_2}{\sigma} \tag{7.5}$$

In order to keep the analysis tractable we consider a particular case of factor intensity rankings satisfying assumptions 1 and 2.

---

[10] These are inputs which have to be in place before production can begin. See in Atkinson and Stiglitz (1980).

Assumption 3: The factor intensities are the same in the variable and the fixed component of the clean goods, that is, $\frac{a_{Kf}}{a_{Lf}} = \frac{a_{K2}}{a_{L2}}$.

Note that together with (7.2) and (7.5), assumption 3 implies that s_2 is fixed in the long run. This significantly simplifies the algebra and the implications for the long run are also clear-cut—clean production increases in the long run if and only if the number of clean firms rises. We must stress that this assumption is for convenience and nothing substantial hinges on it. The following equation summarises the factor intensity rankings:

$$\frac{a_{KF}}{a_{LF}} < \frac{a_{Kf}}{a_{Lf}} = \frac{a_{K2}}{a_{L2}} < \frac{a_{K1}}{a_{L1}}. \tag{7.6}$$

Pollution Emission

We assume that a dirty (clean) brand emits $\phi(\chi)$ units of pollution per unit of output. The total pollution E is the sum of pollution emitted from production of all brands and given by:

$$E = \phi n_1 s_1 + \chi n_2 s_2, \ \phi > \chi$$

where $n_1 s_1$ and $n_2 s_2$ are aggregate domestic production of dirty and clean brands respectively. We also assume that there is an upper limit of emission $\bar{E}$. Without loss of generality we assume that $\chi = 0$, which implies that emission/pollution increases if and only if aggregate dirty production increases.

Market Clearing

The market clearing equation for labour (L) and capital (K) are given by:

$$a_{L1}n_1 s_1 + a_{L2}n_2 s_2 + a_{LF}n_1 + a_{Lf}n_2 = \bar{L} \tag{7.7}$$
$$a_{K1}n_1 s_1 + a_{K2}n_2 s_2 + a_{KF}n_1 + a_{Kf}n_2 = \bar{K} \tag{7.8}$$

where $\bar{L}$ and $\bar{K}$ are supplies of labour and capital respectively. In addition to the two-factor market clearing conditions, there are three goods market clearing conditions—one each for dirty brands

(s_1), clean brands (s_2) and foreign imports (x^*). Equations (7.9), (7.10) and (7.11) are the market clearing equations for a dirty brand, clean brand and an imported brand respectively:

$$s_1 = p_1^{-\sigma} P^{\sigma-1} z + p_1^{-\sigma} P^{*(\sigma-1)} z^* \tag{7.9}$$

$$s_2 = p_2^{-\sigma} P^{\sigma-1} z + p_2^{-\sigma} P^{*(\sigma-1)} z^* \tag{7.10}$$

$$x^* = [p^*(1+t)]^{-\sigma} P^{\sigma-1} z^* \tag{7.11}$$

The national income of this economy (z) is given by

$$z = w\bar{L} + r\bar{K} + \pi + t n^* p^* x^* \tag{7.12}$$

where π is the profit (if any) accruing to firms producing differentiated goods. In the long run, free entry drives the profits down to zero, while in the short run firms might earn non-zero profits. The government levies a tariff at a rate t on the imported varieties and rebates the tariff revenue $t n^* p^* x^*$ in a lumpsum manner to domestic residents. This completes the specification of the model. We now turn to the effects of reduction in tariff—first in the short run and then in the long run.

Trade Liberalisation

Suppose the domestic government reduces tariff on all imported brands. We examine whether lowering trade barriers increases the production of 'dirty' goods.[11] In our framework there are

---

[11] Note that in the presence of imperfect competition, a reduction in tariff rates could lower real income. In a small open economy with labour as the sole factor of production, Venables (1982) showed that if domestic brands are non-tradeable, a tariff can raise home welfare. In our framework that is not necessarily the case since there are two crucial differences from Venables (1982): (a) domestic brands are traded; and (b) there are two factors of production (labour and capital). Indeed, trade liberalisation increases real income in our framework for a wide range of parameterisations, and under these same parameterisations the possibility—increase in dirty production in the short run and decline of the same in the long run—remains.

two factors of production and effectively three 'lines of production', namely, the variable cost component and the fixed cost
component of the dirty brands, and variable component of the
clean brand. In the short run, since the fixed cost components are
given, the model works like a standard two-goods, two-factor
model. In the long term version, when the number of factors
(two) is less than the 'lines of production' (three in our framework), factor intensities in value terms—that is, shares in cost (the
θ_{ij}'s)—will differ from the physical intensities—that is, shares of
an input used in a 'line of production' (the γ_{ij}'s), and this plays
an important role in our set-up.

Short Run

As mentioned before, in the short-run version of the model we
assume that the number of clean and dirty brands is fixed. Differentiation of pricing equations (7.2) and (7.3) and solving for
$\hat{w}$ and $\hat{r}$ in terms of $\hat{p}$ gives (a 'hat' over a variable denotes a
percentage change, for example, $\hat{x} = dx/x$):

$$\hat{w} = \frac{\theta_{K2}\hat{p}_1 - \theta_{K1}\hat{p}_2}{\theta_{L1} - \theta_{L2}}, \tag{7.13}$$

$$\hat{r} = \frac{\theta_{L1}\hat{p}_2 - \theta_{L2}\hat{p}_1}{\theta_{L1} - \theta_{L2}}, \tag{7.14}$$

where θ_{ij} denotes the cost share of factor i in production of a
unit of j. Using (7.13) and (7.14), and noting that the dirty
brand is the capital-intensive one, we get the standard Stolper-
Samuelson result:

$$\frac{\hat{w} - \hat{r}}{\hat{p}_1 - \hat{p}_2} = \frac{1}{\theta_{L1} - \theta_{L2}} < 0 \tag{7.15}$$

that is, an increase in the relative price of the dirty goods lowers
the wage–rental ratio—the relative price of the factor intensively
used in the production of clean brands.

In the short run, since n_1 and n_2 are given and the fixed costs
are incurred upfront, the relevant labour and capital supplies

respectively are $\tilde{L} = \bar{L} - a_{LF}n_1 - a_{Lf}n_2$ and $\tilde{K} = \bar{K} - a_{KF}n_1 - a_{Kf}n_2$. We assume that a_{iF} and a_{if} ($i = L, K$) are fixed in the short run and no capital–labour substitution is possible.[12] Logarithmically differentiating the two-factor market clearing equations ([7.7] and [7.8]), substituting for $\hat{w}$ and $\hat{r}$ from (7.13) and (7.14), and solving for $\hat{s}_1$ and $\hat{s}_2$ yields:

$$\hat{s}_1 = \frac{\tilde{\gamma}_{K2}[\sum_{i=1,2} \tilde{\gamma}_{Li}\theta_{Ki}\varepsilon_i] + \tilde{\gamma}_{L2}[\sum_{i=1,2} \tilde{\gamma}_{Ki}L_{Li}\varepsilon_i]}{(\theta_{Ls} - \theta_{Lq})(\tilde{\gamma}_{Ls} - \tilde{\gamma}_{Ks})}(\hat{p}_1 - \hat{p}_2) \qquad (7.16)$$

$$\hat{s}_2 = -\frac{\tilde{\gamma}_{L1}[\sum_{i=1,2} \tilde{\gamma}_{Ki}\theta_{Li}\varepsilon_i] + \tilde{\gamma}_{K1}[\sum_{i=1,2} \tilde{\gamma}_{Li}\theta_{Ki}\varepsilon_i]}{(\theta_{Ls} - \theta_{Lq})(\tilde{\gamma}_{Ls} - \tilde{\gamma}_{Ks})}(\hat{p}_1 - \hat{p}_2) \qquad (7.17)$$

where $\tilde{\gamma}_{Li}(\tilde{\gamma}_{Ki})$ and ε_i denote the physical share of labour (capital) and the elasticity of substitution respectively in production of a unit of i, $i \in \{1, 2\}$. Subtracting (7.17) from (7.16) and rearranging yields:

$$\frac{\hat{s}_1 - \hat{s}_2}{\hat{p}_1 - \hat{p}_2} = \frac{\sum_{i=1,2} \tilde{\gamma}_{Li}\theta_{Ki}\varepsilon_i + \sum_{i=1,2} \tilde{\gamma}_{Ki}L_{Li}\varepsilon_i}{(\theta_{L1} - \theta_{L2})(\tilde{\gamma}_{L1} - \tilde{\gamma}_{L2})} > 0 \qquad (7.18)$$

Given that in a standard 2×2 model, the factor intensity rankings of the commodities in terms of cost shares and physical shares are identical, equations (7.17), (7.18) and (7.20) essentially say that supply curves are upward sloping—an increase in the relative price of dirty goods raises the production of 'dirty' output and lowers 'clean' production.

To analyse the demand side, we now turn to market clearing equations for brands. Differentiating (7.9) and (7.10), and subsequently subtracting one from the other and rearranging gives:

$$\hat{s}_1 - \hat{s}_2 = -\sigma(\hat{p}_1 - \hat{p}_2) + (\eta_1 - \eta_2)[(\sigma - 1)\hat{P} + \hat{z}] \qquad (7.19)$$

where η_1 (respectively η_2) is the domestic share in total consumption of dirty (clean) brands. Interpreting from a partial

---

[12] This is a simplifying assumption. Nothing substantial hinges on it.

equilibrium perspective, (7.19) says that for a given P and z, the relative demand for dirty goods is decreasing in relative price. Substituting (7.18) in (7.19) and using $\hat{x}^* + \sigma\hat{T} = (\sigma - 1)\hat{P} + \hat{z}$ — which follows from the differentiation of the market clearing equation of the imported brand—yields the following relationship:

$$\frac{\hat{p}_1 - \hat{p}_2}{\hat{T}} = \frac{(\eta_1 - \eta_2)}{A + \sigma}\left(\frac{\hat{x}^* + \sigma\hat{T}}{\hat{T}}\right) \tag{7.20}$$

where $A \equiv \dfrac{\displaystyle\sum_{i=1,2}\tilde{\gamma}_{Li}\theta_{Ki}\varepsilon_i + \sum_{i=1,2}\tilde{\gamma}_{Ki}L_{Li}\varepsilon_i}{(\theta_{L1} - \theta_{L2})(\tilde{\gamma}_{L1} - \tilde{\gamma}_{L2})} > 0$. Given that the small

open economies we are interested in are developing economies embarking on trade liberalisation, which has little environmental regulation in place, it is natural to assume that domestic share in consumption of dirty brands is higher than that of clean brands, that is, $\eta_1 > \eta_2$. Provided σ is not too large, $\dfrac{\hat{x}^* + \sigma\hat{T}}{\hat{T}} < 0$, since the imports (x^*) increase due to trade liberalisation. This in turn implies $\dfrac{\hat{p}_1 - \hat{p}_2}{\hat{T}} < 0$. That is, the relative price of dirty goods increases from trade liberalisation. From the supply relationships [see (7.16) and (7.17)] it immediately follows that production of dirty goods increases as well. Thus, in the short run lowering trade barriers increases dirty production.

The intuition is simple. Lowering trade barriers increases real income, which in turn increases the relative demand for dirty goods, assuming that the domestic share of consumption in the dirty varieties is larger than that in the clean ones. With a standard upward sloping supply relationship, the outward shift in relative demand leads to an increase in relative price in dirty goods and production of dirty output.

Proposition 1: Assume that a small tariff-ridden open economy is initially in long-run equilibrium. A reduction in tariff raises the aggregate production of the dirty brands and accordingly increases pollution.

Long Run

In the long run there is free entry and exit, and hence the number of dirty and clean brands produced, n_1 and n_2, are no longer exogenous. Corresponding to these two new variables, n_1 and n_2 respectively, there are two zero-profit conditions given by (7.4) and (7.5) respectively. Differentiation of these and rearrangement yields:

$$\hat{s}_1 = \frac{\theta_{LF} - \theta_{L1}}{\theta_{L1} - \theta_{L2}} (\hat{p}_1 - \hat{p}_2) \tag{7.21}$$

$$\hat{s}_2 = \frac{\theta_{Lf} - \theta_{L2}}{\theta_{L1} - \theta_{L2}} (\hat{p}_1 - \hat{p}_2) = 0 \tag{7.22}$$

where θ_{iF} (respectively θ_{if}) is the cost share of factor i ($= L, K$) in production of the fixed component F (respectively f). Note that s_2 does not change with a change in relative price because $\theta_{Lf} - \theta_{L2} = 0$, which follows from Assumption 3. Subtracting (7.22) from (7.21) gives:

$$\frac{\hat{s}_1 - \hat{s}_2}{\hat{p}_1 - \hat{p}_2} = \frac{\theta_{LF} - \theta_{L1}}{\theta_{L1} - \theta_{L2}} \tag{7.23}$$

The variable cost components respectively of the dirty goods is the least labour intensive, while the fixed cost component of the same is most labour intensive (see Assumption 3) . That is, $\theta_{LF} - \theta_{L1} > 0$ and $\theta_{L1} - \theta_{L2} < 0$, which in turn implies the following result:

Lemma 1: s_1/s_2 is decreasing in p_1/p_2.

This is different from the short run where, on the supply side, s_1/s_2 is always increasing in p_1/p_2. However, it is important to note that the negative relationship, captured in (7.23), is at the firm level for a given number of clean and dirty firms. To assess the impact of price changes on the aggregate dirty and clean production as a whole, we need to examine the changes in number of firms. Differentiating the two-factor market clearing equations

(7.9) and (7.10), substituting $\hat{s}_2 = 0$, and $\hat{w}$ and $\hat{r}$ from (7.21), (7.13) and (7.14) respectively, and rearranging yields:

$$(\gamma_{L1}+\gamma_{LF})\hat{n}_1+(\gamma_{L2}+\gamma_{Lf})\hat{n}_2+\gamma_{L1}\hat{s}_1=\frac{\sum\limits_{i=1,2,F,f}\gamma_{Li}\theta_{Ki}\varepsilon_i}{\theta_{L1}-\theta_{L2}}(\hat{p}_1-\hat{p}_2) \quad (7.24)$$

$$(\gamma_{K1}+\gamma_{KF})\hat{n}_1+(\gamma_{K2}+\gamma_{Kf})\hat{n}_2+\gamma_{K1}\hat{s}_1=-\frac{\sum\limits_{i=1,2,F,f}\gamma_{Ki}\theta_{Li}\varepsilon_i}{\theta_{L1}-\theta_{L2}}(\hat{p}_1-\hat{p}_2) \quad (7.25)$$

Using (7.21), (7.22), (7.24) and (7.25), we find the following relationship between the aggregate supply of dirty goods and relative prices:

$$\hat{n}_1 + \hat{s}_1 = \frac{A_1}{(\theta_{L1} - \theta_{L2})[(\gamma_{L1} + \gamma_{LF}) - (\gamma_{K1} + \gamma_{KF})]}(\hat{p}_1 - \hat{p}_2) \quad (7.26)$$

$$\hat{n}_2+\hat{s}_2=\hat{n}_2=-\frac{A_2}{(\theta_{L1} - \theta_{L2})[(\gamma_{L1} + \gamma_{LF}) - (\gamma_{K1} + \gamma_{KF})]}(\hat{p}_1-\hat{p}_2) \quad (7.27)$$

where

$$A_1 = \sum_{i=s_1, s_2, F, f}[\gamma_{Li}\theta_{Ki}(\gamma_{K2} + \gamma_{Kf}) + \gamma_{Ki}(\gamma_{L2} + \gamma_{Lf})\theta_{Li}]\,\varepsilon_i + (\theta_{LF}$$
$$- \theta_{L1})\,[\gamma_{LF}(\gamma_{K2} + \gamma_{Kf}) - \gamma_{KF}(\gamma_{L2} + \gamma_{Lf})]$$

$$A_2 = \sum_{i=s_1, s_2, F, f}[\gamma_{Li}\theta_{Ki}(\gamma_{K1} + \gamma_{KF}) + \gamma_{Ki}(\gamma_{L1} + \gamma_{LF})\theta_{Li}]\,\varepsilon_i + (\theta_{LF}$$
$$- \theta_{L1})\,[\gamma_{LF}(\gamma_{K1} + \gamma_{KF}) - \gamma_{KF}(\gamma_{L1} + \gamma_{LF})]$$

The factor intensity rankings in different lines of production given by (7.6) imply that and $(\theta_{LF} - \theta_{L1}) > 0$, $[\gamma_{LF}(\gamma_{K2} + \gamma_{Kf}) - \gamma_{KF}(\gamma_{L2} + \gamma_{Lf})] > 0$ and $\gamma_{LF}(\gamma_{K1} + \gamma_{KF}) - \gamma_{KF}(\gamma_{L1} + \gamma_{LF}) > 0$. Thus, both A_1 and A_2 are strictly positive. Then, from the aggregate supply relationships, given by (7.26) and (7.27) respectively, it is easy to see that aggregate dirty production increases with trade liberalisation if both (*a*) and (*b*) hold or if neither of them holds: (*a*) $\dfrac{\hat{p}_1 - \hat{p}_2}{\hat{T}} < 0$; and (*b*) $(\theta_{L1} - \theta_{L2})[(\gamma_{L1} + \gamma_{LF}) - (\gamma_{k1} + \gamma_{KF})] > 0$.

Both (*a*) and (*b*) hold in the short run. Income gains from trade liberalisation create excess demand for the dirty goods—and this in turn leads to higher relative prices for dirty goods. The second one—point (*b*)—is trivially satisfied since the variable cost component is the only relevant one in the short run and the rankings of the two lines of production in terms of factor intensities is the same for cost shares (θ_{ij}) and physical shares (γ_{ij}).

In the long run the relative price of the dirty goods might decline. The key to understanding this result is the inverse relationship between s_1/s_2 and p_1/p_2, given by (7.23). Unlike the upward-sloping short-run supply curve, here the relative supply of the dirty goods (at the firm level) is downward sloping in $(s_1/s_2, p_1/p_2)$ space. The demand relationship is still given by (7.19) and is downward sloping as well. Hence, if the relative supply function is flatter than the demand, an outward shift in demand created due to trade-induced income gains would lead to decline in relative prices in the dirty goods. This shows up in (7.28), which we obtain from combining (7.23) and (7.19):

$$\frac{\hat{p}_1 - \hat{p}_2}{\hat{T}} = \frac{(\eta_1 - \eta_2)}{\sigma - \left(1 + \dfrac{\theta_{Lf} - \theta_{LF}}{\theta_{L1} - \theta_{L2}}\right)} \left(\frac{\hat{x}^* + \sigma\hat{T}}{\hat{T}}\right) \tag{7.28}$$

If the demand relationship is steeper than the supply curve in $(s_1/s_2, p_1/p_2)$ space, the following holds:

$\sigma < -\dfrac{(\theta_{LF} - \theta_{Lf}) - (\theta_{L1} - \theta_{L2})}{\theta_{L1} - \theta_{L2}} \equiv \left(1 + \dfrac{\theta_{Lf} - \theta_{LF}}{\theta_{L1} - \theta_{L2}}\right)$. Thus, if we consider (as we did in the short run) that, $\dfrac{\hat{x}^* + \sigma\hat{T}}{\hat{T}} < 0$ and $\eta_1 > \eta_2$ then, trade liberalisation leads to lower the relative price of the dirty goods. The increase in relative price of the clean goods brings in more clean firms. This in turn increases clean production (or equivalently lowers aggregate dirty production) provided (*b*) holds.

However, the decline in the relative price of dirty goods is not necessary for an increase in clean production in the long run. One might even say that the decline in the relative price of the exportable goods is a perverse possibility. So now we consider another important channel, referred to in the introduction, through which trade liberalisation can lead to an increase in clean production. Assume that $\sigma > \left(1 + \dfrac{\theta_{Lf} - \theta_{LF}}{\theta_{L1} - \theta_{L2}}\right)$, that is relative price of dirty goods increases with trade liberalisation and $(\theta_{L1} - \theta_{L2})$ $[(\gamma_{L1} + \gamma_{LF}) - (\gamma_{K1} + \gamma_{KF})] < 0$. Even though variable cost component of the dirty brand is capital intensive $(\theta_{L1} < \theta_{L2})$, the share of overhead capital might be so low in the production of the dirty goods that, overall, dirty goods actually can turn out to be labour intensive $(\gamma_{L1} + \gamma_{LF} > \gamma_{K1} + \gamma_{KF})$. If this is the case, then even if relative price of the dirty goods increases, aggregate dirty production declines.

The intuition is simple. For a given configuration of firms, an increase in relative price of the dirty goods a causes a decline in its supply [see(7.23)]. This increases the available capital–labour ratio for other lines of production. Since clean goods is capital intensive in this case, an increase in the available capital–labour ratio encourages entry in the clean sector, which in turn leads to an increase in aggregate clean production.

Proposition 2: Assume that a small tariff-ridden open economy is in long-run equilibrium and the share of tariff revenue in the national income is small. Then a reduction in tariff lowers the aggregate production of dirty goods, if and only if exactly one of the following holds:

(1) $\sigma < \left(1 + \dfrac{\theta_{Lf} - \theta_{LF}}{\theta_{L1} - \theta_{L2}}\right)$; or

(2) $sgn\,(\theta_{L1} - \theta_{L2}) = -sgn\,[(\gamma_{L1} + \gamma_{LF}) - (\gamma_{K1} + \gamma_{KF})]$.

The difference in short-run and long-run effects suggests that policy makers need to exercise caution in addressing environmental concerns arising from trade liberalisation. For example, a myopic government might adopt too stringent an environmental policy, without realising that some of the 'dirtyness' will wither away (through the exit of dirty firms) in the long run. Note that we deliberately set aside any strategic policy making by the governments—emission quotas, pollution taxes—to focus on one channel, namely, entry and exit in the long run. Needless to say, in the presence of endogenous policies, the rise in incomes due to trade liberalisation would create demand for a cleaner environment, which would raise the environmental standards.

Conclusion

The beneficial effect of trade liberalisation in the literature works through an income effect, and typically in a competitive framework. We have provided a new channel for trade liberalisation to affect the environment. When the market was small (in the presence of trade-reducing high tariffs), there were too few clean firms (since these come with high fixed costs). When trade is liberalised but no entry is allowed, dirty firms expand. But with a higher market size, entry means cleaner production. So the answer as to whether trade is dirty or clean for the environment is that it is both—dirty in the short run and clean in the long run. As mentioned in the introduction, this is not just the conclusion of an arcane theoretical model—it is supported by historical evidence.

References

Atkinson, Anthony B. and Joseph E. Stiglitz. 1980. *Lectures in Public Economics*, New York: McGraw-Hill.
Copeland, B.R. 1994. 'International Trade and the Environment: Policy Reform in a Polluted Small Open Economy', *Journal of Environmental Economics and Management*, 26: 44–65.
Copeland, B.R. and M. Scott Taylor. 1994. 'North–South Trade and the Global Environment', *Quarterly Journal of Economics*, 109: 755–87.

Copeland, B.R. and M. Scott Taylor. 2003. *Trade and the Environment*. Princeton University Press.

Ethier,W. 1982. 'National and International Returns to Scale in the Modern Theory of International Trade', *American Economic Review*, 72: 389–405.

Grossman, G.M. and A.B. Krueger. 1995. 'Economic Growth and the Environment', *Quarterly Journal of Economics*, 353–77.

Helpman, E. and P.R. Krugman. 1985. *Market Structure and Foreign Trade*. Cambridge, MA: MIT Press.

Krugman, P.R. 1979. 'Increasing Returns, Monopolistic Competition and International Trade', *Journal of International Economics*, 9 (1979): 469–79.

Lopez, R. 1994. 'The Environment as a Factor of Production: The Effects of Economic Growth and Trade Liberalization', *Journal of Environmental Economics and Management*, 27: 163–84.

Rauscher, M. 1997. *International Trade, Factor Movements and the Environment*. Oxford: Clarendon Press.

Sen, P., A. Ghosh and A. Barman. 1997. 'The Possibility of Welfare Gains with Capital Inflows in a Small Tariff-distorted Economy', *Economica*, 64: 345–52.

Smulders, S. 2001. 'Growth and Environment', Keynote Lecture, Annual Conference of the European Association of the Environmental and Resource Economics, Southampton.

Stokey, N. 1998. 'Are there Limits to Growth?', *International Economic Review*, 39: 1–31.

Ulph, A.M. 1996. 'Environmental Policy and International Trade when Governments and Producers Act Strategically', *Journal of Environmental Economics and Management*, 30: 265–81.

Venables, A.J. 1982. 'Optimal Tariffs for Trade in Monopolistically Competitive Commodities', *Journal of International Economics*, 12: 224–41.

8

Smallholders and the Forest Logging Industry in the Brazilian Amazon

Frank Merry and Gregory S. Amacher

Introduction

Since 1995 almost 600,000 migrant families have officially settled in Brazil,[1] of which approximately 56 per cent have settled in the region described as the 'Legal Amazon'. The lot settled by these migrants is 100 hectares, giving an estimated total area currently occupied by smallholders in the Brazilian Amazon of 32.5 million hectares; the unofficial settlement area is widely regarded to be much greater. Within these settlements the forest resource is not viewed as an efficient producer of wealth (Macqueen 2004; Macqueen et al. 2003). Instead, most smallholders clear land, burn the forest stock, and plant agricultural crops in a classic cycle of slash-and-burn systems. This has led to widespread deforestation of native forest stocks. Moreover, an ignorance of forest management practices by smallholders, coupled with lack of secure property rights,[2] has eliminated potential rents that could be captured by both smallholders and the government (through tax revenue collections).

[1] See http://www.incra.gov.br.

[2] Forest management plans, approved by the Instituto Brasileiro do Meio Ambiente e dos Recusros Naturais Renováveis (IBAMA; the

Recently, a new type of relationship between the forest industry practising sustainable forest management and smallholders is emerging in migrant settlements. Smallholders have begun to enter into formal forest management contracts with the logging industry. These are market-based agreements, where large capital-based firms contract to clear land and harvest timber from the 'legal deforestation' area of smallholder plots,[3] while implementing forest management plans for the remainder of the lot according to legislation designed by the Instituto Brasileiro do Meio Ambiente e dos Recusros Naturais Renováveis (IBAMA).[4] Smallholders with these contracts benefit throughout the year from labour savings from income generation (that is, the loggers' capital investment reduces the time needed by the smallholder to clear land), and the community may benefit if logging improves infrastructure through building of roads needed for timber removal and processing. Labour savings could allow diversion of family members towards other productive activities, and infrastructure may increase access to markets and off-farm income-generating opportunities. The end result of these contracts may be to ultimately change the decision making of smallholders regarding land clearing and agricultural crop production, both of which are leading causes of deforestation in Amazonia. It is no wonder that these contracts have recently been identified as a promising new forest management tool for promoting sustainable forest practices (for example, see Lima et al. 2003; Merry et al. 2004; Nepstad et al. 2004; Nepstad et al. in press).

Brazilian Institute of the Environment and Renewable Natural Resources, which is responsible for all aspects of environmental regulation and control in Brazil), require formal documentation of landownership—even a temporary title, or *protocolo*, will suffice—which is rarely present in settlements (Alston et al. 1999). This hurdle makes forest management planning by smallholders on their lots difficult.

[3] Brazilian legislation provides for the legal deforestation of 20 per cent of the lot. The remainder must stay as forest and can only be used for forest management with approved management plans.

[4] This type of contract is commonplace on the frontiers, but in the past has been entirely biased to suit the timber industry due to information externalities and high smallholder discount rates associated with

This paper investigates the importance of smallholder forest industry contracts to productivity, labour allocation and land clearing (deforestation) decisions. The empirical approach here follows existing literature by addressing incomplete labour markets present in the sample region, but also goes beyond to show how forest industry contracts affect household labour decisions.[5] The analysis examines a full set of labour choices for smallholders. It is certainly possible that labour choices depend on these contracts, and understanding this dependence will provide a clearer picture of smallholder economic activity.

Model of Smallholder Decisions

Let us examine the importance of forest management contracts to smallholder labour use, production of crops and land clearing. We construct a household-based model relevant for our data to show how these decisions depend on forest management contracts, wealth, demographic factors and other variables such as the opportunity cost of time.

We examine a subsistence household employing its own labour and producing goods, but facing constraints on labour time and production. Similar approaches applied to smallholders in other Latin American contexts can be found in Pattanayak and Sills (2001); Pendleton and Howe (2002); and Shivley (2001). There are also numerous related models applied to fuelwood collection in arid countries, including Bluffstone (1998); Cooke (1998a, 1998b); Kohlin (1998); Kohlin and Amacher (2005); and Kohlin and Parks (2001). While our modelling of the labour market is similar, our work differs from other smallholder studies in that we consider forest industry contracts, and we consider different types of labour allocation decisions. Furthermore, wood is not a limiting household resource in the Amazon; thus, the forest

---

life on the frontier. The difference in the emerging contracts is equal information and formal written contracts.

[5] Most of the focus on smallholder behaviour has been on land clearing or on migration patterns and household cycles (Barbier and Burgess 2001; Caviglia 2000; Perz and Walker 2002).

management contracts we examine differ considerably from the community forestry arrangements studied in fuelwood-based development literature.

Household labour in Brazilian smallholder communities is allocated in two distinct phases. In the wet season, a period of four to six months, the smallholder uses labour for crop production activities. During the dry season labour is used primarily for land clearing and burning of forested land. Other activities, such as non-timber forest product collection or off-farm labour, can span both seasons. Male adult labour is the main type of labour for household productive activities, and it is normally the oldest adult male that serves as the primary decision maker for the household.

Let the index $c = 1, 0$ denote whether or not a representative smallholder has entered into a formal contract with the forest industry. Suppose the representative smallholder receives utility from consumption of forest-related goods (hunting and collection of non-timber forest products) (F), other goods (x), agricultural goods (Q_c) and leisure time $(T - L)$,

$$U(F, x, Q_c, T - L; \Omega) \tag{8.1}$$

where Ω is a vector of smallholder household-specific factors that affect utility. Utility is increasing in all arguments.

The amount of forest land left uncleared will be denoted $\bar{A} - A$, where A is land cleared for agriculture and $\bar{A}$ is the smallholder endowment of land. In the language of the Brazilian government, $\bar{A} - A$ is the 'legal reserve', and A is land cleared according to 'legal deforestation'. The government limits allowable land clearing so that this represents a constraint, $\bar{A} - A \leq H$, where H is the limit. For most smallholders in our sample, as discussed later, this constraint is not binding.

The variable L in (8.1) is total household time allocated in all production activities and is constrained by total time available T and leisure time l, that is:

$$L = L_E + L_A + L_F + L_o + L_c + L_t = T - l \tag{8.2}$$

where L_E is labour exchanged with other households, L_A is labour used for agricultural production, L_F is labour used for non-timber forest product collection, L_o is off-farm labour if any, L_c is labour devoted to land clearing, and L_t is labour devoted to transport of household-produced goods to markets. It is possible that having a forest management contract changes labour devoted to land clearing. The time constraint (8.2) is a distinguishing feature of the household models noted earlier.

The smallholder household engages in production of crops on cleared land with a production vector defined by the following concave production function:

$$Q = Q \, (A, L_A, L_{HD}, K_A, L_E, R) \tag{8.3}$$

where A measures hectares of land cleared on the smallholder's plot during the period of our data, L_{HD} is labour hired by the smallholder if any, K_A is capital used in crop production (or the value of capital items as a proxy), and R is a vector of land characteristics important to crop yields.

The land clearing choice A is a complex function of household preferences and labour opportunities. It is not an explicit choice per se, but rather follows from labour and capital decisions—this is also true in Pendleton and Howe (2002). Consequently, land clearing depends on labour use and availability, prices and capital, but it may also be a function of logging contracts. The precise specification of the land clearing function is addressed later.

The household faces the following cash budget constraint which requires total purchases and spending to equal total income generated through household production activities plus any exogenous income received:

$$I = [P_c A + M + P_A(Q - Q_c) + wL_b] - [P_x X + wL_{HD} + rK_A \\ + t(Q - Q_c, L_t, c)] = 0 \tag{8.4}$$

The terms in the first bracket measure household income components, including land clearing income if the smallholder sells wood to the forest industry ($c = 1$), exogenous income M, sale of crops not consumed (third term) (P_A is the price of crops and Q_c is crops consumed), and off-farm wage income if the smallholder travels away to urban areas during the year (w is the off-farm wage rate). The second set of bracketed terms measures expenditures of the smallholder—these include other goods consumed in the market (first term) (P_x is the price of other goods), any labour that the smallholder might have access to hiring (second term), capital used (third term) (r is the cost of capital), and transport costs for selling produced agricultural goods in the nearest market (last term).

The transport cost function in (8.4), $t(Q - Q_c, L_t, c)$ reflects the fact that smallholders must devote resources (time and money) to travelling to markets for sale of produced goods—in our survey, households sold and consumed some of what was produced, so that $Q > 0$ and $Q_c > 0$, and thus all households reported a price for products sold (indicating that an assumption of complete output markets seems reasonable for our data). Transport cost is increasing in the amount sold in the market and labour time. The inclusion of the index c reflects the possibility that the forest industry's presence in the area improves the quality of roads needed for the movement of wood out of the region, and thus that

$$\frac{\partial t(.)}{\partial c} \leq 0.$$

Thin Labour Markets

Smallholders do not have unobstructed access to hiring labour or supplying their own labour off farm during the production season. Settlements are spread out over hundreds of kilometres, and to find off-farm work the male head of household must often travel away to larger markets (where abundant labour opportunities exist) for extended periods of time.[6] Farm labour comes primarily from the household's own labour, or it is arranged through an exchange with other households in the immediate area. The presence of this exchange, where an individual works a number of days for a neighbour in return for the equivalent number of days provided by the recipient, is a feature of every smallholder in our data and is also an indication that labour markets are either incomplete or that transactions costs for hiring are

[6] When off-farm work was reported in our sample, this was typically due to the smallholder head of household travelling and staying away for several months.

high. Finally, and importantly, smallholders in our sample use their own labour uniquely for some productive activities, such as hunting and non-timber forest products collection.

These observations imply that labour markets in smallholder settlements are not fully complete and this will affect our empirical approach. To wit, in our sample, discussed later, many small-holders do not report (or know) market wages for off-farm labour. Labour is, therefore, not supplied and hired freely at a single wage rate. In cases like this previous work has shown that households make labour decisions according to an opportunity cost of time that is an unobserved function of household preferences. Production and consumption decisions also become non-separable, that is, functions of preferences.[7]

The literature further establishes that the value marginal product (VMP) of household production is an appropriate instrument for the opportunity cost of time. We will follow this literature closely here (for general examples, see: Bluffstone 1995; Jacoby 1993; Thornton 1994; also see Amacher et al. 1996, 1999; Cooke 1998a and b; Kohlin and Parks 2001; Pattanayak and Sills 2001; Pendleton and Howe 2002; Shivley 2001). Assuming that households allocate labour optimally, any important production activity can be used to define the value marginal products for the household. The VMPs are called 'shadow wages' and are important to both production and consumption decisions with non-separability.

Shadow wages can be computed by estimating the production function (8.3) and then calculating the value of marginal product for labour time using the market price of goods. This VMP is then used in the empirical analysis as the opportunity cost of labour time. The precise interpretation of the shadow wage comes from the first order conditions of the smallholder's utility maximisation problem.

---

[7] The idea is similar to a model where constraints on labour use exist, but here our constraint arises due to the travel time (that is, transactions cost) required for the smallholder to access off-farm labour markets—this reduces time available from the right hand side of equation (8.2).

Smallholder Decisions

We will focus primarily on labour supply decisions and production. To obtain the first order conditions of the smallholder's utility maximisation problem, we maximise (8.1) subject to the cash budget constraint (8.4), the time constraint on labour (8.2), the production function for agriculture (8.3), and the land clearing constraint, while also implicitly assuming the smallholder is constrained in providing off-farm labour, $L_o = 0$ (hired labour may still be positive if it is available and the relevant cost of it is the wage paid). The household's choices are labour allocated to various activities, including land clearing, capital use and consumption of market goods (x), as well as produced goods (Q_c).

The Lagrangian for the problem is:

$$\zeta = Max_{L,F,x,L_{hd}} \{U(F, x, Q_c, T - L; \Omega) + \lambda I + \mu(L - T + l)$$
$$+ vQ + \xi(\overline{A} - A - H)\} \tag{8.4}$$

where the multipliers on the constraints (λ, μ, v, ξ) are all assumed to be non-negative. In (8.5) λ is the multiplier on the budget constraint in (8.4), μ is the multiplier on the labour time constraint of (8.2), and it represents the opportunity cost of household time (it is sometimes called a shadow wage). For simplicity in narration, assume that agricultural output is strictly positive and that the constraint on land clearing is not binding. Then, the first order conditions for production and labour supply include (8.2), (8.3), (8.4) and the following equations for smallholder labour supply allocated to selected activities:

$$L_c : -\frac{\partial U(.)}{\partial L_c} + \mu - \lambda[P_A \frac{\partial Q(.)}{\partial A} \frac{\partial A(.)}{\partial L_c}] = 0 \tag{8.6}$$

$$L_A : -\frac{\partial U(.)}{\partial L_A} + \mu - \lambda P_A[\frac{\partial Q(.)}{\partial L_A}] = 0 \tag{8.7}$$

$$L_E : -\frac{\partial U(.)}{\partial L_E} + \mu - \lambda[P_A \frac{\partial Q(.)}{\partial A} \frac{\partial A(.)}{\partial L_E} + P_A \frac{\partial Q(.)}{\partial L_E}] = 0 \tag{8.8}$$

$$L_F : -\frac{\partial U(.)}{\partial F}\frac{\partial F}{\partial L_F} - \frac{\partial U(.)}{\partial L_F} + \mu = 0 \qquad (8.9)$$

$$L_t : -\frac{\partial U(.)}{\partial L_t} + \mu - \lambda\frac{\partial t(.)}{\partial L_t} = 0 \qquad (8.10)$$

The opportunity cost of time is present in these conditions through the labour time constraint multiplier. Further, all labour time equations include, as the marginal cost of time, a value marginal product term that represents the marginal cost of employing labour time for each activity. Condition (8.6) shows that the smallholder allocates land clearing labour so that the marginal disutility of labour plus the shadow wage equals the marginal benefit of labour in terms of production of goods produced from additional land cleared. The second condition (8.7) shows that crop labour is allocated so that the marginal disutility of labour time equals the marginal value product of goods produced and sold in the market. Equation (8.8) shows that exchange labour time is chosen by equating the shadow value of time less disutility of labour, equal to the value marginal product of having additional labour in production (term in brackets). Finally, transportation labour time in equation (8.10) is chosen to balance the opportunity cost of time less disutility of work, with the marginal benefit of additional income (third term). The importance of a forest management contract, denoted by $c > 0$, is implicit in all of these conditions.

The opportunity cost of time is represented by the shadow price of the labour time constraint, μ. This measures the marginal benefit of an additional unit of labour time to household utility and is endogenous to the equations given earlier. Rewriting (8.6) and assuming again that leisure time is zero, we have $\mu = \lambda$ $[P_A \frac{\partial Q(.)}{\partial A}\frac{\partial A(.)}{\partial L_c}] - \frac{\partial U(.)}{\partial L_c}$. From this it is obvious that the shadow value of labour time used in land clearing is a function of preferences (through utility) and the value marginal products of smallholder household labour in important production activities (through the production function). The shadow wage is, therefore, determined simultaneously with other choices made by the smallholder.

Econometric Specification

The first order conditions can in principle be solved for a vector of labour supplies and production possibilities:

$$L^* = L(P_A, P_x, r, w, \hat{w}, R, M, c; \Omega) \tag{8.11}$$

$$Q = Q\,(A, L_A, K_A, L_{HD}, L_E, R) \tag{8.12}$$

where the * denotes optimal choices for the labour decisions, and the production function (8.12) follows from (8.3). The optimal labour choices from (8.11) determine the realised level of labour-intensive land clearing on the smallholder's lot:

$$A^* = A(L_F^*, L_E^*, L_{HD}^*, c) = A(P_A, P_x, r, w, \hat{w}, R, M, c; \Omega) \tag{8.13}$$

As the arguments of the optimal choices and land clearing equations are derived from the first order conditions, these choices will depend on explanatory variables such as the vector of agricultural prices, preference variables, forest management contracts, and characteristics of the resource stock that might affect land clearing. From the first order conditions (8.6) to (8.10), the parameter $\hat{w}$ denotes the shadow wage and must also be included in the labour supply choice (see Jacoby 1993). As discussed earlier, this can be instrumented using a value marginal product obtained from (8.12):

$$\hat{w} = \frac{\partial Q(.)}{\partial L_A} \tag{8.14}$$

We should point out that market wages should still be used to represent the cost of hired labour, or to define the income the male family labour in our sample earns through off-farm work. Hence, as Jacoby (ibid.) shows, there are two wages that will affect (8.11) and (8.13), the market wage and the shadow wage in (8.14).[8]

[8] Given that we assume households are optimising, the shadow wage would equal the market wage if labour markets were complete.

Forest management contracts are also present in these equations. They affect smallholder income directly (see equation [8.5]) and indirectly through transportation and labour time savings. In order to evaluate their importance, we must obtain an econometric specification by developing reduced forms for (8.11) to (8.14). Incomplete labour markets imply that the model is nonseparable, and thus each decision depends implicitly on household preferences as well as production factors in addition to the shadow wage. The formal comparative statics of such a system have been shown repeatedly in the literature to be unsolvable. Thornton (1994) made some progress using a method of principle components applied to a reduced set of decisions, but he was only able to conduct comparative statics for two household choices.

Despite this, the first order conditions do define the estimable equations and the explanatory variables that should be present in each equation. We expect smallholder labour supplies (8.11) to be a positive function of output prices, capital and land characteristics favourable for agricultural production, and a negative function of opportunity costs of time, a forest management contract and exogenous income. The production function (8.12) should be a positive function of labour and capital units, as well as resource factors important to production such as land cleared. The amount of land cleared (8.13) should be a positive function of output prices and the forest management contract, and a negative function of opportunity costs of time, transport costs and exogenous income. These assumptions are consistent with labour supplies being positively related to own price effects and negatively related to cross price effects for substitute activities. Shadow wages affect labour as an opportunity cost.

Precise estimation procedures for (8.11) to (8.14) follow Jacoby (1993) and Thornton (1994). Rather than repeating their derivations here, we describe the procedure. First, one assumes the existence of an optimal vector of inputs consistent with the first order conditions (8.6) to (8.10). The maximum profit function for a smallholder conditioned on these decisions is then defined, using these optimal choices, and inserted into the cash budget constraint (8.5) so that net income is defined at the optimal input choices. The utility maximisation first order conditions, using this new budget constraint, are then solved for conditional consumption demands. All of the optimal decisions from this maximisation are again substituted into the cash constraint, which must hold at equilibrium household choices. Given that certain linearity conditions hold in the vicinity of this optimum, the conditional input (labour) supplies are then derived using Hotelling's lemma applied to the modified cash constraint. If households are optimising, which is always assumed, then all of the smallholder household's choices are a function of exogenous income and preference-related variables, as well as all relevant prices and costs.[9]

Functional forms follow from assumptions about the utility and production functions. If we assume a Stone–Geary utility function and a Cobb–Douglas production function, as the previously discussed household studies did, then the maximum profit function used to derive the estimable equations is log linear. This implies that our labour supply functions in (8.11) and land clearing (8.13) are log linear specifications, while the production function (8.12) is a log-log specification (Amacher et al. 1999; Thornton 1994).

The system of equations (8.11) to (8.14) also contains endogenous regressors, such as crop income, shadow wage and land clearing (present in the labour supply function). Endogeneity will be handled with the usual instrumental variable estimation procedure. A suitable instrument in our data for the income variable is exogenous (non-production) income and remittances, and following the literature an instrument for the endogenous shadow wage in the labour supply and land clearing functions is the value marginal product in (8.14). To estimate the land clearing equation, we will use a two-stage least squares procedure (Greene 1997), where first the land clearing equation is estimated using the shadow wage and exogenous income, as well as the other explanatory variables. This first-stage regression is used to determine a prediction for land clearing in our data. The prediction is then

---

[9] We would also have consumption decisions in a full model, but it is not necessary to estimate these decisions because our main objective is to investigate how forest management contracts impact labour and productivity decisions.

used in a second-stage regression where the labour supply regressions are estimated. Potential heteroskedasticity in the data will be corrected using White's method ex ante to estimation (ibid.).

Data and Results

Data to estimate the model come from an enumerated interview questionnaire applied to a random sample of 360 smallholders in 19 communities of the INCRA (National Institute for Colonisation and Agrarian Reform) settlements Moju I and II along feeder roads of the BR 163 (Santarém–Cuiaba highway) between kilometre markers 101 and 145 south of Santarém. One principal enumerator was trained by the authors at the Instituto de Pesquisa Ambiental da Amazônia (IPAM), and accompanied to the field between March and June 2003. Interviews were conducted with the head of household, using a recall instrument based on smallholder decisions over the past one year.

Descriptive statistics for important variables used in the regressions, along with others of interest, are presented in Table 8.1. There were an average of 3.74 dependents and other members of the family ($sd = 2.23$, $n = 360$). Only 11 per cent of the sample stated that they held definite title to the land, while 60 per cent of the lots ($n = 339$) had been officially settled under INCRA rules; 12 per cent had been illegally squatted ($n = 339$) and 28 per cent ($n = 339$) of lots had been purchased. Respondents had been living on the lots for an average of 6.8 years ($sd = 6.3$, $n = 355$), but the range of residence was from 26 years to 2 months. The average lot size was 94 hectares ($sd = 13$, $n = 357$) and located 26 km ($sd = 18$, $n = 356$) from the BR 163 highway. Upon settling, smallholders found an average of 2.5 hectares deforested ($sd = 5.9$, $n = 356$), and each smallholder cleared an average of 8.8 hectares ($sd = 11.7$, $n = 351$) for a total average clearing of 11.25 hectares ($sd = 12.77$, $n = 352$), roughly 13 per cent, well under the legal 20 per cent limit set by INCRA.

In the case of total land clearing, older communities appear to have deforested a greater area, but it also appears that younger communities clear land at a higher rate. The average value of agricultural products sold and consumed was (Real) R$ 1,064

Table 8.1
Descriptive Statistics of Variables Used in Regressions

	Unit	Mean	Standard Deviation	Minimum	Maximum	n
Number of Dependents		3.74	2.23	0.00	14.00	360
Logging Contract	%	0.20	0.40	0.00	1.00	360
Age of Resident	Years	46.00	12.46	20.00	77.00	307
Distance to Water	m	313.43	635.74	0.00	5,000.00	357
Distance to Major Highway	km	26.15	18.16	0.15	82.00	356
Distance to All-weather Dirt Highway	km	17.99	9.77	0.00	42.00	356
Area Deforested (Present Owner)	hectare	8.80	11.73	0.00	90.00	351
Gently Sloping Land	Y/N	0.61	0.49	0.00	1.00	360
Years on Lot	Years	6.77	6.27	0.10	26.00	355
Settled by INCRA	Y/N	0.60	0.49	0.00	1.00	339
Planted Area Last Year	hectare	1.64	1.55	0.00	20.00	355
Transport Cost (per Sack)	R$	2.24	0.65	1.50	10.00	194
Transport Time	Hours per Trip	4.98	1.26	2.00	8.00	174

(Table 8.1 continued)

(*Table 8.1 continued*)

	Unit	Mean	Standard Deviation	Minimum	Maximum	n
Hours Worked per Day	Hours	7.31	2.08	0.00	14.00	345
Man-Days Hired	Days/Year	59.55	124.79	0.00	900.00	348
Days Exchanged	Days/Year	59.07	43.40	0.00	210.00	317
Days Worked Off Farm	Days/Year	44.75	73.40	0.00	300.00	349
Days Hunting	Days/Year	21.08	35.41	0.00	240.00	349
Days Collecting NTFPs	Days/Year	15.31	27.99	0.00	192.00	319
Monthly Purchases	R$/Month	150.72	100.48	20.00	600.00	351
Crop Value	R$	1,900.90	2,993.31	0.00	28,166.00	316
Exogenous Income	R$/Year	1,524.14	2,049.80	0.00	12,000.00	348
Shadow Wage	R$/Year*	270.91	440.03	0	4,854.58	305

Note: *The shadow wage in the table is the estimated value marginal product measured per year for an average hour of extra work per day spent in the field.

(*sd* = 2,184, *n* = 316) and R$ 836 (*sd* = 1,313, *n* = 316) respectively (R$ 1 = USD$ 0.34). There was no significant difference between the two means using a two-sample t-test. For the most part, agricultural products are sold in the nearest market town (Santarém). The average area harvested in the past year was 1.64 hectares (*sd* = 1.6, *n* = 355). Crop production was completed without the use of fertiliser (only 1 per cent reported use) or pesticides (5 per cent reported use), a result consistent with Scatena et al. (1996). The most common form of transportation used to access markets was a bus; all of the agricultural products sold were transported in 60 kg sacks. The average costs of transport per sack was R$ 2.24 (*sd* = 0.65, *n* = 194), and the average time per trip was 5 hours (*sd* = 1hr 15 minutes, *n* = 174).

On average smallholders worked in the fields 7.31 hours per day, which included an average of 7.61 hours per day (*sd* = 2:05, *n* = 345) in the dry season and 6.17 hours (*sd* = 2:10, *n* = 345) in the wet season (this is a significant difference at $p \leq 0.05$). Forty-six per cent (*n* = 360) of the smallholders hired labour, but many reported not having the ability to hire labour for all activities. Fifty-four per cent of respondents exchanged labour with their neighbours for an average of 59 days per year. As noted earlier, the presence of this exchange labour is an indication of the constraint smallholders face on hiring labour.

About 45 per cent of the respondents were able to find periodic off-farm employment (*n* = 358). However, this employment was not steady or easy to obtain, and in most cases it involved travel and periodic residence in an urban area. Indeed, the mean number of days worked off farm per month in the dry season was only 4.5 (*sd* = 7.5, *n* = 350), and in the wet season 3.2 (*sd* = 5.6, *n* = 349)—significant difference between means at $p \leq 0.05$. Annual exogenous income and remittances from family members not living on the farm averaged R$ 1,524 (*sd* = 2,049, *n* = 357). Finally, smallholders collected non-timber forest products (NTFPs) on 0.5 days per month during the dry season (*sd* = 1.1, *n* = 319) and 2.1 days per month during the wet season (*sd* = 4.2, *n* = 320)—significant difference between means at $p \leq 0.05$. Only 13 per cent of the respondents thought that timber harvesting affected NTFPs. Fifty-four per cent indicated they hunted (*n* = 177), on an average of 21 days per year.

Tables 8.2 to 8.5 contain all results from estimating (8.11) to (8.14). But first, word about some variables in the regressions. Crop production is measured in R$ and is a wet season activity, while land clearing is a dry season activity. The regression variable 'crop value' is a weighted average of crop values for goods produced and serves as a proxy for output price. 'Area deforested' is an endogenous variable measuring land cleared in the crop production function as per equation (8.12). This should not be confused with the 'planted area last year' variable, which is exogenous to this year's decisions and is a measure of the size of the smallholder's crop operation. The variable 'value of capital items' is used as a proxy for either the cost of capital or the amount of capital used, as in other household studies. The variable 'logging contract' is a dummy variable for whether or not the smallholder has a contract. Finally, the 'shadow wage' variable is the endogenous estimated value marginal product, following equation (8.14).

Table 8.2 reports estimation of the agricultural production function (equation [8.12]). The dependent variable for the production function is the annual value of crops produced—we used this so that different crops could be aggregated. Significant variables in the production function include hours worked per day (+), days of exchange labour used for production (+), off-farm labour time (if taken by the smallholder) (−), hired labour time in days (+), time spent on the lot (+), planted land area (+), whether the smallholder had received a formal logging contract (−), and whether the lot was part of a formally organised INCRA settlement (−). The positive labour and land area variable signs make sense (that is, additional land and labour increase crop value), and exchange labour is clearly important to production, indicating again that our shadow wage approach is valid. But the most interesting variables are time that the smallholder has resided on the lot, and whether the smallholder has a formal logging contract. The former indicates that learning increases the value of production over time—also, those smallholders who have held their land longer have better developed crop gardens and larger areas deforested. The latter suggests that those smallholders who obtain the additional income from logging contracts produce fewer crops

Table 8.2
Agricultural Production

Description	Coefficient	T-value	Significance
	7.01	(2.7)	***
Value of Capital Items	0.12	(0.9)	
Distance to Major Highway	0.08	(0.5)	
Distance to Water Source	0.05	(0.5)	
Age of Resident	−0.89	(1.6)	
Area Deforested	−0.03	(0.2)	
Number of Dependents	−0.16	(0.8	
Hours Worked per Day (Wet Season)	0.86	(2.8)	***
Days Exchanged (Wet Season)	0.19	(1.1)	**
Off-farm Labour (Wet Season)	−0.29	(2.0)	**
Hired Labour	0.27	(2.2)	**
Years on Lot	0.50	(2.1)	*
Planted Area Last Year	0.46	(1.9)	*
Gently Sloping Land	−0.14	(0.5)	
Settled by INCRA	−0.56	(1.8)	*
Logging Contract	−1.12	(3.0)	***

$N = 140$
$R^2 = 0.33$
Adjusted $R^2 = 0.25$
$F[15,124] = 4.16$, $p = 0.00$

Notes: *** <0.01, ** <0.05, * <0.10; functional form: log-log.

from their lots. Greater income affords the smallholder with more time for non-marketed activities (such as hunting and NTFP collection—discussed later). It also reduces the need to use crop income for family support. This is consistent with other work which argues that smallholders employ labour in crop production to reach some minimum income target that is defined by preferences—our results suggest that the logging contract relaxes this constraint.

Table 8.3 reports estimates of the area deforested (land cleared) for crop production by smallholders (equation [8.13]). One might surmise that forest management contracts induce more deforestation because, as discussed earlier, large capital firms increase the quality of land clearing for the smallholder. Interestingly, this

Table 8.3
Area Deforested by Present Owner (hectares)

Description	Coefficient	T-value	Significance
	16.33	(1.5)	
Value of Capital Items	0.27	(0.6)	
Logging Contract	−1.09	(0.4)	
Age of Resident	0.05	(0.5)	
Distance of All-weather Dirt Highway	−0.27	(1.5)	
Daily Time for Water Collection	0.76	(0.5)	
Years on Lot	1.27	(6.0)	***
Transport Cost	0.32	(0.2)	
Number of Days Exchanged (Dry Season)	−0.05	(0.5)	
Off-farm Wage (Dry Season)	−0.01	(0.1)	
Wage Paid for Hired Labour	−1.36	(1.6)	
Crop Value	−0.00[a]	(2.2)	**
Shadow Wage	−0.02	(2.5)	**
Exogenous Income	0.00	(0.6)	
$N = 141$			
$R^2 = 0.49$			
Adjusted $R^2 = 0.43$			
$F[13,127] = 9.27$, $p = 0.00$			

Notes: *** <0.01, ** <0.05, * <0.10, [a] −0.0017; functional form: OLS.

is not the case for our data. Referring to Table 8.3, formal logging contracts do not have a significant effect on area deforested. Of course, this is consistent with the effect of forest industry contracts on decreasing crop production as found earlier; the smallholder who receives income from forest contracts does not have to devote more land area to increase income. Although this result is preliminary, it does allay a potential fear that forest industry–smallholder interactions in migrant settlements might increase deforestation through access to heavy machinery—at least for the type of (sustainable) forest management contract present in our sampled settlements. Other significant variables in the deforestation equation include years of land tenure by the smallholder on the lot (+) and the shadow wage (−). The shadow wage has a

Table 8.4

Crop Production Labour (Dry Season) and Transport Labour Time

	Dependent Variable: Labour Allocation	
	Crop Production Labour	Crop Transport Labour
Constant	1.95 (3.1)***	2.36 (4.83)***
Value of Capital Items	−0.04 (1.0)	−0.02 (0.8)
Crop Value	−0.08 (2.4)***	−0.02 (0.6)
Distance to All-weather Dirt Highway	0.03 (0.7)	0.04 (1.0)
Distance to Water Source	0.00 (0.2)	−0.01 (0.7)
Age of Resident	−0.06 (0.4)	−0.07 (0.6)
Area Deforested	0.03 (0.7)	−0.05 (1.2)
Number of Dependents	0.06 (1.0)	0.01 (0.3)
Years on Lot	−0.13 (2.0)***	−0.05 (0.9)
Planted Area Last Year	−0.02 (0.2)	0.05 (0.7)
Logging Contract	0.16 (1.6)	−0.18 (2.2)***
Other (Off-farm) Goods Value	0.02 (0.3)	−0.05 (1.0)
Exogenous Income	0.00 (0.4)	0.00 (1.0)
Shadow Wage	0.19 (4.8)***	0.02 (0.8)
	$n = 147$	$n = 147$
	$R^2 = 0.47$	$R^2 = 0.47$
	Adj. $R^2 = 0.42$	Adj. $R^2 = 0.42$
	$F[13,134] = 9.23,$	$F[13,134] = 9.23,$
	$p = 0.00$	$p = 0.00$

Notes: *** <0.01, ** <0.05, * <0.10.

Table 8.5
Annual Labour Time in Other Activities

	Off farm	Exchanged	Hired	NTFP Collection	Hunting
		Dependent Variable: Labour Days per Year			
Constant	6.34 (2.5)	15.4 (5.5)	-10.21 (3.2)	7.24 (3.2)	5.90 (2.5)
Value of Capital Items	-0.10 (0.7)	-0.32 (1.9)**	0.42 (2.2)***	0.07 (0.5)	-0.29 (2.0)***
Crop Value	0.11 (0.8)	-0.08 (0.5)	0.31 (1.8)**	-0.20 (1.4)	-0.23 (1.7)**
Distance to All-weather Dirt Highway	0.02 (0.1)	0.36 (1.8)**	0.01 (0.5)	0.01 (0.0)	0.41 (2.3)***
Distance to Water Source	0.03 (0.3)	-0.06 (0.6)	0.00 (0.5)	0.04 (0.5)	0.06 (0.7)
Age of Resident	-1.82 (3.2)***	-3.16 (4.8)***	1.13 (1.5)	-1.26 (2.4)***	-1.13 (2.0)***
Area Deforested	-0.88 (0.5)	-0.36 (1.8)**	0.00 (0.0)	-0.45 (2.9)***	0.06 (0.3)
Number of Dependents	0.72 (3.2)***	-0.04 (0.9)	-0.25 (0.8)	-0.04 (0.2)	0.02 (0.1)

	(1)	(2)	(3)	(4)	(5)
Years on Lot	-0.44 (1.7)**	0.75 (2.6)***	-0.09 (0.3)	0.48 (1.9)**	0.04 (0.2)
Planted Area Last Year	0.56 (2.1)***	0.15 (0.5)	0.30 (0.9)	0.09 (0.4)	0.00 (0.0)
Logging Contract	-0.20 (0.5)	0.36 (0.4)	0.79 (1.6)*	-0.12 (0.3)	0.26 (0.7)
Off-farm Goods Value	0.19 (0.8)	-0.22 (0.4)	0.41 (1.3)	-0.32 (1.4)	0.19 (0.8)
Exogenous Income	0.33 (7.9)***	0.04 (0.9)	0.20 (3.8)***	0.07 (1.9)**	-0.02 (0.4)
Shadow Wage	-0.12 (0.7)	0.15 (0.8)	0.01 (0.1)	0.28 (1.7)**	0.28 (1.9)***
	$n = 147$	$n = 148$	$n = 145$	$n = 134$	$n = 146$
	$R^2 = 0.47$	$R^2 = 0.25$	$R^2 = 0.27$	$R^2 = 0.18$	$R^2 = 0.15$
	Adj. $R^2 = 0.42$	Adj. $R^2 = 0.17$	Adj. $R^2 = 0.20$	Adj. $R^2 = 0.09$	Adj. $R^2 = 0.06$
	$F[13,134] = 9.23$,	$F[13,134] = 3.36$,	$F[13,131] = 3.70$,	$F[13,120] = 2.07$,	$F[13,132] = 1.80$,
	$p = 0.00$	$p = 0.00$	$p = 0.00$	$p = 0.02$	$p = 0.04$

Notes: *** <0.01, ** <0.05, * <0.10.

reasonable sign, as a higher opportunity cost reduces the amount of time used for land clearing, given that labour is productive in non-clearing uses. Finally, most smallholders clear land more heavily early in their tenure; thus, it is also reasonable to expect that deforestation will decrease the longer a smallholder has resided on the lot.

Table 8.4 reports labour time of the household devoted to on-farm dry season production activities.[10] For on-farm labour the shadow wage variable is positive and significant, as expected, because a higher productivity increases the cost of diverting labour away from crop production activities. Furthermore, higher crop value and the number of years on the lot have negative impacts on dry season labour, which suggests that over time, as the agricultural production investment matures, less time is devoted to land clearing activities.

It was earlier discussed that the forest industry contracts could have spillover effects on communities through improvement of infrastructure and possibly increased access to distant markets where some produced goods are sold. This was embodied in the transportation cost term of equation (8.4) and the first order condition (8.10) (see the third term). Table 8.4 presents the transportation cost labour time allocation for smallholders in our sample. Interestingly, the only significant variable in the regression is whether the smallholder had a forest management contract. The presence of the forest industry in the area suggests, according to the results, that the elasticity of labour time is roughly 2 hours per trip in time savings.

Finally, Table 8.5 presents the results for other annual labour allocation decisions by the smallholder for off-farm, exchange, hiring, NTFP collection and hunting activities. Off-farm labour allocation decisions are affected by age (–), family size (+), years on the lot (–), planted crop area (+) and exogenous income (remittances) (+). The presence of a logging contract did not affect off-farm labour allocation, which suggests that the mere presence of

[10] Recall that labour in the dry season is mostly allocated to land clearing activities, while in the wet season labour is directed to crop production.

logging may not provide additional off-farm opportunities. Exchange labour is not affected by the shadow wage, which would point to an equal exchange process in which the value of an individual's day, in terms of opportunity cost, is close to that of the person with whom it is exchanged. There are also strong social pressures to participate in exchange labour within established communities, which would explain the positive and (highly) significant sign in the exchange labour regression for years on the lot. Exchange labour depends positively and significantly on quality of the roads—making travel between lots, and thus exchange, easier. Although the logging contract itself has no direct effect on exchange labour, it may have an indirect effect by improving access to other household labour. Wealthier households exchange less labour, and older individuals with smaller crop areas also exchange less labour. These trends show that newer settlers, and those with capital limitations, participate in labour exchange as a means of overcoming periods where labour constraints are binding. In the hired labour equation, we see that all of the variables that add income to the household, including access to a logging contract, increase the number of days labour is hired by the household.

Table 8.5 also shows labour allocated to collection of NTFP and hunting. Time spent collecting NTFP depends significantly on age of the smallholder (–), previous deforestation undertaken on the lot (–), years the smallholder less resided on the lot (+), exogenous income of the smallholder household (+) and shadow wage, which is barely significant at the 10 per cent level. These signs make sense. A higher deforested area implies less available land for hunting—most smallholders in our sample hunt monkeys, deer and other small mammals that are dependent on forested area. Increases in exogenous income imply more labour time available to NTFP collection, perhaps because this activity is jointly produced with leisure or the release of a financial constraint. Greater land tenure, measured by time on the lot, implies that the smallholder has learned about the importance and uses of non-timber products from forests, and thus their collection increases.

We also find that possession of logging contracts does not seem to imply that smallholders shift towards harvesting uses of forests—in fact, smallholders with these contracts do not devote any more or less labour to NTFP collection than those without. This is an important result given that the presence of the forest industry could imply that there are more opportunities to harvest from the smallholder's legal reserve—an area that is used for NTFP collection.

Finally, hunting is an important alternative for own food consumption in the smallholder household, and it may be a weak form of leisure. Referring to the Table, significant variables at the 5 per cent level include value of crops (–), value of capital items owned by the smallholder (–), road quality (+), age of the smallholder (–) and the shadow wage (+). These results generally make sense because, as the value of capital used in crop production or the value of crops increases, more labour time shifts away from non-crop activities. Wealthier households are able to purchase the goods (meat) produced by hunting. The shadow wage for own labour in both the hunting and the NTFP collection equations is positive, which may indicate a preference for the individual's own labour in these activities.

Discussion

Smallholder forest use in the Brazilian Amazon has been haphazard and poorly managed, as most land is simply cleared and burned for crop production. A lack of understanding about the rent-earning potential of forests and lack of formal land titles result in disincentives for sustainable long-term forest management or forest protection. One solution may be found in forest firms practising reduced impact logging on smallholder lots (Lima et al. 2003; Nepstad et al. 2004). These firms negotiate formal logging contracts with smallholders. Communities with these contracts may benefit from increased infrastructure and increased access to markets. Smallholders with contracts also learn about the volume and value of trees on their lot through these interactions.

The influence of these contracts has not been studied among smallholder communities in Amazonia, but it will clearly be important to the future of deforestation. This paper has focused on what effects, if any, formal logging contracts have had on important decisions smallholders make concerning labour time, land clearing and productivity.

These contracts are relatively recent, but we find definite short-term effects on smallholder behaviour. Forest management contracts lead them to decrease crop production. We also find, contrary to what one might think, that these interactions between smallholders and industry have not led to increased deforestation through greater land clearing. Smallholders in our sample also benefit from decreased transportation costs in settlements where the forest industry has begun to harvest timber. One might expect that forest industry interaction would lead smallholders to lean towards more harvesting-based uses of the forest area held on their lots, as they learn that there are values associated with harvested trees, or as they obtain more information about the quality and species made available on their land through contracts with the forest industry. However, this was not found to be the case. Instead, the labour time that smallholders devote to NTFP collection and hunting is not adversely affected by having a forest management contract. Thus, the sum of these results means that logging contracts probably will not, at least in the short term, lead to the degradation of remaining 'legal reserve' forest areas.

We began originally with the premise that labour markets are thin, following from the observations in our sample that (non-monetarily compensated) exchange labour is important, and the fact that these spread out settlements imply few smallholders actually have off-farm opportunities unless they travel away to large towns for extended periods of time. To this end we find some interesting results concerning labour decisions. The opportunity cost of time measured through shadow wage is significant to many labour decisions, supporting our initial assumption regarding labour markets being thin. Other recurring important variables to labour decisions include the time the smallholder has lived on their lot, as well as access to and distance from markets. Land tenure promotes NTFP collection activity, increases the likelihood of using uncompensated exchange labour for land clearing with other households, increases crop value produced, and decreases deforestation area (although this last effect may simply be because most land clearing is done by a smallholder early on). As smallholders move further away from markets where goods are sold, this serves to increase use of their forests for non-consumptive and hunting reasons, and, again in support of our labour market assumptions, significantly increases exchange labour use, given that hired labour becomes scarce.

We have shown that forest management contracts are important to smallholder decisions. We have also shown how other important decisions depend on variables such as land tenure. An important next step of this research would be to estimate the welfare effects of having forest management contracts for the representative smallholder, and to then use this information to conduct a benefit-cost analysis of these emerging contracts for smallholders on the Amazon frontier to assess the social desirability of these arrangements. While our results suggest that these contracts show some promise, this study is only a first attempt at understanding how they are important in migrant communities.

References

Alston, L.J., G.D. Libecap and B. Mueller. 1999. *Titles, Conflict, and Land Use: The Development of Property Rights and Land Reform on the Brazilian Amazon Frontier*. Ann Arbor, MI: University of Michigan Press.

Amacher, G.S., W.F. Hyde and K. Kanel. 1996. 'Household Fuelwood Demand and Supply in Nepal: Choice Between Cash Outlays and Labor Opportunity', *World Development*, 24(11): 1725–36.

———. 1999. 'Nepali Fuelwood Production and Consumption: Regional and Household Distinctions, Substitution, and Successful Intervention', *Journal of Development Studies*, 2(3): 138–63.

Barbier, E. and J. Burgess. 2001. 'The Economics of Tropical Deforestation', *Journal of Economic Surveys*, 15: 413–21.

Bluffstone, R. 1995. 'The Effect of Labor Market Performance on Deforestation in Developing Countries Under Open Access: An Example from Rural Nepal', *Journal of Environmental Economics and Management*, 29(1): 42–63.

———. 1998. 'Reducing Degradation of Forests in Poor Countries When Permanent Solutions Elude Us: What Instruments Do We Really Have?', *Environment and Development Economics*, 3: 295–317.

Caviglia, J. 2000. *Sustainable Agriculture in Brazil: Economic Development and Deforestation*. New York: Edward Elgar Press.

Cooke, P. 1998a. 'The Effect of Environmental Goods Scarcity on Own Farm Labor Allocation: The Case of Agricultural Households in Rural Nepal', *Environment and Development Economics*, 3: 443–69.

———. 1998b. 'Intrahousehold Labour Allocation Responses to Environmental Good Scarcity: A Case Study from the Hills of Nepal', *Economic Development and Cultural Change*, 46: 807–30.

Greene, W. 1997. *Econometric Analysis*. New Jersey: Prentice Hall.

Jacoby, H. 1993. 'Shadow Wages and Peasant Family Labor Supply: An Econometric Application to the Peruvian Sierra', *Review of Economic Studies*, 60: 903–21.

Kohlin, G. 1998. 'The Value of Social Forestry in Orissa, India', Ph.D. thesis. Sweden: Gothenberg University, Ekoinomiska Studies 83.

Kohlin, G. and G. Amacher. 2005. 'Welfare Implications of Social Forestry Projects: The Case of Orissa, India, *American Journal of Agricultural Economics*, 87(4): 855–69.

Kohlin, G. and P. Parks. 2001. 'Spatial Variability and Incentives to Harvest: Deforestation and Fuelwood Collection in South Asia', *Land Economics*, 77: 206–18.

Lima, E., A. Leite, D. Nepstad, K. Kalif, C. Azevedo-Ramos, C. Pereira, A. Alencar, U. Lopes and F. Merry. 2003. *Florestas Familiares: Um Pacto Sócio-ambiental Entre a Indústria Madereira e a Agricultura Familiar na Amazônia*. Belém, Brazil: Instituto de Pesquisa Ambiental da Amazônia.

Macqueen, D.J. 2004. *Forest Ethics: The Role of Ethical Dialogue in the Fate of the Forests*. Edinburgh: IIED.

Macqueen, D.J., M. Grieg-Gran and H. Baumüller. 2003. *Trade and Forests: Why Forest Issues Require Attention in Trade Negotiations—Policy Views on Trade and Natural Resource Management*. London: IIED and ICTSD.

Merry, F., O. Almeida, E. Lima, G. Amacher, A. Alves and M. Guimares dos Santos. 2004. 'Overcoming Marginalization in the Brazilian Amazon through Community Association: Case Studies of Forests and Fisheries'. IIED Project Report, Edinburgh.

Nepstad, D., A. Alencar, A.C. Barros, E. Lima, C. Azevedo-Ramos, S. Rivero and P. Lefebvre. In press. 'Governing the Amazon Timber Industry', in D. Zarin et al. (eds), *Working Forests in the American Tropics: Conservation through Sustainable Management?* Columbia University Press.

Nepstad, D., C. Azevedo-Ramos, E. Lima, D. McGrath, C. Pereira and F. Merry. 2004. 'Managing the Amazon Timber Industry', *Conservation Biology*, 18: 1–3.

Pattanayak, S. and E. Sills. 2001. 'Do Tropical Forests Provide Natural Insurance? The Microeconomics of Nontimber Forests Product Collection in the Brazilian Amazon', *Land Economics*, 77: 595–612.

Pendleton, L. and E. Howe. 2002. 'Market Integration, Development, and Smallholder Forest Clearance', *Land Economics*, 78: 1–19.

Perz, S. and R. Walker. 2002. 'Household Life Cycles and Secondary Forest Cover Among Small Farm Colonists in the Amazon', *World Development*, 30: 1009–27.

Scatena, F.N., R.T. Walker, A.O.K. Homma, A.J. Conto, C.A.P. Ferreira, R.A. Carvalho, A.C.P.N. Rocha, A.I.M. Santos and P.M. Oliveira. 1996. 'Cropping and Fallowing Sequences of Small Farms in the "Terra Firme" Landscape of the Brazilian Amazon: A Case Study from Santarém, Pará', *Ecological Economics*, 18: 29–40.

Shivley, G. 2001. 'Agricultural Change, Rural Labor Markets, and Forest Clearing: An Illustrative Case from the Philippines', *Land Economics*, 77: 268–84.

Thornton, J. 1994. 'Estimating the Choice Behavior of Self-employed Business Proprietors: An Application to Dairy Farming', *Southern Economic Journal*, 87(4): 579–95.

9

Bio-diesel as Alternative Fuel

D.K. Tuli

Introduction

India's consumption of energy and transportation fuels is extremely modest by world standards. In 2001 the annual gasoline (petrol) and diesel consumption was 9 litres per capita. The Chinese and the US figures were around four times and 120 times the Indian figure (*Earth Trends* 2005). Yet even this consumption is met at considerable costs. The country is plagued by shortages and high fuel prices. In the US petrol prices per gallon (3.8 litres) currently fluctuate between US$ 2.5 and 3 (*Economist* 2005). In purchasing power parity terms this translates to around Rs 4.5 to 5.5 per litre compared to about Rs 45 to 50 per litre in India. India imports about 70 per cent of its petroleum demand and, therefore, bears a huge risk from wildly fluctuating world prices of oil. The petroleum import bill is currently about US$ 13 billion (about 30 per cent of the total import bill) compared to the current trade deficit of about US$ 11 billion. Given that economic growth is positively correlated with growth in energy consumption, at its current low level of per capita income India needs new sources of cheap fuel. However, its high population density of around 328 persons per sq. km. (2.5 and 10 times that of China and the United States respectively) implies that conventional fuels like diesel and petrol cannot entirely meet this need (even in the case of sufficient supplies) as pollution disbenefits are significantly magnified by a

higher population density. India, therefore, needs to find a source
of abundant cheap and clean fuel. Among the alternate fuels for
the transportation sector, ethanol and bio-diesel have been explored on a large scale. While ethanol is a suitable blending component for gasoline, bio-diesel is a choice component for addition
to diesel.

The concept of bio-diesel came to the forefront in 1900 when
the inventor of the diesel engine, Rudolph Diesel, ran his engine
on a large number of fuels including peanut oil in the Paris Show.
As Hobbs says, the concept of bio-fuels has been in vogue in
human society since the middle ages, as farmers used cultivated
crop to run their organic engines (horses). In 1912 Rudolph Diesel
stated: 'The use of vegetable oils for engine fuels may seem insig-
nificant today. But such oils may in the course of time become as
important as petroleum and coal tar products of current time'
(www.sustainablebusiness.org).

Bio-diesel is a renewable diesel substitute (component) and it
also enhances the combustion characteristics of diesel. Reduction
in unburnt hydrocarbons, almost no sulphur oxide emissions, and
lower carbon monoxide emissions are associated with the use of
bio-diesel. When compared to petro-diesel, it reduces emission
of particulate matter by 40 per cent, unburned hydrocarbons by
68 per cent, carbon monoxide by 44 per cent, sulphates by 100
per cent, polycyclic aromatic hydrocarbons (PAHs) by 80 per cent,
and the carcinogenic nitrated PAHs by 90 per cent on an average.
Tests have shown that bio-diesel has similar or better fuel consumption, horsepower, and torque and haulage rates as conventional diesel.

After filtering out suspended matter and paying attention to
oil quality, discarded vegetable oils or their esters are quite adequate as engine fuels, even after considering the need for city
environmental maintenance and resource recycling (Box 9.1).
The Netherlands, Germany, Belgium and Austria (combined) dis-
card, and recycle as animal feed, a total of 107,000 tonnes of used
vegetable oil annually. Box 9.2 outlines the chronological history
of development of bio-diesel in Austria. The United States discards
about a million tonnes of used vegetable oils from restaurants
and food processing plants, and most of this is used as animal
feed. In Japan approximately 200,000 tonnes of vegetable oils

Box 9.1
Oil-producing Plants

Corn	Coffee	Calendula
Cashew	Linseed	Cotton
Oat	Hazelnut	Hemp
Palm	*Euphorbia*	Soyabean
Lupine	Pumpkin seed	Rapeseed
Rubber seed	Sesame	Olive tree
Kenaf	Sunflower	Castor bean
Rice	Macadamia nut	Jojoba
Safflower	Brazil nut	Pecan
Peanut	Avocado	Oil Plam
Tung oil tree	Coconut	Macuba plam
Jatropha		

are discarded annually from public facilities, and this is reused as animal feed. Every year many million tonnes waste cooking oils are collected and used in a variety of ways throughout the world. This is a virtually inexhaustible source of energy, which might also prove to be an additional line of production for 'green' companies.

India being a diesel-run country, the requirement of diesel is almost six times that of gasoline. Presently, we use about 42 million (MMT) of diesel, which will rise to 52 MMT in 2006–7 and to 65 MMT in 2011–12. This diesel is processed mainly from imported crude oil as the domestic production is less than 30 per cent of crude requirements. Following the example of Brazil, which has successfully used petrol–ethanol blends, India has also introduced the commercial use of 5 per cent ethanol-blended petrol. With encouraging results from users, the government of India has drawn up plans to increase the level of blending to 10 per cent in the near future. However, in order to meet its rapidly expanding diesel requirements, an alternative to conventional diesel is required.

Bio-diesel made from the *Jatropha* plant may be the answer. The next section discusses the features of the plant and its suitability as a source of bio-diesel. This is followed by a brief description of Indian efforts in producing bio-diesel.

Box 9.2
Bio-diesel Chronology: The Austrian Example

1982:	Initial transesterification experiments using rapeseed oil at the Institute of Organic Chemistry, Graz, Austria.
1983:	Early experiments using waste cooking oil.
1985:	First pilot plant worldwide for the production of rapeseed oil methyl ester at Silberberg Agricultural College, Styna, Austria.
1987:	Engine and emission tests using methyl ester from waste cooking oils with VL List GmbH, Graz, Austria.
1988:	First patent taken for transesterification process.
1989–90:	Government-supported research project on high-quality fuel from waste cooking oils.
1991:	Austrian innovation award for bio-diesel from waste cooking oil. Large-scale esterification experiments using 100 per cent waste cooking oil, in cooperation with the Technical University of Graz. Further patents for esterification and preparation of glycerol phase.
1994:	Start of industrial bio-diesel production from 100 per cent waste cooking oil at Mureck, Austria.
1995:	Patent for re-esterification to increase yield to 100 per cent.
1998:	Start-up of first bio-diesel plant worldwide capable of processing animal fats with up to 20 per cent free fatty acids at 100 per cent yield.

Jatropha: A Source of Bio-diesel

The bio-diesel programme of the West is entirely based on edible oils, for which they have surplus production capacity. The Indian picture is entirely different as we are the largest importers of edible oils. However, there are several natural species of non-edible seeds that have traditionally been grown in our country. *Jatropha* and *Pangomia* are the front-runners in this category. These plants can be grown in all parts of the country, and require minimal input and care. Therefore, a serious initiative to develop bio-diesel from non-edible oils in India was initiated at the beginning of

2000–2001. The main drivers of the bio-diesel programme include an integrated rural development programme, part replacement of imported crude, emission benefits, and a related boost to the agricultural/employment sector.

Jatropha (*Jatropha curcas*) is a genus of approximately 175 shrubs and trees from the family *Euphorbiaceae*. Plants from the genus natively occur in Africa, North America and the Caribbean. The *Jatropha* plant originated in the Carribean and was later taken to Africa and Asia by Portuguese traders. It is already being used in India: the rail line between Mumbai and Delhi is planted with *Jatropha* and the trains run on 15–20 per cent bio-diesel made from the plant. (for details see Wikipedia, the online encyclopaedia).

The plant has many advantages: low-cost seeds with high oil content, small gestation period, ability to grow on even degraded soils under all levels of precipitation, and a small plant size which makes collection of seeds very convenient. This plant makes recycling of carbon possible as it utilises carbon dioxide in the atmosphere to grow and yield oil kernels. When oil manufactured from *Jatropha* seeds is used as a fuel, it produces carbon dioxide. Thus, the net amount of carbon dioxide added to the atmosphere is approximately zero. For every unit of energy required for the production of bio-diesel there are at least 2.5 units of energy contained in the fuel because of the use of free energy from the atmosphere (Hobbs 2003).

According to the Centre for Jatropha Promotion in Churu, India, the cost of producing bio-diesel is currently around Rs 17.5 per litre, but should go down to Rs 12 with large-scale production. This is much lower than the import price of conventional diesel (Rs 24 per litre). Each hectare of land is expected to yield around 1.6 tonnes of bio-diesel. Given the ability of this plant to grow on wasteland (approximately 10 million hectares across the country) with negligible precipitation, there is a strong possibility of using *Jatropha* for large-scale production of bio-diesel. Even successful use of 50 per cent of our wasteland area will enable us to meet 12.5 per cent of our projected diesel requirements in 2011–12 and lead to savings of US$ 4 billion (at current prices) in our import bill. The use of this plant will also help check soil erosion and the spread of wastelands, and generate employment (see Centre for Jatropha Promotion).

The gestation period in *Jatropha* cultivation is not long. A seedling starts yielding seeds after a year of its plantation. Moreover, 2,500 plants can be grown on just 1 hectare. The rate of mortality is around 20 per cent implying that 2,000 plants survive to yield oil. From the second year onwards *Jatropha* cultivation generates an income of Rs 25,000 per hectare. Its ability to grow under all agro-climatic conditions implies that very little uncertainty is associated with it. The machines used to produce oil can be viable even on a small scale so that commercial production is available almost immediately. One expeller is required for a minimum of 100 hectares of *Jatropha*, and one esterification plant is required for 1,000 hectares. Short gestation periods and low risk imply very little discounting of returns, as also only short-term finance. Small viable and economic scales of operation imply that if its production is properly planned, transportation costs associated with this fuel may be minimal.

Progress of the Indian Bio-diesel Programme

The successful launch of ethanol as a blending component of petrol provided the necessary boost to the development of bio-diesel. Commercial R&D units, for example, Indian Oil Corporation (IOC) R&D and Mahindra & Mahindra, also joined in the efforts to explore the possibility of large-scale development of bio-diesel for the transportation sector. The Indian Railways at their R&D wing in Lucknow tested the bio-diesel made from *Jatropha* by IOC R&D in stationary energies and successfully completed a trial run of the prestigious Shatabdi train that was powered by this fuel. Thus, R&D efforts in converting non-edible oils (mainly *Jatropha* and Karanjia) to bio-diesel suitable for transportation were fairly successful.

Taking note of the development of bio-diesel in several countries, especially the EU, which had set a target of a minimum biofuel share of 5.75 per cent in all transportation fuels by year 2010, the government of India commenced an Indian initiative on biofuels. NGOs such as SUTRA of the Indian Institute of Science, Bangalore, and Winrock International played an important role in this regard.

The Planning Commission took a giant step and constituted a set of committees in July 2002 to study all issues relating to the development and use of bio-diesel from non-edible oils. These committees, headed by eminent people from government research institutes, industry and regulatory bodies, had the following major terms of reference.

- current levels of bio-fuel availability;
- issues regarding blending of bio-fuels with mineral fuels;
- commercial-scale development on relative costs and benefits;
- specifications for bio-fuels and quality standards;
- identification of R&D needs;
- marketing strategies; and
- mobilising financial resources.

Several committees immediately started working on the focused tasks scheduled to be completed in a period of six months. The Planning Commission submitted a comprehensive report on the development of bio-diesel to the government in July 2003. This report outlines the national mission on bio-fuel and gives recommendations regarding all aspects of development of bio-diesel. The overall targets recommended include launching of a national mission on bio-diesel with the objective of producing enough for blending up to 20 per cent in high speed diesel by year 2011–12.

A demonstration project is to be taken up in mission mode with the [micromissions]. The Ministry of Rural Development will be the nodal agency for plantation activities and the demonstration project will be completed by 2007. The funds necessary for the project, covering an area of 400,000 hectares in compact lots, each having 50,000 to 60,000 hectares, will be made available through government subsidy and loans. The estimated financial requirements for the demonstration project is Rs 150 million. A coordination committee will decide the manner in which the funds are to be mobilised. The report proposes that transesterification units be set up by oil companies with their own funds or with the help of financial institutions. The administrative expenses of the mission will be borne by the government, which will also provide dedicated funds for R&D (Rs 6.8 million).

The second phase of the mission is expected to begin in 2007 and will be a self-sustaining exercise. A model of institutional networking has also been proposed in which close cooperation between the plantation sector, production sector, marketing and R&D has been ensured.

Conclusion

India, being an agro-based economy, has great potential in biofuel. Along with ethanol, bio-diesel is the most promising renewable fuel derived from vegetable sources that can be used as a substitute or component of diesel.

The suitability of non-edible oils, especially *Jatropha* and Karanjia, as feedstock for bio-diesel production has been fairly well established. There exists enough waste or marginal land for cultivating these crops. The Planning Commission has taken a bold initiative to promote bio-diesel on a large scale within a well-defined time schedule. It is expected that a large quantity of oilseeds will soon reach the market (www.renewingindia.org). During this lead time issues regarding collection of seed, oil extraction, transesterification and marketing need to be sorted out. High-yielding species of oilseed crops should be developed and extensive services provided to farmers. Designing of commercial transesterification plants of medium capacity should also be completed before the crops arrive in the market.

References

Hobbs, Steven. 2003. 'Bio-diesel: Farming for the Future'. Invited presentation, 11th Australian Agroeconomic Conference.
Economist. 2005. 'A Nasty Whiff of Inflation', 22 September.
Wikipedia. 'Jatropha', http://en.wikipedia.org/wiki/Jatropha.
Centre for Jatropha Promotion. http://www.jatrophaworld.org/
Earth Trends. 2005. 'World Resources Institute', http://earthtrends.wri.org/datatables/index.cfm? theme=6

10

Efficiency, Jevons' Paradox and the Evolution of Complex Adaptive Systems

Mario Giampietro and Kozo Mayumi

Introduction

The question whether or not an increase in energy efficiency leads to the promotion of energy saving has been debated since the 1973 OPEC oil embargo. Many environmentalists suggest that improving the efficiency of energy use is an effective policy instrument to reduce global carbon dioxide emissions. On the other hand, the advocates of the 'rebound effect' (or 'Khazzoom-Brookes postulate') maintain that an increase in energy efficiency, as characterised at the microeconomic level, leads to an increase in energy use when considering the macroeconomic level rather than to a reduction (Brookes 1979; Herring 1999; Khazzoom 1980; Saunders 2000). An empirical investigation of the relation between improvements in energy efficiency and the rebound effect has to face three conceptual problems yet to be fully explored: (a) how to define and measure energy efficiency; (b) how to distinguish energy efficiency due to a change in technological coefficients from a price-induced substitution; and (c) how to separate the effect of an increase in population from energy efficiency at the macroeconomic level. In relation to this task, there is a promising empirical work based on historical data to cope with these difficult problems (Polimeni and Polimeni 2006).

The purpose of this paper, however, is to provide a different perspective on the link between increases in efficiency and sustainability. We provide a thermodynamic and epistemological framework to make the following points: (*a*) that an increase in energy efficiency promotes sustainability is a myth; and (*b*) an alternative approach to dealing with circular causations is necessary when representing and analysing evolving systems organised in nested hierarchies (which are termed as *complex adaptive systems*, CAS for short).

Surprisingly enough, looking at the history of the rebound effect, such a concept was closely examined in 1865 by none other than William Stanley Jevons, one of the four founders of neoclassical economics (a quartet that includes Gossen!). For this reason, this concept is referred to as Jevons' paradox (Jevons 1990). Jevons' paradox is discussed in the next section by introducing the two concepts of intensive and extensive variables. These are crucial in understanding the inherent difficulty in predicting future behavioural patterns of CAS. In fact, CAS are operating on different hierarchical levels and scales simultaneously, and changing their identities at various temporal modes. We then look at the nature of Jevons' paradox in terms of the two types of efficiency in physical terms. That is, Jevons' paradox is reflecting the existence of a natural tension between two contrasting principles (minimum entropy production and maximum energy flux). These two principles refer to two legitimate but contrasting drivers of the evolution of CAS expressed on different scales. The next section of this paper deals more systematically with the epistemological challenge faced when perceiving, representing and analysing the evolution of CAS. We make the point that Jevons' paradox is not a paradox at all. It appears so only because conventional scientific analytical tools are not adequate to deal with the evolution of CAS. Several important concepts (emergence, multiple levels and scales, impredicativity) are introduced to justify a call for alternative methodological tools required to deal with the evolution of CAS.

Jevons' Paradox Revisited

Jevons' paradox (Alcott 2005; Jevons 1990; Mayumi et al. 1998) was first enunciated by Jevons in his 1865 book *The Coal Question*. Briefly, it states that an increase in output–input ratio—the 'efficiency' in using a resource—leads, in the medium to long term, to an increased use of that resource rather than to a reduction. At that time Jevons was discussing possible trends of future consumption of coal and reacting to scenarios advocated by technological optimists. In fact, contemporaries of Jevons were urging to dramatically increase the efficiency of engines in order to reduce coal consumption. In the face of such a claim, Jevons correctly indicated that more efficient engines would have expanded the possible uses of coal for human activities. Therefore, increases in efficiency would have boosted the rate of consumption of existing coal reserves rather than reducing it.

Jevons' paradox proved to be true not only with regard to demand for coal and other fossil energy resources, but also with regard to demand for resources in general. Doubling the efficiency of food production per hectare over the last 50 years (the Green Revolution) did not solve the problem of hunger; it actually made the problem worse since it increased the number of people needing food and the absolute number of the malnourished (Giampietro 1994). In the same way, doubling the area of roads did not solve the problem of traffic, it made the traffic condition worse since it encouraged the use of more personal vehicles (Newman 1991). As more energy-efficient automobiles were developed as a consequence of rising oil prices, American car owners increased their leisure driving (Cherfas 1991). Not only did the expected performance of cars improve, but the number of miles increased as well. US residents are now increasingly driving mini-vans, pickup trucks and four-wheel drives. More efficient refrigerators have become bigger (Khazzoom 1987). A promotion of energy efficiency at the micro level of economic agents tends to increase energy consumption at the macro level of the whole society (Herring 1999). In economic terms we can describe these processes as increases in supply boosting the demand in the long term, much stronger than the so-called Say's law.

Jevons' paradox has different names and different applications: 'rebound effect' in energy literature and 'paradox of prevention' in relation to public health. In the latter case the paradox is that the amount of money 'saved' by prevention of a few targeted diseases leads to a dramatic increase in the overall bill of the health sector in the long term. Due to the fact that humans sooner or later must die (which is a fact that seems to be ignored by *ceteris paribus* efficiency analysts), any increase in the lifespan of a population directly results in an increase in health care expenses. Besides the higher fraction of retired persons in the population who need more health care, it is well known that the hospitalisation of the elderly is much more expensive than of young adults.

This last example leads us to the heart of the paradox. Technological improvements in efficiency of a process represent improvements in *intensive variables* defined as 'improvement' per unit of something and under the *ceteris paribus* hypothesis that everything else remains the same. However, an increase in efficiency could translate into savings on the requirement of inputs only if CAS would not modify their portfolio of behaviours in response to changes in efficiency. As a matter of fact, CAS, especially human systems, tend to adapt quite fast and effectively to any changes. As soon as technological improvements are introduced in a society, more room is generated for either: (*a*) a further expansion of current levels of activity (for example, more people make more use of their old cars) within the original setting; and/or (*b*) an expansion of the option space with the addition of new possible types and activities (for example, new models of cars including new features such as air-conditioning or more space per person). The former expansion refers to a change in *extensive variables within a given formal identity assigned to the system under analysis*. By formal identity we mean the given set of attributes and proxy variables used for characterising the performance and behaviour of a modelled system. That is, the dimension of the process gets bigger within the same option space and when characterising the change from within the original formal identity for the system (for example, the same car with more driving). The latter expansion refers to a qualitative change in the formal identity to represent the system under analysis (for example, a new type of car with more functions and gadgets).

In this discussion we are defining in general terms: (*a*) *extensive variables* as additive variables, which are used to quantify the size of a system in relation to a relevant observable quality; and (*b*) *intensive variables* as non-additive variables, which are used to quantify a relevant quality of a system per unit of its size.

This distinction has important implications for the modeller in relation to another distinction:

1. Quantitative changes can be handled in formal models by keeping the same set of attributes in the formal identity of the modelled systems (the same set of extensive and intensive variables). These quantitative changes only require an update of the value taken by the selected variables.
2. On the other hand, qualitative changes cannot be handled by using the old formal identity of the system under investigation. The modeller must add new attributes to obtain a new quantitative characterisation of the modelled system.

Getting back to the example of the evolution of cars, the introduction of more efficient car engines has implied that air-conditioning became a standard feature of modern cars. It has implied the addition of a new expected attribute to their identity. Increases in efficiency have also made it possible to introduce new categories of cars such as the mini-van or SUV (sport utility vehicles). This represents an increase in the diversity of possible options within the set of accessible states for consumers. This expansion of the option space has added new meanings to the original identity associated with the word car. The introduction of these new meanings can be viewed as the emergence of new couplings between: (*a*) external referents; and (*b*) symbols used in the mathematical representation adopted in the models.

Therefore, there is a logical bifurcation with regard to the possibility of interpreting and forecasting the effect of an increase in efficiency in the process of evolution, which can be characterised as follows:

1. When assuming that the formal identity used in the model will remain relevant and useful in the future, we can say that increasing efficiency over the given set will lead to a decrease in energy consumption. That is, on this side of the logical bifurcation, we are operating under the *ceteris paribus* assumption when making predictions about the effect of an increasing efficiency.

2. When assuming that the formal identity to be used in models will change over time, then we must admit that there is a systemic problem with the semiotic interpretation of the meaning of the word car. That is, the set of attributes and epistemic categories required to capture relevant features when modelling cars is open and expanding. In this case, increasing the efficiency of the various functions associated with a given formal identity of a car will provide a window of opportunity to add new features and attributes (new meanings for the storyteller) to such a formal identity. A more efficient car will unavoidably expand its current performance. This will require a different formal identity in the model in the future in order to reflect the increased ability of cars to perform more functions and express more behaviours. Therefore, on this side of the logical bifurcation we are operating under the assumption that the phenomenon of emergence is something unavoidable when dealing with the evolution of CAS. It is not possible to make predictions about the effect of an increase in efficiency using the original formalisation of the concept of efficiency. Emergence entails that the original formal identity used in a model will have to be replaced by another formal identity.

The important point for our discussion is how the system will expand and what consequences will emerge because of this expansion. These questions cannot be answered by those studying the system from within the original formal identity. That is, these questions cannot be answered by making inferences based on the given set of attributes associated with the original formal identity under the *ceteris paribus* assumption. Put another way, when maximising the efficiency of a given process, we are actively boosting the likelihood of emergence. The more effective the formalisation of efficiency used for boosting improvements, the quicker it will become obsolete. This is why, when dealing with the analysis of the evolution of CAS, it is crucial to adopt complementing views about their change: (a) a steady state view, which makes it possible to deal with concepts such as efficiency, better design and reliability at one scale; and (b) an evolutionary view, which makes it possible to deal with alternative useful concepts such as adaptability, diversity and uncertainty on a different scale.

Two Types of Efficiency and Jevons' Paradox: The Minimum Entropy Production and the Maximum Energy Flux

Following Kawamiya (1983) we can define two types of efficiency in physical terms that are useful to study the nature of Jevons' paradox:

1. **Efficiency of Type 1 (EFT1):** This refers to the ratio of output to input. EFT1 does not consider the time required to obtain the output.
2. **Efficiency of Type 2 (EFT2):** This refers to the output per unit time. EFT2 does not consider the amount of input required to obtain the output.

If the thermal efficiency of a Carnot engine is regarded as the output, then EFT1 is the maximum achievable efficiency for this class of engine, even though it must be less than 1 because of the entropy law. If the speed of a piston is regarded as the output, then EFT2 is infinitesimal (zero for practical purposes). Starting from this extreme condition and moving into the realm of real thermal engines, it is well known that any increase in EFT2 will result in reduction of EFT1. Getting into a more familiar example, if we want to increase the speed of our car above the recommended threshold for fuel economy, we will consume more gasoline per kilometre. Even though most drivers know that a higher EFT2 will imply a lower EFT1, they often prefer going for a higher EFT2 in terms of speed of the car rather than for a higher EFT1 in terms of lower fuel consumption.

Thermodynamic considerations can help in understanding the differences in logic behind the optimisation of these two types of efficiency by social and economic systems. A lower input requirement, implied by an increase in EFT1, has beneficial effects *on the stability of boundary conditions*. The consequent reduction in the requirement of the input consumed by a society is ecologically benign. It decreases the speed of depletion of natural resources and the stress on the environment associated with the expression of a given formal identity. On the other hand, a higher speed of throughput, implied by an increase in EFT2, has beneficial effects *on the ability of the socio-economic system to express more complex behaviours and enlarge its domain of action*. This higher speed of the biophysical throughput associated with the economic process is benign since it can be related to a higher level of production and consumption of goods and services by a given society. That is, EFT1 is related to the scale of the socio-economic system (for example, the size of the biophysical metabolism of a given society) when compared with the biophysical metabolism of the ecosystems embedding it. Therefore, EFT1 should be considered carefully when natural capital becomes a limiting factor in economic growth (Daly 1995). In thermodynamic terms, EFT1 is concerned with the minimum energy throughput required to sustain a particular structure/function of a given society.

The minimisation of EFT1 has been formalised by the Prigogine school in relation to the analysis of dissipative systems as the minimum entropy production principle (Glansdorff and Prigogine 1971; Nicolis and Prigogine 1977). This principle states that 'linear systems obey to a general inequality implying that at a steady non-equilibrium state, entropy production becomes a minimum compatible with the constraints applied on the system' (Nicolis and Prigogine 1977: 45). It is crucial to observe that even if this principle has been developed within the field of non-equilibrium thermodynamics, its validity requires the assumption that the system under analysis must be operating very close to steady state. To formalise this kind of stability, scientists use a Liapunov function typical of control theory. Learning how to reduce internal consumption is definitely positive for CAS. The higher the EFT1, the lower the quantity of input taken from the environment (less depletion of natural resources) and the less waste released into the environment (less environmental pollution).

On the other hand, lowering the flow of throughput associated with a dissipative system implies lowering the diversity of options and behaviours that can be expressed by that system. Consequently, also in ecological theory, the concept of maximisation of energy flows within ecosystems has been proposed as one of the general principles of evolution for CAS: the maximum energy flux (Lotka 1922), and the maximum power principle (Odum and Pinkerton 1955).

The apparent contradiction between these two principles can be easily reconciled when considering the fact that they refer to different and non-equivalent perceptions and representations of relevant features of CAS.

1. The minimum entropy production principle, associated with the metaphor of EFT1, refers to a perception of the characteristics of CAS obtained *from inside the system*, that is, on the interface between the two levels of analysis: level n (focal level—the whole) and level $n - 1$ (lower level— the parts).

2. The maximum energy flux principle, associated with the metaphor of the EFT2, refers to a perception of the characteristics of CAS obtained *from outside the system*, that is on the interface between the two levels of analysis: level $n + 1$ (higher level—the context) and level n (focal level— the whole).

When describing a system belonging to CAS at a higher level, the maximum energy flux principle indicates the continuous process of generation of new complexity through co-evolution. That is, this principle points to the need to increase the mutual compatibility and adaptability of interactive CAS. On the larger scale the distance from thermodynamic equilibrium of the whole is high. This entails the emergence of unpredictable behaviours and the need to change the formal identities used to define what efficiency is. 'When a dissipative structure is near such instability its entropy production reaches a relative maximum and it becomes sensitive to small fluctuations' (O'Neill et al. 1986: 105).

When describing a system belonging to CAS at lower levels, the minimum entropy production principle indicates a trend towards a continuous reduction of quantities of energy and matter required to sustain a particular function—an increase in efficiency. However, this increase in efficiency at lower levels (reduction of entropy generation per unit of mass of the dissipative adaptive system) will result in a higher stability of that function in the long term only if the free energy 'spared' at lower levels by higher efficiency is moved up in the hierarchy (Margalef 1968) and invested in the emergence of new structures/functions. This explains the phenomenon of emergence in the higher levels of CAS.

Put another way, the two trends of maximisation of energy flux for the whole system—detected when describing the process of interaction of the whole with its context—and minimisation of entropy production per unit of lower level component—detected when describing the process of metabolism at a lower hierarchical level—are not contrasting or exclusive of each other. Rather, they are operating in parallel on different scales. The final outcome of these two parallel contrasting trends is a better integration of CAS with its environment. In this way internal and external characteristics of interacting CAS are adjusted to each other in the process of co-evolution.

When interpreting sustainability within the concept of co-evolution (among different socio-economic systems and ecological systems), the yin–yang tension entailed by the Jevons' paradox leads to an increased compatibility among the various systems of control operating on different space–time scales in CAS. These systems of control are operating on different scales both within the CAS under analysis (for example, a given economy) and within their environment determining the favourable boundary conditions (for instance, the ecosystem embedding it). Understanding this mechanism should lead to a balance between the priority given to these two principles. Unfortunately, in the case of economic systems, there is a tendency to give excessive attention to the short-term increase in EFT2: increasing the speed of throughput in terms of production and consumption of goods and services. In the narrative of neo-classical economics this translates into a clear priority given to the maximisation of economic growth in order to be able to boost the material standard of living. In this perspective the opposite concern with EFT1 is often neglected. This results in a lower priority given to the goal of reducing the rate of depletion of natural resources and the actual levels of environmental pollution. The final result of this imbalance between these two principles is the definition of development policies based on a myopic rule: the faster the throughput (for example, GDP) the better.

The Epistemological Challenge:
Perceiving, Representing and Analysing
the Evolution of Complex Adaptive Systems

The foregoing discussion on Jevons' paradox indicates the difficulty in predicting the future of CAS based on the *ceteris paribus* hypothesis. That is, assuming that the given mix of goals, the perceived initial conditions and boundary conditions, and the available technical options, together with resource constraints, existing institutional settings, as well as the selected criteria and indicators, will remain the same in the future. Here we examine more systematically why perceiving, representing and analysing the evolution of CAS brings us serious epistemological challenges that are not encountered within the conventional scientific paradigm.

The basic characteristics of CAS, in our view, can be summarised as follows:

1. CAS are operating in non-equilibrium thermodynamic conditions (Glansdorff and Prigogine 1971; Nicolis and Prigogine 1977). They are maintaining *and creating* their own structures and functions through interaction with their environment.
2. CAS are hierarchically organised and operating across multiple levels and various spatial-temporal scales (Allen and Starr 1982; Koestler 1967, 1969, 1978; O'Neill 1989; O'Neill et al. 1989).

The Prigogine school refers to the first characterisation of CAS as dissipative systems or self-organising systems (Glansdorff and Prigogine 1971; Nicolis and Prigogine 1977). Similarly, Kampis (1991), putting emphasis on the self-evolving aspect, refers to the same characterisation of CAS as self-modifying systems. We should be aware of the subtle difference between the characterisation of CAS given by the Prigogine school, and the one of autopoietic (capable of self-production) systems conceptualised by Maturana and Varela (1980, 1998). Maturana and Varela put emphasis on: (*a*) the network of processes of production; and (*b*) the closure, in terms of functionality, for autopoietic systems, which are capable of producing themselves. This is in contrast with allopoietic systems, such as a car factory, which use raw materials (components) to generate a car (an organised structure) that is something *other* than itself (a factory). When dealing with economic systems, we find that they are made of allopoietic systems (for example, car factories). However, it has to be noted that at the level of the whole, there is an emergent property of the economic process that has its peculiar ability to *produce the production processes*: 'It is this sector [process production]...that constitutes the fountainhead of the growth and further growth' (Georgescu-Roegen 1974: 251). To make it clear, individual processes of production of individual commodities are not guaranteeing the sustainability of an economy. Rather, it is the emergent ability of an economy to *create* (innovate as well as maintain) its own structures and functions through an informed and controlled interaction with the environment that is crucial.

Due to this key characteristic, CAS are always qualitatively as well as quantitatively evolving or co-evolving with their environment. This is why they are always 'becoming' something else (Prigogine 1987). To make things more challenging for the analyst, their speed of 'becoming something else' often exceeds the speed at which humans can learn how to update their perception, representation and analysis. As noted before, the process of evolution of CAS is associated with *emergence*, meaning that it is practically impossible to have *a substantive formal representation* of it.

Here we should recall Georgescu-Roegen's (1976: xxi–xxii) severe verdict on the usefulness of economic models to make predictions about the future:

> Even more crucial is the absence of any concern for whether the formula thus obtained will also fit other observations. It is this concern that is responsible for the success natural scientists have with their formulae. The fact that econometric models of the most refined and complex kind have generally failed to fit future data—which means that they failed to be predictive—finds a ready, yet self-defeating, excuse: history has changed the parameters. If history is so cunning, why persist in predicting it?

In this passage Georgescu-Roegen criticises the performance of econometric models in the case in which the basic formalisation remains valid (the problem is with the inability to choose the right values of parameters). However, as noted before, the predicament faced by those modelling the future of CAS is even more severe.

Due to the incessant emergence of new functions and structures within CAS, modellers are facing an unavoidable dose of uncertainty and ignorance. This entails that arithmomorphic models, particularly dynamic models, cannot be an adequate tool for representing and simulating their evolving behaviour (Giampietro et al. 2005). CAS always require a continuous updating of the following items *even when operating under a given objective*: (*a*) the set of causalities *believed to exist* within CAS; (*b*) the set of relevant attributes associated with types used to represent the perceived causalities within CAS; (*c*) the set of functional relationships believed to exist among relevant attributes of types; (*d*) the set of proxy variables used to characterise relevant attributes of types; (*e*) the choice of how to define variables and parameters within the chosen set of proxy variables; (*f*) the selection of an adequate set of measurement schemes; and (*g*) the formal inferential system (axioms, production rules and algorithms).

The second characteristic of CAS—hierarchically organised and operating across multiple levels and various spatial-temporal scales—seems to be an advantage for scientists. Representing CAS as a hierarchical system helps, since 'comparatively little information is lost by representing [nearly decomposable systems] as hierarchic' (Simon 1962: 477). Simon (ibid.) states: 'If there are important systems in the world that are complex without being hierarchic, they may to a considerable extent escape our observation and our understanding.' This analysis is certainly correct. However, it does not fully address the epistemological challenge associated with perceiving and representing systems organised across hierarchical levels and scales. In fact this second characteristic is at the core of the conundrum addressed by the hierarchy theory (Allen and Starr 1982). When dealing with the perception, representation and analysis of CAS, the role of the observer becomes crucial: 'Hierarchy theory is a theory of the role of the observer and the process of observation in scientific discourse. It is a theory of the nature of complex questions that focuses on observations as the interface between perception and learning' (Ahl and Allen 1996: 27). This entails that, as observed by Rosen (1977: 229), in any CAS there are many subsystems 'that are all present in the original [hierarchical] system' . . . 'which one we actually "see" is specified entirely by how *we* choose to interact with the system' (emphasis added). That is, what is observed when perceiving and representing a CAS in a formal model depends not only on the characteristics of what is observed but also on: (*a*) the choices made by the observer; and (*b*) the characteristics of the observation process. When dealing with hierarchically organised systems, alternative yet perfectly legitimate methods of description can coexist (Whyte et al. 1969). To make things more difficult, the characteristic structural and functional patterns expressed at different hierarchical levels by an observed CAS are evolving at various speeds on different scales (Giampietro 2003).

Finally, there is another epistemological predicament of CAS, namely, *impredicativity* (or circular causality). This is a characteristic that has been systematically ignored by traditional scientific treatment. Impredicativity has to do with the familiar concept of the 'chicken–egg problem', or what Bertrand Russel called the 'vicious circle' (quoted in Rosen 2000: 90). The definition of impredicativity is as follows: 'When a set M and a particular object m are so defined that on the one hand m is a member of M, and on the other hand the definition of m depends on M, we say that the procedure (or the definition of m, or the definition of M) is impredicative' (Kleene 1952: 42). Therefore, such a definition has no meaning and so cannot belong to logic: 'impredicativity entails untypedness' (Lietz and Streicher 2002). However, it should be noticed that the latest developments of theoretical physics— for example, superstring theory—represents an important step towards the acknowledgment of such a concept. A renowned physicist, Gell-Mann (1994), made a clear reference to the bootstrap principle (based on the old saying about the man who could pull himself up by his own bootstraps) by describing the concept as follows: 'The particles, *if assumed to exists*, produce forces binding them to one another; the resulting bound states are the same particles, and they are the same as the ones carrying the forces. Such a particle system, *if it exists*, gives rise to itself' (ibid.: 128, emphasis added).

However, Gell-Mann's statement gives us a hint of how to deal with the conundrum of impredicativity within CAS. The passage basically means that as soon as the various elements of a self-entailing process—defined in parallel on different levels—are all present and at work, then such a process will be able to stabilise itself. This process of autopoiesis will then arrive at a point generating a predictable and detectable entity. By entity we mean something that can be distinct from noise by an observer who has an interest in learning about it.

The impossible formalisation of an impredicative loop derives from the fact that the various elements generating the self-entailing process can only be perceived and represented by adopting different spatial-temporal scales and, therefore, different descriptive domains. That is, such a process cannot be formalised in substantive terms. Moreover, impredicative loops violate the rule of linear causation typical of reductionism. For example, when adopting a given scale, we can perform an analysis that clearly indicates that the number of predators is determining the number of prey. However, when adopting a larger scale, we can develop an analysis clearly indicating that it is the number of prey determining the number of predators. This process of impredicativity has been clearly proved in quantitative terms in ecology (Carpenter and Kitchell 1987). In the same way, the concept of 'consumers' democracy' claims that the selection of goods produced by an economy is determined by the choices made by consumers. However, when adopting a local scale of analysis (getting into a narrative based on a smaller space–time domain), it is obvious that a consumer can only choose among products that have already been produced.

Exactly because of this peculiar epistemological challenge, conventional analytical tools cannot handle the representation of impredicative loops in substantive terms. Conventional analytical tools are developed within a paradigm assuming that all phenomena of reality can be explained by adopting a linear definition of cause and effect. In technical jargon we can say that conventional analytical tools are assuming that all the phenomena of reality can be perceived and represented within the same descriptive domain, referring to the same substantive definition of space and time and by using a set of reducible models (Rosen 2000). This assumption excludes the possibility of having two or more relevant narratives about the same event that are logically independent and therefore providing contrasting but useful explanations. That is, the conventional approach claims that it is possible to single out 'the' right perspective to be adopted in defining the optimal action among the universe of alternatives. We do not believe that this is possible.

Because of these peculiar characteristics of CAS, scientists should not concentrate their attention only on the rigorous application of a formal system of inference that must be based on a pre-analytical choice of a formal identity for the modelled system. Such a mathematical model can only represent an expected behaviour of that specific formal identity on the given scale. Rather, scientists have to keep an eye on the evolution of a sound relationship between a selected set of narratives and the resulting set of selected models. That is, not only does the selected model have to be pertinent in relation to the chosen narrative, but it must also provide a relevant result for the observers/agents who will use the result of the model. As stated by Box (1979), 'all models are wrong, some are useful'.

In this second check, the identity of the storyteller—who decides the relevance of the narratives—does matter. In fact for a model there is something that is much worse than being wrong. A model can be based on an irrelevant narrative. If a model is wrong in its simulations but still based on a sound selection of relevant narratives and attributes, sooner or later practitioners in the field will learn how to better calibrate or patch it. On the contrary, when the selection of the underlying narrative is wrong, the model will keep providing irrelevant and misleading results.

Conclusion

As emphasised earlier, before making any formal analysis of CAS—before attempting to model their evolution—an analyst must start with examining the relevance of selected narratives about CAS in relation to the goals of the analysis. This is useful to address explicitly why we make an analysis of CAS in the first place. This will help reveal legitimate but contrasting views of different observers (or storytellers). These various views about CAS cannot be fully perceived and represented by using only a formal model at the time, no matter how complicated the inferential system selected for doing it (Giampietro 2003; Giampietro et al. 2006; Mayumi and Giampietro 2006; Rosen 1985, 2000). Any given perception/representation of reality based on a particular formal model does necessarily reflect a set of choices made by a special storyteller about the selection of a relevant narrative for a given state of affairs in relation to a given set of goals. As Schumpeter (1954: 42) aptly remarked: '*Analytical work begins with material provided by our vision of things, and this vision is ideological almost by definition*'.

Funtowicz and Ravets (1990) developed a new epistemological framework they called post-normal science (PNS). In PNS uncertainty, the storytelling associated with different stakeholders and their value conflicts should be considered as crucial elements in the process of decision making. The adjectives 'post-normal' indicates a departure from curiosity-driven or puzzle-solving exercises of normal science in the Kuhnian sense (Kuhn 1962). Normal science was successfully extended from the laboratory of core science to the conquest of nature through applied science. However, the same scientific approach is no longer appropriate for the solution of sustainability problems. In fact, the social, technical and ecological dimensions of sustainability problems are so deeply connected that it is simply impossible to consider these dimensions separated, one at the time, as done in the narratives of conventional disciplinary fields.

Because of this new challenge we proposed an alternative use of quantitative analyses in the field of sustainability (Giampietro 2003; Mayumi 2001; Mayumi and Giampietro 2006). This requires new methodological approaches and a new strategy for research. Rather than using models and numbers to predict the future and to find 'optimal solutions' and 'best courses of action', we propose to use models and numbers to check the quality of the selected narratives in the pre-analytical step. This translates into a check on the quality of problem structuring and issue definition used to characterise a given situation or to define possible scenarios. This paradigm shift follows the suggestion of Simon (1976, 1996): when dealing with governance and sustainability, science should move away from substantive rationality and search for procedural rationality. Such a change of paradigm obviously requires a dramatic change in both the procedure and the analytical toolkit adopted for the analysis.

References

Ahl, V. and T.F.H. Allen. 1996. *Hierarchy Theory: A Vision, Vocabulary, and Epistemology*. New York: Columbia University Press.

Alcott, B. 2005. 'Jevons' Paradox', *Ecological Economics*, 54: 9–21.

Allen, T.F.H. and T.B. Starr. 1982. *Hierarchy*. Chicago: University of Chicago Press.

Box, G. 1979. 'Robustness is the Strategy of Scientific Model Building', in R.L. Launer and G.N. Wilkinson (eds), *Robustness in Statistics*. New York: Academic Press.

Brookes, L.A. 1979. '*A Low-energy Strategy for the UK* by G. Leach et al.: A Review and Reply', *Atom*, 269: 3–8.

Carpenter, S.R. and J.F. Kitchell. 1987. 'The Temporal Scale of Variance in Limnetic Primary Production', *American Naturalist*, 129: 417–33.

Cherfas, J. 1991. 'Skeptics and Visionaries Examine Energy Saving', *Science*, 251: 154–56.

Daly, H. 1995. 'Consumption and Welfare: Two Views of Value Added', *Review of Social Economy*, 53: 451–73.

Funtowicz, S.O. and J.R. Ravets. 1990. 'Post-normal Science: A New Science for New Times', *Scientific European*, 266: 20–22.

Gell-Mann, M. 1994. *The Quark and the Jaguar*. New York: Freeman.

Georgescu-Roegen, N. 1974. 'Dynamic Models and Economic Growth', in *Energy and Economic Myths: Institutional and Analytical Essays*. New York: Pergamon Press.

———. 1976. *Energy and Economic Myths: Institutional and Analytical Essays*. New York: Pergamon Press.

Giampietro, M. 1994. 'Using Hierarchy Theory to Explore the Concept of Sustainable Development', *Futures*, 26(6): 616–25.

———. 2003. *Multi-scale Integrated Analysis of Agro-ecosystems*. Boca Raton: CRC Press.

Giampietro, M., K. Mayumi and D. Pimentel. 2005. 'Mathematical Models of Society and Development: Dealing with the Epistemological Predicament of Complexity', *Encyclopedia of Life Support Systems*. (Topic 6.3.9: Editor of Theme 6.3 [Mathematical Models] Jerzy Filar).

Giampietro, M., K. Mayumi and G. Munda. 2006. 'Integrated Assessment and Energy Analysis: Quality Assurance in Multi-criteria Analysis of Sustainability', *Energy*, 31: 59–86.

Glansdorff, P. and I. Prigogine. 1971. *Thermodynamics Theory of Structure, Stability, and Fluctuations*. New York: John Wiley.

Herring, H. 1999. 'Does Energy Efficiency Save Energy? The Debate and its Consequences', *Applied Energy*, 63: 209–26.

Jevons, F. 1990. 'Greenhouse: A Paradox', *Search*, 21: 171–72.

Jevons, W.S. 1865. *The Coal Question.* (reprint of third edition, 1906). New York: Augustus M. Kelley.

Kampis, G. 1991. *Self-modifying Systems in Biology and Cognitive Science: A New Framework for Dynamics, Information and Complexity*. New York: Pergamon Press.

Kawamiya, N. 1983. *Entropii to Kougyoushakai no Sentaku* (in Japanese) (Entropy and Future Choices for Industrial Society). Tokyo: Kaimei.

Khazzoom, J.D. 1980. 'Economic Implications of Mandated Efficiency Standards for Household Appliances', *Energy Journal*, 1(4): 21–39.

———. 1987. 'Energy Saving Resulting from the Adoption of More Efficient Appliances', *Energy Journal*, 8(4): 85–89.

Kleene, S.C. 1952. *Introduction to Metamathematics*. London: D. Van Nostrand.

Koestler, A. 1967. *The Ghost in the Machine*. New York: MacMillan.

———. 1969. 'Beyond Atomism and Holism: The Concept of the Holon', in A. Koestler and J.R. Smythies (eds), Beyond Reductionism. London: Hutchinson.

———. 1978. *Janus: A Summing Up*. London: Hutchinson.

Kuhn, T.S. 1962. *The Structure of Scientific Revolutions*. Chicago: University of Chicago Press.

Lietz, P. and T. Streicher. 2002. 'Impredicativity Entails Untypedness', *Mathematical Structures in Computer Science*, 12: 335–47.

Lotka, A.J. 1922. 'Contribution to the Energetics of Evolution', *Proceedings of National Academy of Sciences*, 8: 147–51.

———. 1956. *Elements of Mathematical Biology*. New York: Dover Publications.

Margalef, R. 1968. *Perspectives in Ecological Theory*. Chicago: University of Chicago Press.

Maturana, H.R. and F.J. Varela. 1980. *Autopoiesis and Cognition: The Realization of the Living*. D. Reidel Publishing.

————. 1998. *The Tree of Knowledge: The Biological Roots of Human Understanding*. Boston: Shambhala Publications.

Mayumi, K. 2001. *The Origins of Ecological Economics: The Bioeconomics of Georgescu-Roegen*. London: Routledge.

Mayumi, K. and M. Giampietro. 2006. 'The Epistemological Challenge of Self-modifying Systems: Governance and Sustainability in the Post-normal Science Era', *Ecological Economics*, 57(3): 382–99.

Mayumi, K., M. Giampietro and J.M. Gowdy. 1998. 'Georgescu-Roegen/Daly versus Solow/Stiglitz Revisited', *Ecological Economics*, 27: 115–17.

Newman, P. 1991. 'Greenhouse, Oil and Cities', *Futures* (5): 335–48.

Nicolis, G. and I. Prigogine. 1977. *Self-organization in Nonequilibrium Systems*. New York: John Wiley.

Odum, H.T. and R.C. Pinkerton. 1955. 'Time's Speed Regulator: The Optimum Efficiency for Maximum Power Output in Physical and Biological Systems', *American Scientist*, 43: 321–43.

O' Neill, R.V. 1989. 'Perspectives in Hierarchy and Scale', in J. Roughgarden, R.M. May and S. Levin (eds), *Perspectives in Ecological Theory*. Princeton, NJ: Princeton University Press.

O'Neill, R.V., D.L. DeAngelis, J.B. Waide and T.F.H. Allen. 1986. *A Hierarchical Concept of Ecosystems*. Princeton, NJ: Princeton University Press.

O' Neill, Robert V., A.R. Johnson and A.W. King. 1989. 'A Hierarchical Framework for the Analysis of Scale', *Landscape Ecology*, 3: 193–205.

Polimeni, J. and Polimeni, R.I. 2006 (in press). 'Jevons' Paradox and the Myth of Technological Liberation', *Ecological Complexity*.

Prigogine, I. 1987. *From Being to Becoming*. San Francisco: Freeman.

Rosen, R. 1977. 'Complexity as a System Property', *International Journal of General Systems*, 3: 227–32.

————. 1985. *Anticipatory Systems: Philosophical, Mathematical and Methodological Foundations*. New York: Pergamon Press.

————. 2000. *Essays on Life itself*. New York: Columbia University Press.

Salthe, S.N. 1985. *Evolving Hierarchical Systems*. New York: Columbia University Press.

Saunders, H. 2000. 'A View from the Macro Side: Rebound, Backfire, and Khazzom-Brookes', *Energy Policy*, 28 (6–7): 439–49.

Schumpeter, J.A. 1954. *History of Economic Analysis*. London: George Allen & Unwin.

Simon, H.A. 1962. 'The Architecture of Complexity', *Proceedings of the American Philosophical Society*, 106: 467–82.
———. 1976. 'From Substantive to Procedural Rationality', in S. J. Latsis (ed.), *Methods and Appraisal in Economics*. Cambridge: Cambridge University Press.
———. 1996. *The Sciences of the Artificial*. Cambridge, MA: MIT Press.
Whyte, L.L., A.G. Wilson and D. Wilson (eds). 1969. *Hierarchical Structures*. New York: American Elsevier Publishing.

Notes on Contributors

Gregory S. Amacher is Associate Professor, College of Natural Resources, and Director, International forestry Center, at Virginia Polytechnic Institute and State University. He has worked in the area of natural resource economics and development for the past 12 years in Asia, Africa and Latin America, publishing over 100 articles, books and monographs. Amacher has served as editor and associate editor of several natural resources and forestry journals, and his articles have appeared in publications such as the *Journal of Environmental Economics and Management, Land Economics, Journal of Economic Development, Journal of Development Studies, American Journal of Agricultural Economics, Natural Resource Modeling* and *World Development.*

Arghya Ghosh teaches and researches at the University of New South Wales, Sydney, Australia. He obtained his doctoral degree from the University of Minnesota, USA. His research interests are in industrial organisation, international economics and political economy. He has several publications to his credit in peer-reviewed journals such as the *Review of Development Economics* and *Economica.*

Mario Giampietro is affiliated to the Istituto Nazionale di Ricerca per gli Alimenti e la Nutrizione, Italy. He has a chemical engineering degree, *laurea* in biological sciences, a master's degree in food system economics, and a Ph.D. in social sciences from Wageningen University. He has been a visiting scientist at Cornell University (1987–89 and 1993–95), Wageningen University (1997), European Commission Joint Research Center, Ispra, (1998), Universitat Autonoma Barcelona (1999–2000), Wisconsin University, Madison (2002) and Penn State University (2005–6). He has published over 100 papers, and a book entitled *Multi-scale Integrated Analysis of Agro-ecosystems*.

Roger Guesnerie is presently Chair of Economic Theory and Social Organisation at Collège de France. He has had a long and distinguished career in research, policy and teaching. He was co-editor of *Econometrica* from 1984 to 1989, president of the European Economic Association in 1994, and president of the Econometric Society in 1996. He is also a member of the American Academy of Arts and Science. He has been visiting fellow at many universities in Europe as well as the United States.

S.C. Gulati is Professor and Head of the Population Research Centre, Institute of Economic Growth, Delhi; and President of the Indian Association for the Study of Population (IASP). He specialises in applied econometrics and population-environment studies, and has contributed to several national and international journals. Dr Gulati has authored and co-authored several books including *Migration, Common Property Resources and Environmental Degradation; Fertility in India: An Econometric Analysis of a Metropolis; Women's Status and Reproductive Health Rights; Contraceptive Use in India; Reproductive Health in Delhi Slums*. His forthcoming book is entitled *Socio-economic Root Causes of Biodiversity Loss in Chilika Lake*.

Jean-Charles Hourcade has a double doctorate in economics and social sciences. He is a member of the advisory board of the European Climate Forum and has served as a member of several high-level government research committees. He was the lead author of the Fourth Assessment Report of the Intergovernmental Panel of Climate Change. He has been a professor at EHESS, Paris, since 1999 and has several research publications to his credit in leading international journals.

Ngo Van Long is James McGill Professor at McGill University, former professor of economics at the Australian National University and former co-editor of the *Canadian Journal of Economics*. He is associate editor of the *Review of International Economics*.

His most recent articles appeared in *Economic Theory* and *Journal of Economic Dynamics and Control*. He is a co-author of several books, including *Optimal Control Theory and Static Optimization in Economics* (1992) and *Differential Games in Economics and Management Science* (2000).

Kozo Mayumi graduated from the Graduate School of Engineering at the Department of Applied Mathematics and Physics of Kyoto University. Between 1984 and 1988 he studied bioeconomics at the Department of Economics of Vanderbilt University under Professor Nicholas Georgescu-Roegen. Mayumi has been working in the field of energy analysis, ecological economics and complex hierarchy theory. He is a professor at the University of Tokushima and an editorial board member of *Ecological Economics* and *Organization and Environment*. In 2001 Mayumi published *The Origins of Ecological Economics: The Bioeconomics of Georgescu-Roegen*.

Frank Merry is with the Woods Hole Research Center (WHRC) specialising in the economics of frontier households and large-scale modelling of land use, with particular reference to the timber industry of the Amazon. He is part of the Amazon Scenarios team at the WHRC, which is a large-scale economic and ecological model of land use and land use change in the Amazon. He also works in the linkage between natural resources and poverty in Mozambique, and the economic effects of the national park on surrounding communities.

Siddhartha Mitra is Reader, Gokhale Institute of Politics and Economics. He completed his Ph.D. at the University of Maryland at College Park. He specialises in development economics, political economy, labour economics and agricultural economics. He has served as consultant to the National Council of Applied Economic Research, New Delhi, besides completing short stints as visiting faculty, Indian Statistical Institute, New Delhi, visiting fellow, Center for Development Research, Bonn, and senior fellow, University of Melbourne. He has contributed extensively to academic journals (such as the *Journal of Environmental Economics and Management* and *American Journal of Agricultural Economics*) and leading newspapers.

M.N. Murty is Professor of Economics, Institute of Economic Growth, Delhi. He was a Visiting Ford Foundation Fellow at University of Birmingham, UK (1991–92) and a senior research associate, Project on Indian Fiscal Systems, University of Warwick, UK (1980–82). He has also served as consultant to the World Bank, International Crop Research Institute, and ESCAP. He has published seven books, undertaken 10 research projects and has regularly published in international journals such as *Environment and Development Economics* and *Economics Letters*.

J. Barkley Rosser, Jr., is Professor of Economics and Kirby L. Kramer, Jr., Professor of Business Administration at James Madison University, with an economics Ph.D. from the University of Wisconsin-Madison. Author of over 100 published papers, he has authored several books including *From Catastrophe to Chaos: A General Theory of Economic Discontinuities* and *Complexity in Economics*. He is on several journal editorial boards and is editor of the *Journal of Economic Behavior and Organization*.

Partha Sen earned his doctoral degree from the London School of Economics in 1984. He is currently a professor of economics at Delhi School of Economics. He has also taught at the Indian Statistical Institute, London School of Economics, National University of Singapore. City University, Hong Kong, University of Washington, University of Michigan and University of Bristol. He has published in international journals such as *International Economic Review* and *Journal of International Economics*, and served as consultant to the ADB and WHO.

Ajit Sinha has a Ph.D. in economics from the State University of New York at Buffalo. He is professor and Director of the Gokhale Institute of Politics and Economics, Pune, and is presently visiting Collège de France as Maitre de conférences associé.

Prior to this he has taught at the LBS National Academy of Administration, India, and University of Newcastle, Australia. Apart from this he has held important visiting positions. He has to his credit a large number of academic papers published in reputed journals across the world.

D.K. Tuli holds a Ph.D. in synthetic chemistry. He has over two decades of varied experience in research and development in the hydrocarbon industry and a special interest in synthetics and biotics. Tuli has to his credit 14 US, two European and over 20 Indian patents. He has also published 50 research papers in professional journals. He has a special interest in the subject of bio-fuels. He is currently the chief executive officer of Indian Oil Technologies Limited, a subsidiary of Indian Oil Corporation.

Index

trade liberalisation, 151, 157–65;
income from, 163; price of
dirty goods, 163; short- and
long-run effects, 164–65
trans-border pollution, controlling, 14–15

UN methodology of Integrated
Environmental and Economic
Accounting, 109
UNCTAD group, 62

US and energy consumption, 75;
biggest polluter in the world,
75; -like arrangements, 80–85;
sulphur dioxide experiments,
79

waste disposal services, 92
water contamination/pollutants,
25–26; Shafik on, 25–26
water-borne wastes, 26
welfare maximisation, 64
WTO, link with, 70–71, 84

Printed in the United Kingdom
by Lightning Source UK Ltd.
117559UKS00003B/10-21

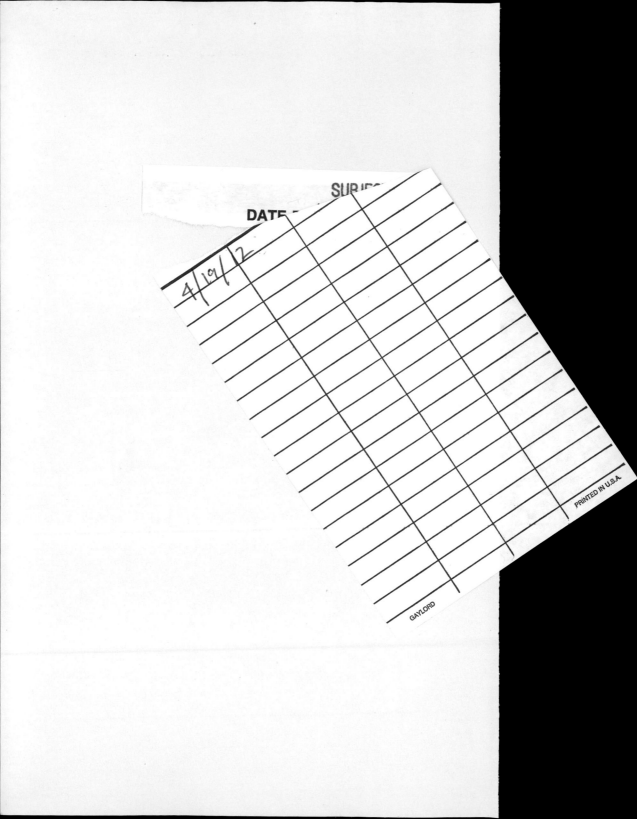

SUBJECT

DATE

4/19/12

GAYLORD

PRINTED IN U.S.A.